G000055348

Police
Suicide
Is Police Culture Killing
Our Officers?

Police Suicide

Is Police Culture Killing Our Officers?

Edited by
Ronald A. Rufo, EdD

CRC Press
Taylor & Francis Group
Boca Raton London New York

CRC Press is an imprint of the
Taylor & Francis Group, an **informa** business

CRC Press
Taylor & Francis Group
6000 Broken Sound Parkway NW, Suite 300
Boca Raton, FL 33487-2742

© 2016 by Taylor & Francis Group, LLC
CRC Press is an imprint of Taylor & Francis Group, an Informa business

No claim to original U.S. Government works

Printed on acid-free paper
Version Date: 20150622

International Standard Book Number-13: 978-1-4822-3499-2 (Paperback)

This book contains information obtained from authentic and highly regarded sources. Reasonable
efforts have been made to publish reliable data and information, but the author and publisher cannot
assume responsibility for the validity of all materials or the consequences of their use. The authors and
publishers have attempted to trace the copyright holders of all material reproduced in this publication
and apologize to copyright holders if permission to publish in this form has not been obtained. If any
copyright material has not been acknowledged please write and let us know so we may rectify in any
future reprint.

Except as permitted under U.S. Copyright Law, no part of this book may be reprinted, reproduced,
transmitted, or utilized in any form by any electronic, mechanical, or other means, now known or
hereafter invented, including photocopying, microfilming, and recording, or in any information stor-
age or retrieval system, without written permission from the publishers.

For permission to photocopy or use material electronically from this work, please access www.copy-
right.com (http://www.copyright.com/) or contact the Copyright Clearance Center, Inc. (CCC), 222
Rosewood Drive, Danvers, MA 01923, 978-750-8400. CCC is a not-for-profit organization that provides licenses and registration for a variety of users. For organizations that have been granted a photocopy license by the CCC, a separate system of payment has been arranged.

Trademark Notice: Product or corporate names may be trademarks or registered trademarks, and are
used only for identification and explanation without intent to infringe.

Visit the Taylor & Francis Web site at
http://www.taylorandfrancis.com

and the CRC Press Web site at
http://www.crcpress.com

Printed and bound in Great Britain by
TJ International Ltd, Padstow, Cornwall

I would like to dedicate this book to my granddaughter Alinah, who makes me very happy and is very special in so many ways. I love being her Papa. Even at a very young age, she is thoughtful and considerate. To my three wonderful daughters Rita, Laura, and Cara, who touch my heart, each in a different way, and who I love with all of my heart.

To my Dad, who influenced me in so many ways and who passed away at a young age, I know he would have been proud of me. To my beautiful wife Debbie, who has always been supportive and patient in my effort to complete my book and to get my crusade about the importance of being emotionally stable to all police officers on and off the job. Debbie has always been my inspiration to reach for the stars and never look back.

Contents

Foreword

By Robert E. Douglas, Jr.

When Dr. Ron Rufo (Chicago police officer) asked me to write this foreword for his book, I was extremely humbled by his request. As executive director and founder for the National Police Suicide Foundation since it was founded in 1997, I have traveled worldwide speaking about mental health suicide prevention for our law enforcement officers along with our military personnel. What I have seen should be alarming to law enforcement leadership in our country. We have been seeing over the past 25 years an ever-increasing concern for line officers dealing with posttraumatic stress disorder (PTSD), as well as officer-related suicides to every in-line-of-duty death according to the 2014 report put out by the International Association of Chiefs of Police, on June 6, 2014 (IACP National Symposium on Law Enforcement Officer Suicide and Mental Health: Breaking the Silence on Law Enforcement Suicides).

With these pressing issues facing the 18,000 law enforcement agencies in our country, it is extremely important that we focus on preventive measures by our administrative and supervisory training programs to address them within our ranks. Dr. Rufo has aggressively addressed all these issues and much more in his book, *Police Suicide: Is Police Culture Killing Our Officers?*

It is my professional opinion that the greater enemy that our officers struggle with each day is not the suspect on the street but instead the enemy that lives with officers attempting to effectively address their emotional trauma that impacts their daily lives! Dr. Rufo provides the psychological and departmental roadmap in helping leadership as well as the officers to navigate through this maze of emotional and physical issues they will face each day while on the street as well as at home. I strongly believe that Dr. Rufo is a true "difference maker" (as John Maxwell, author of numerous books on leadership, would say), as he addresses our leadership issue in charting the course for law enforcement agencies to make great decisions on helping and assisting their personnel strive to serve their communities throughout this country. Never forget that change is unavoidable! The only thing certain about our tomorrow is the decision we make today.

Dr. Rufo's book illustrates that such positive and creative change must happen first within us before it can happen around us!

By John Mayer, PhD

The suicide and attempted suicide of police officers is a mental health concern that has been neglected for too many years. The stigma of discussing mental health is slowly, but steadily, being lifted in many segments of our society and in many occupations, but in those occupations that carry with them the duties of protecting others, the idea of attending to one's own mental health remains heavily stigmatized. There are many reasons given for the denial of mental health care in these professions, and some of them have been the peer culture within the occupation, the role models available to the workers, ineffective coping mechanisms, and poor preventive measures within the occupation. In the culture of the police officer, one of the most prevailing reasons for the inattention to emotional or personal self-care is the mind-set among their fellow police peers that such concerns identify them as weak and not fit to handle the rigors of the job. Appearing weak in front of their fellow officers makes them vulnerable, and being vulnerable will get them ridiculed and shunned by the other officers.

In police work, in addition to these prevailing forces keeping police officers away from mental health prevention, Rufo, in this book, delves into specific forces in the lives of police officers that create a peer culture that puts low priority on mental health prevention and the officer's emotional life. Sadly, in the 25 weeks of training in the police academy, there is no attention paid to the coping mechanisms needed to handle the large amount of stress and negativity that the police officer faces on the job each day. This formal personal preparation should be an integral part of the police officers' toolkits as they approach their jobs each day. The lack of formal preparation not only perpetuates the stigma against mental health services but it also leaves the officer no other opportunity to learn personal coping mechanisms other than through peer observation, informal mentoring, on-the-job training, or fending for one's self through some other means such as investing in a book like this to augment training. And, of course, it also opens up the great possibility that the police officer will cope with strenuous work through negative behaviors and emotions.

This is where Rufo's book becomes invaluable as a tool for police officers because it supplements what prevention they are getting elsewhere. For that reason, this book is a *must read* for every officer, every administrator, every chief everywhere to cope with the complexities of modern police work.

Let me talk about this book for it is not only a book for police officers but also a book for police administrators, municipal officials, police family members, and everyone who wants to understand the pressures and coping mechanisms of a municipal police officer. The book is well researched, thorough, well presented, and well organized. It covers all one would need to know to understand the problem of police suicide. *Police Suicide: Is Police*

Culture Killing Our Officers? takes us from what the cadet experiences in the police academy through the daily job stress and even to the aftermath of a police suicide. No other book is as comprehensive as this. Rufo gives us a look into the police academy and the training that cadets receive. Here we get our first glimpse of the fact that the personal life of police officers is not addressed nor are there coping mechanisms or emotional preparedness for this job that put so much strain on the psyche of officers.

Some time ago, I wrote a book on the lives of Catholic priests titled *Grace under Pressure*. As a result of an extensive research project where I interviewed priests from across the United States, I learned a great deal about what it takes to be a successful Catholic priest. What I learned in that research reminds me of the preparation and lifestyle of police officers. At that time, I discovered that priests were not receiving training in the emotional tools necessary to cope with their roles as leaders of often multimillion-dollar corporations so soon after their ordination. With the shortage of priests in the Catholic Church, a priest is quickly thrust early in his career into the highly stressful position of being a pastor of an organization that can have a budget upward of millions of dollars, a building or buildings that often need constant repair and care, or a congregation teeming with spiritual needs, and he is often alone in doing this as the diocese (name for the district administration) doesn't have the manpower to assign an assistant priest to help out. In fact, I often found one priest heading multiple parishes alone, so multiply this stress by three or four. The most glaring aspect of this research, again at that time, was that the priest received no training on business administration or finance. And, as I pointed out, they were not given preparation on how to cope with all this stress. Even more remarkable is that within the seminary and ordination process, the priests' natural coping resources, their families, were purposely and directly discouraged from being a part of the priests' lives. To badly paraphrase a statement made at the ordination ceremony, "You give your sons now to the work of the Lord and they are no longer yours but ours. So, alone and coping with tremendous pressures, they are not trained to handle and stripped of the logical coping mechanism that groomed one to follow this calling (the family). It is no wonder many priests cannot cope with such pressures. In fact, it is remarkable that so many of these men do make this all work for them."

Why this comparison? I outline this here as a strong example of exactly what we face in the profession of being a police officer. The same elements setting up the police officer to fail, to crack under this pressure, are in the training process, the peer culture of police, and the on-the-job experiences of police officers. We need to do a better job of preparing police for this stress and a better job caring for our officers throughout their careers. If we do so, we will have better police officers and we will be better served as a society. This book is a primer in that direction.

I have known Ron Rufo for many years. Our paths have crossed in our work and often in our personal life. In every encounter, I have always observed Ron to rise to the occasion. If it was on duty, Ron was the consummate professional police officer. If it was personal, Ron was affable, engaging, and positive. What this tells me about this man is that he copes with life well. He has a wide bandwidth of personal interests, a rich and full family life, and a passionate professional life. Ron and I have always been kindred spirits in all those ways. I understand Ron and his approach to his job and to life itself. I can't think of a better authority to author such an important book than Dr. Ronald Rufo Chicago Police Department. He has been on the streets as a Chicago police officer for years, he studied and obtained a doctorate, he is a passionate family man, and he is a well-balanced, emotionally stable individual. All of these are the credibility that Ron brings to this book.

Acknowledgments

To Julie Diaz, who is not only an exceptional proofreader but also a dear friend who has been committed and steadfast in her effort to make this book a success. She has proven to be an invaluable teammate in preparing this manuscript for publication. Julie has worked extremely hard in correcting and organizing the many pages of script that I have sent her, without ever complaining. Her suggestions were clearly remarkable and well thought out. She has assisted me in putting my message on police suicide and police culture in a clear and organized perspective. She must have gone through a few red pens on my manuscript, and I could not begin to thank her for her dedication to my book. Thanks again, Julie. You truly are the best!

To the following four contributors of this book, who agreed to write their own chapters:

- Kent Williams is an insightful and dynamic personality in law enforcement who takes a proactive approach to the problems police officers face on a daily basis. Thank you for writing Chapter 2.
- Tom Cline, a dear friend of mine with a gentle and kind disposition, has a tremendous outlook on life. He has taught many recruits about the importance of emotional wellness. Thank you for writing Chapter 3.
- Dr. Bobby Smith, truly an inspirational person and speaker who I have had the pleasure to meet. He is in every sense of the word a policeman's policeman. He is renowned for his dedication and courage after facing a devastating injury in the line of duty as a Louisiana State Trooper. Chapter 8 is a chapter taken from Dr. Bobby Smith's book *The Will to Survive*.
- John Marx, a well-known authority in the field of suicide prevention. Thank you for writing Chapter 10.

I want to personally acknowledge every person in this book who has contributed to making this book a success. To the many experts in the health-care profession, the clergy, and the law enforcement who I personally interviewed and who were gracious enough to share their thoughts, opinions, and insight for my book on the effect of police culture as it relates to police suicide. Again, my sincere thanks to everyone.

Health-Care Professionals

- Denis Adams, Licensed Clinical Social Worker, is a clinical therapist for the professional Counseling Service Employee Assistance Program (EAP) of the Chicago Police Department.
- Dr. Carl Alaimo, Sr., retired after 26½ years of service as the director and chief psychologist of the Mental Health Services Department of Cermak Health Services of Cook County, Illinois. Dr. Alaimo has worked closely with the State of Illinois Division of Mental Health, the Circuit Court of Cook County–Criminal Justice Division, and the Chicago Police Department Crisis Intervention Team. He currently is teaching at the Cook County Training Institute.
- Dr. Alexis Artwohl is a well-respected expert in the field of police suicide. She is an internationally recognized behavioral science consultant working with law enforcement as a trainer, researcher, and author. She has written a book entitled *Deadly Force Encounters: What Cops Need to Know to Mentally and Physically Prepare for and Survive a Gunfight.*
- Dr. Frank Campbell is compassionate and concerned about the many survivors of police suicide. He works with the survivors and victims of attempted suicide, and he is the former executive director of the Baton Rouge Crisis Intervention Center and the Crisis Center Foundation in Louisiana. He is currently senior consultant for Campbell and Associates Consulting where he consults with communities on forensic suicidology cases. He introduced his Active Postvention Model, most commonly known as the Local Outreach to Suicide Survivors (LOSS) Team.
- Dr. Jack Digliani is a well-known authority on police culture and the problems and issues that officers experience. He is a licensed psychologist and a former law enforcement officer. Dr. Digliani has a wealth of knowledge and experience and is an expert in the field of police psychology and police peer support. He is the author of *Reflections of a Police Psychologist* and has written the *Police and Sheriff Peer Support Team Manual*, the *Law Enforcement Critical Incident Handbook*, and the *Law Enforcement Marriage and Relationship Guidebook.*

- Dr. Marla Friedman has a vision to incorporate emotional wellness to the many police chiefs throughout the nation. It is an honor and pleasure to have her thoughts in this book. She is a licensed clinical psychologist and has written an article about the complex subject of police suicide for *Command Magazine*, a publication of the Illinois Association of Chiefs of Police.
- Bruce Handler, MD, has been involved in Crisis Intervention Team (CIT) training of more than 6000 law enforcement and correctional officers in Illinois.
- Dr. John Mayer is a very good friend. I appreciate his time and effort in making my book a success. He is a prolific author of 20 books about mental health issues and a well-known psychologist with more than 30 years of experience in the Chicagoland area. He is a consultant to many law enforcement agencies throughout the country. John also cowrote the foreword of this book.
- Victoria Poklop, MS, is a dedicated and compassionate licensed professional counselor at the Des Plaines Police Department, Des Plaines, Illinois.
- Dr. Ellen Scrivner is a highly respected police psychologist. She has worked extensively with the FBI, other federal agencies, and many police departments across the country, developing programs in risk assessment, police wellness, psychological training, community policing, and law enforcement coordination.
- Dr. Bryan Vila is extremely knowledgeable on the subject of sleep deprivation and the detrimental effects it has on police officers. He is well known in law enforcement and has been involved in numerous sleep-related studies throughout his career.
- Dr. John Violanti has written 15 books on the subject of police suicide. He was a New York State Trooper for 23 years and a criminal investigator and coordinator of the Psychological Assistance Program for the New York State Police. Dr. Violanti has been involved in the design, implementation, and analysis of police stress and health studies throughout his career.
- Lisa Wimberger is well known in police circles for her relaxation techniques and coping mechanisms that enhance a person's emotional well-being. Wimberger founded the Neurosculpting® Institute that is used by many law enforcement agencies throughout the country, especially for an officer's emotional survival.
- Dr. Nancy Zarse is a distinguished clinical psychologist and professor of the Forensic Department at the Chicago School of Professional Psychology. Dr. Zarse is well known for her clinical work and critical incidence training with law enforcement personnel throughout the United States.

Clergy

- Father Dan Brandt is amazingly easygoing and has a great sense of humor. As police chaplain, he is dedicated to the men and women of the Chicago Police Department.
- Father Tony Pizzo is a dear and personal friend who is kindhearted and compassionate to everyone. He is a Jesuit priest from St. Rita's Parish and has counseled many police officers throughout his career.
- Father Charles Rubey is well known around the world for his work and dedication to those who have lost a loved one to suicide, especially through the support group The Compassionate Friends.

Law Enforcement

- Dr. Dean Angelo Sr. has been in law enforcement for 34 years and is currently the president of the Chicago Fraternal Order of Police Lodge 7.
- Pam Church is the chief of police of the Western Springs Police Department, Western Springs, Illinois.
- Phil Cline is the former police superintendent of the Chicago Police Department.
- Robert Douglas, Jr., is a sincere and dedicated professional who works tirelessly to prevent suicide among law enforcement officers. He is the executive director of the National Suicide Foundation, Inc. and a former police officer. Bob was also gracious enough to cowrite the foreword of this book.
- John Barney Flanagan spoke candidly and openly about the loss of his son to suicide. Thank you for sharing your feelings. Barney is a retired assistant deputy superintendent and spent 35 years as a Chicago police officer. He retired as a first deputy superintendent, Chicago Police Department.
- Douglas Fuchs is the police chief of the Redding Police Department, Redding, Connecticut.
- Hiram Grau retired as a deputy superintendent after 28 years in the Chicago Police Department, and in 2011, he became the director of the prestigious Illinois State Police.
- Lt. Colonel Dave Grossman is an internationally recognized scholar, author, soldier, and speaker who is one of the world's foremost experts in the field of human aggression and the roots of violence and violent crime. Lt. Col. Grossman specializes in the study of the psychology of killing, and he has written the books *On Killing* and *On Combat*,

which are required reading at the FBI academy and numerous other academies and colleges.

- Terry Hillard is extremely well respected in the law enforcement community. He is the former superintendent of police for the city of Chicago and has spent more than three decades in law enforcement.
- Bill Hogewood is a renowned and trusted authority as a peer support innovator and instructor in law enforcement. He began his career as a Prince George's County police officer and proudly served the citizens of Maryland for 28 years. He became training program manager for crisis negotiation and peer support in the Bureau of Alcohol, Tobacco, Firearms and Explosives (ATF). He has trained and consulted in the United States and internationally in hostage negotiations, peer support, suicide recognition and intervention, and stress management.
- Michael Holub is the police chief of the La Grange Police Department, La Grange, Illinois.
- Garry McCarthy is the current superintendent of police for the Chicago Police Department.
- Jeff Murphy worked as a police officer for more than 40 years, retiring as a lieutenant in the Chicago Police Department. He was instrumental in developing the Critical Incident Training (CIT) Program for the Chicago Police Department and surrounding law enforcement departments.
- Sean Riley is an inspirational, open, and caring fellow police officer who was honest about the issues he experienced on the job as a police officer and what he has done to change his life. He is the founder and executive director of *Safecallnow.org*. Riley is also a former police officer of the San Diego County Sheriff's Department and Kirkland Police Department and past union president.
- Steve Stelter is the chief of police for Brookfield, Illinois, and has 35 years of experience in law enforcement.
- Barry Thomas is the captain of the Story County Sheriff's Department, the second vice president of the FBI National Academy Associates, and the chair of the executive board for Safe Call Now.
- Brad Woods is recognized for his leadership and dedication to helping police officers in emotional crisis within the Chicago Police Department. He retired as a commander of the Personnel Division. While in charge of the Personal Concerns and the Behavioral Intervention Unit, he developed an early warning system that would get help to an officer before the officer's situation became worse.

Special thanks to

- Beverly Anderson, PhD, Police Suicide: Understanding Grief and Loss, Metropolitan Police EAP (www.giftfrom within.org).
- Scott Affholter, a retired lieutenant, Wyandotte Michigan Police Department.
- Augie Battaglia, retired police officer, Chicago Police Department.
- Cheryl Brown, Suicide Finding Hope, a website that deals with the survivors and coping with loss from suicide.
- Dr. Kevin Gilmartin.
- Dee Hatos, thank you for writing about police and the media in the Introduction.
- Phil Hasket, retired police officer, Chicago Police Department.
- Tim J. Freesmeyer, founder and president of Etico Solutions.
- Dr. Olivia Johnson, founder of the Blue Wall Institute and Illinois State representative for the National Police Suicide Foundation. She is the author of *Brass Versus Officers: Distrust Gets Us Nowhere.*
- Dr. Robin Kroll, a clinical psychologist and the director of interventions, specializes in police psychology. Dr. Kroll's concentration includes working with police officers in individual, group, and family therapy for issues related to addiction, mood disorders, work-related matters, and posttraumatic stress disorder.
- Kevin McNulty, police officer, Chicago Police Department.
- Brian O'Neil, writer for the Tacoma News Tribune.
- Jay Padar, sergeant with the Chicago Police Department. Jay coauthored the book *On Being a Cop* with his father, Jim Padar.
- Jim Padar worked as a Chicago police officer for more than 29 years, retiring as a lieutenant.
- Justin Roa, an extremely talented young man who did an excellent job on the book cover. Your artwork was an inspiration for the title of the book.
- Donald Simmons, police officer, Chicago Police Department.
- Lt. Matt Walsh, Cook County Sheriff's police.

Editor

Dr. Ron Rufo is a highly decorated Chicago police officer with over 20 years' service, which includes a Life Saving Award, Department Accommodation, and Unit Meritorious Award. He has 23 honorable mentions and over 100 letters of appreciation as a Chicago police officer. Ron began his career in the 9th District, was assigned to the prestigious Ambassador program, and was eventually assigned to the Preventive Programs Unit, where he has served as a crime prevention speaker for over 13 years. For most of his career, Ron has been actively involved as a peer support team leader for the Employee Assistance Program (EAP) section of the Chicago Police Department. He has had specialized training in suicide prevention and is a member of the Critical Incident Team. Ron has been on numerous calls responding to police officers in crisis and has been involved in the aftermath of police suicides. He is currently assigned to the 18th Police District.

Ron received his bachelor of arts degree in criminal social justice from Lewis University in 2000, graduating with highest honors and as a scholar of the university. He earned his master of arts degree in organizational leadership from Lewis University in 2002. He received his doctorate degree in organizational leadership from Argosy University in 2007. His dissertation was "An Investigation of On-Line Sexual Predation of Convicted Male Offenders". His first book, *Sexual Predators Amongst Us*, was released in December 2011. He coauthored a second book, *Police and Profiling in the United States: Applying Theory to Criminal Investigation*, with Dr. Lauren Barrow in July 2013.

Ron has contributed a chapter on sexual predator investigations to a book geared toward police detectives and crime scenes. He has also contributed a chapter on building safety for a property manager's guide to a book on terrorism and property management. Ron has taught criminal social justice in the master's program at Kaplan University since 2008.

Introduction

If I commit suicide, it will not be to destroy myself but to put myself back together again. Suicide will be for me only one means to put myself back together again. Suicide will be for me only one means of violently reconquering myself, of brutality invading my being, of anticipating the unpredictable approaches of God. By suicide, I reintroduce my design in nature; I shall for the first time give things the shape of my will.

Antonin Artaud, French poet

Introduction: Life's Journey

This book will provide a realistic insight into the life of a police officer through a police officer's eyes. I have been a Chicago police officer for over 20 years and will give graphic details of what an officer goes through to survive on the streets, but what he or she gives up in return.

Early in childhood many people will ask, "What do you want to become when you grow up?" I am not completely sure when I thought about becoming a police officer. I never said to anyone that I would like to be a police officer until my late twenties. It was always in the back of my mind, but I never acted on it until my early thirties. I am not sure what exactly persuaded me to take the necessary steps to become a police officer; it may have been my demeanor to help others. No one in my family was in law enforcement. My encounters with police officers were rare and infrequent.

I truly believe a person finds a career path he or she is destined for. I use the word "destined" because I believe a higher power puts us where he wants us to be. I had a few different professions before I actually focused on becoming a policeman. I was divorced with three children when I traveled to Las Vegas, Nevada, in hopes of becoming a law enforcement officer. I arrived early and took in the spectacular light display of the famed Las Vegas Strip. The next day, I arrived at the Las Vegas Convention Center to take the written part of the exam. I was amazed how many people wanted a job in law enforcement. True to the area, I tried to figure what my odds were of being a metro police officer. The crowd was enormous and growing. For the Las Vegas exam, you must pass each part of the exam to continue on. I passed the written section with flying colors, and I was scheduled to run a mile and a half the next day. I got up early and proceeded to the indoor track where they gave me a nylon yellow pullover with #6 on the front and back. The instructions were clear, and the entire run was videotaped so there would be no mistake to its accuracy. Each candidate must run six laps around the oval track in 12 minutes and 30 seconds or before. If a candidate runs the course in 12 minutes and 31 seconds, they will not go on any farther in the exam process. I soon found out after the first lap that I was not in the best shape to run, especially in the thin air of Las Vegas. There was no excuse on my part; I did not pass the exam. The moderator yelled out "#6 you can stop after five laps." I knew by 12:45 on the clock that it was over. I did not pass, but I did not quit. I ran the full six laps just to prove to myself that I can do it. The next year, I took the Reno exam and made it all the way to the oral boards. My lack of law enforcement procedures was apparent; I failed miserably. My hopes of becoming a police officer were diminishing. Both exams taught me something: if you want the job as a police officer, you better become more prepared. When I returned home from Nevada, I had a goal and was focused on taking the upcoming police exam and becoming one of Chicago's *finest*.

I was 35 years old when I took the Chicago police exam. I joined a health club with a buddy of mine, and we ran every morning. At 35 years old (this was considered old by police standards, but there was no age or educational restrictions back then), I was still pursuing a dream. I remember walking into Curie High School on the south side of Chicago where there were thousands of applicants waiting to get in, very similar to the scene at the Las Vegas Convention Center when I took the Las Vegas police exam. There were six sites offering the police exam that day. The news reported that over 36,000 individuals were vying for only 2000 openings. The odds were a 1–18 chance of being a cop.

After the written test, there were a few hurdles in the process. There was a hiring freeze for a year, and then a discrimination lawsuit was filed by a number of applicants. I thought I would never become an officer. At 39 years old,

I finally was called in for the next segments of the exam. Going through the testing process was long, with the anticipation and waiting for the next step in the process. The agility test was my last obstacle, and I ran the mile and a half in less than 12 minutes on an unusually blistering hot June day. There I was sitting in a room with the other candidates who passed the run, the last segment to starting the academy. We were told to quit our previous jobs and move into the city and that we would be starting the Police Academy on July 5, 1994. We were told to report to the Police Academy at 8 a.m. sharp in a suit and tie.

The night of July 4 was filled with anticipation and the sounds of errant firecrackers exploding what seemed like yards away from my bedroom window. I tossed and turned and could not sleep. I was worried that if I did fall asleep, I might not hear the alarm clock. At 4 o'clock, I got up, took a shower, and proceeded to get dressed. Better that I am early than late. I arrived at the Police Academy at 5 a.m., 3 hours earlier than I was supposed to arrive. The shocked police officer on duty at the front desk asked me bluntly, "What the hell do you want, who are you?" I explained that I was in the next academy class and could not sleep. Shaking his head, the officer directed me to the vending machines in the cafeteria and said, "Welcome to the Chicago Police Department." The rest is history.

Always a Cop

I am amazed when one of my family members or acquaintances introduces me. To this day, most of my friends and family introduce me as Ron, he is a Chicago cop. Rarely do they say hello to Dr. Rufo or even acknowledge my degree. I do not resent being introduced that way; in fact I am very proud of being an officer, but there is more to me than just being a cop. I am a husband, father, professor, and author. I find most medical doctors and attorneys are introduced in the same way; this is Joe, and he is a heart surgeon or Bob is an attorney.

The badge defines who we are. Once the badge goes on, it never comes off, whether anyone else sees it or not. It fuses with the soul, through adversity, fear, and adrenaline. It is a symbol of pride, integrity, and guts. Many of you will never know that feeling of being a cop, a crusader of justice. Even after a good cop leaves the job for a well-deserved retirement, he will know a lifetime of camaraderie that few experience. In law enforcement, there is a lasting partnership or brotherhood even after the uniform has remained isolated in the back of the closet. Police officers will share with other officers their war stories, accomplishments, and burdens of the job. They will share with each other a lifetime of experiences that no citizen could ever dream of. Police friends are for life!

Public Perception of the Police

The public looks to the police for answers and solutions to problems and to be problem solvers. Rarely does the public realize that the police are humans and that we have issues of our own. Most people like the police; a few individuals loathe the police. A majority of people do not enjoy their encounters with the police. The police are called for service when something bad or catastrophic has occurred, for example, a car accident, burglary, or theft report, and the list goes on. Often when the police are involved, there is some form of negative connotation attached to the situation.

Media Perception of the Police

The media, both newsprint and television, will often sensationalize a story that involves the police, more often emphasizing police misconduct over something good that the police have done. News coverage regarding the inappropriate behavior of an officer is often highlighted in the headlines of the daily paper and in the local newscasts. Police should not be above the law or the citizens they are sworn to protect, and that is often the focus of the officer who has abused his or her power in an effort to circumvent the law.

People are curious about how the officer got caught up in the misconduct or situation that they are accused of being involved in. The consensus is the officer abused his power and should be severely punished; there are enough criminals on our streets and the police officer should not be one of them. The Constitution of the United States maintains that anyone accused of any criminal or illegal behavior is *innocent until proven guilty*. It is the general consensus that police officers who are accused of a crime, police misconduct, or inappropriate behavior are most likely guilty (or assumed guilty anyway).

Police officers will get their day in court. Even if the officer is found not guilty in a court of law, the general public will assume the court was influenced by his profession. In the minds of citizens, police officers will protect their own if it means writing favorable reports or looking the other way when it comes down to police misconduct or inappropriate accusations. In the mind-set of the public, police officers *truly are above the law*, in their belief that everyone involved in the criminal justice system will ultimately protect the police officer in some way. The officer accused of misconduct will always carry that stigma of wrongdoing even though he has been exonerated in a court of law. To his friends and colleagues in law enforcement, the stigma of misconduct will overshadow any awards or accolades the officer may have received.

Media Perception by Diane Hatos

Mark Twain once said that a lie can circle the world before the truth can finish tying its shoes.

Let's face it; these days the media is every officer's nemesis. In this fairly new phenomenon, the media uses its influence to directly shape our view of the police world. Police personnel face endless challenges of self-destruction and humiliation now that nearly everyone carries cell phones equipped with video cameras that can and do record at the touch of a button. These videos, which expose situational chaos, largely illustrate unfortunate, out-of-context, citizen encounters featuring police brutality that ultimately gives law enforcement a "black eye."

In all fairness, yes, there are times when force is needed to restore the peace—there are a lot of bad guys out there. This point quickly escapes the public when tweets go out and Facebook news feeds are inundated with video clips featuring the "dark side" of police work. For reasons unknown to me, these isolated, unflattering images take America and the world by storm, receiving hundreds of thousands of "hits" in a relatively short amount of time, while the true, "feel good" stories about the "good guys" in law enforcement fail to grab our attention. Why?

The majority of police officers act courteously and professionally most of the time. There is no shortage of videos showing police officers using excessive force, much less any real discrimination that in many cases portrays law enforcement in a downright false light. At the very least, these exposés are questionable. It takes a keen and willing eye to look for the truth. While successful at capturing an audience, there is no denying that the prevalence of these videos "posted" on social media fails drastically at capturing the positive side of law enforcement. And it's not fair. This phenomenon has become a runaway train with no brakes. Every recorded detail, no matter how false or contrived, one-sided or slanted, is easily believed; there is absolutely no room for disclaimers.

In the early days of television and radio as many of you may remember, everything was subject to a censorship process, fairly strict in comparison to today's standards. Currently, censorship is very limited—there are no filters in social media. Videos taken by individuals do go viral, literally, in a matter of hours. As a result, we have become victims of this "in your face" style of media propaganda.

Sadly, this litany of audio and video recordings exhibiting "cops behaving badly" has had a profound effect, not only on those in law enforcement but also on how the general public views the police. The media has an undeniably powerful influence on how people form their opinions on the police, and they know it. Additionally, this type of pessimistic journalism has a powerful and detrimental effect on police morale.

On any given day in every city in America, the newspapers are alive with local, national, and world news articles featuring police stories. These articles largely accentuate the negative aspects of law enforcement, which, in all honesty, only *truly* happen in a *very minute* segment of the entire police profession. This blatant distortion of factual reporting has infiltrated social media creating a real concern for law enforcement agencies.

The community-oriented policing (COP) initiative is a growing trend in the majority of departments across the country: it focuses on building strong ties with a wide array of community members. These mutually beneficial relationships rely on trustworthy interactions and are not always easily forged. The public can become quickly outraged and begin to believe that all cops are abusive when negative news stories or videos surface. They seriously undermine COP efforts.

The folks in Seattle, Washington, are a prime example of media influence and negative public perception. Recently, the Seattle Police Department underwent a complete transformation after public allegations of racial profiling and police brutality caused the Department of Justice (DOJ) to launch a thorough investigation in 2011. This media-fueled inquiry uncovered a pattern of constitutional violations in the department's use-of-force policies. In efforts to avoid a federal lawsuit, the Seattle Police Department agreed to adhere to a federally drawn plan that included a new training and reporting program, as well as an improved oversight strategy for the entire department.

During the past three years, Seattle PD has endured intense public scrutiny. The department has not only gone through four chiefs but also recently appointed a fifth chief, Kathleen O'Toole, on June 23, 2014. O'Toole, a former chief in Boston, became the first female to hold this position in Seattle.

Chief O'Toole is facing a daunting endeavor; more than 120 Seattle officers have filed a lawsuit challenging the department's new, federally mandated use-of-force policies that were put into place under the terms of the reform program. She has publicly announced not only a firm commitment to restore civic trust but also a willingness to reestablish an acceptable level of pride in the officers of the organization. Chief O'Toole is motivated to win back her officers through an intensive, hands-on approach, sans litigation. This will not be an easy task. The actions of a few coupled with bad publicity have greatly contributed to overall poor citizen perception of this department.

Naturally everyone antes in on the topic when a department suffers such intense media exposure. Restaurants and taverns are filled with people discussing the latest *news reports*. Heated discussions commonly include exclamations of "they need to just fire the chief!" The effects are real; our citizens are full of frustration.

A cloud of doubt and mistrust develops when citizens are repeatedly exposed to the media hammering images into their heads. When the DOJ comes to town and becomes involved in any department's affairs, isn't it only natural for the general public to question and mistrust the local police? There may be a few reports that indicate constitutional violations, where the police have obviously failed to practice professionalism and restraint. The media targets the heated exchanges between police and loud and angry citizens. At that point, is it any wonder that people, out of desperation, want to fire the chief?

Brian O'Neill (2014), a Tacoma police officer and former Tacoma News Tribune contributor of a column known as the *Blue Byline*, has noted that "the legal definition of necessary force does not come complete with a million examples; it's simply one long sentence. That makes it open to interpretation by people with broadly different mindsets. But such is life in a free country." O'Neill has a valid point; many times the political rhetoric behind the scenes spills over the edge of common sense, leaving nothing but a trail of officer dissatisfaction and civil disobedience in its wake. After all, no one wants to be on the receiving end of the *blame game.*

Reporting to work each and every day in a department rife with controversy and political unrest must be extremely difficult. To weather this type of storm, every officer in the department is required to display a bravado of strength at all times. And without question, to deflect all of the residual media blowback on the streets, it is surely an enormous test to perpetually act like "one of the good guys," a "good example," or at the very least field the barrage of personal questions with patience and class. How tiring!

We are all well aware that the media for their actions would be classified as sharks. A moment of poor judgment, or one bad decision, and a good cop can suddenly be demoted or fired for their actions. Regrettably, in the media today, there is a common theme: police officers caught on tape in a serious encounter that inevitably makes the officers look bad, and they are immediately exploited on social media. The media will continuously show the clip over and over again, showing angry crowds gathering at a scene of the alleged incident, often making out more of the story than need be. Often police officers are not given the chance to present their take on the encounter, nor are they even aware that bystanders are capturing their every movement on video or audio. But that's too bad, and once it's out there, no one can unring that bell. Once again, the general public has spoon-fed its mind-set to dislike the cops. What a shame!

In today's world, it takes a unique individual to enter the field of law enforcement; in many ways, it is a gamble with fate. Although every profession has its ups and downs, police work is another story entirely. Things can easily turn on a dime even if an officer does every single thing to the best of his ability, every single day of his career. One negative "tweet," or one out-of-context video that makes its rounds on social media (which ultimately is finding its way via "trending" onto the national news), will negatively influence the way our citizens view a police department and, to some, the entire law enforcement profession.

Ferguson: It's Too Early to Demonize or Canonize by Brian O'Neill

In the conflicting narratives about the shooting of Michael Brown in Ferguson, Missouri, Officer Darren Wilson is either a rogue who killed an unarmed man or a heroic survivor. Brown is either a martyr to the vile practice of racial profiling or else a dangerous felon shot while attacking a cop. Why the need to demonize or canonize at this point? We have heard that Brown, a young African-American man, robbed a convenience store minutes before Officer Wilson stopped him while he and a friend were walking down the middle of a street. We have also been told that Brown shoved Wilson back inside his car, injuring him, and then attempted to take the officer's duty weapon. It supposedly fired and Brown fled. He was then shot numerous times, allegedly while surrendering to Wilson.

Nearly every aspect of the confrontation is disputed by witnesses and police, yet many people have made up their minds about what happened. That defies logic. The dynamic events leading up to a police shooting are a layer of subtle microevents that form a coherent picture only when pieced together. In much the same way, the Big Bang cannot be adequately explained without breaking it into nanoseconds; every nuance leading up to a shooting must be dissected before it can be understood. Let's consider two disputed details: Was Brown unarmed? If it is shown that he did lay his hands on Wilson's duty gun, his lack of a weapon of his own isn't necessarily a decisive factor. (And if he let go of the gun and backed away, should a reasonable person assume he wouldn't try again?) Did Wilson shoot Brown when his hands were raised? If so, it's hard to imagine a justification for the use of deadly force.

As a former police officer, the most frustrating condemnation of police came from columnist Leonard Pitts, Jr. Pitts invoked the spirit of Atticus Finch, demanding that we climb into the skin of another person and walk around in it before rendering judgment. Missing was any admission that cops have skin, too. Two brief examples from my own career: In the first, my partner and I were chasing a wanted felon, a 6-foot, 350-pound gang member known to have carried weapons in the past. I found him first and drew my gun. This massive young man challenged me, closing the distance between us in seconds. Though his hands were empty, at his side he was a step away from putting his hands on my weapon. No time to draw a less lethal weapon, no time to reholster. Do I shoot an unarmed man? Fortunately, my partner arrived. After a lengthy fight, we arrested him. I still do not know what I would have done had he not shown up.

The second incident involved a preteen boy who had allegedly used a knife in a robbery against another kid. When I found the suspect and his mother at home, I politely attempted to address the issue. She heaped abuse on me, calling me a "f-ing pig" and "stupid cracker," among other choice names. I endured it in silence for 10 straight minutes until my sergeant arrived, listened briefly, and then told me to walk away. The score: hatred 1, justice 0. None of this is meant to excuse the police response in Ferguson. The cops share much of the blame for the subsequent riots. We learned in the 1990s, when Tacoma's Hilltop was awash in gunfire and gangs, that handcuffs and jail are merely a tourniquet. The real remedy is a strong partnership between the people and their police. But that kind of partnership takes willingness to step into the skin of another, including the skin in uniform.

The Job Itself

Many officers may feel the stress of the job and are in denial regarding their feelings. Officers may feel overwhelmed by circumstances or problems that have occurred in their career, family, or personal life, and they do not want to speak with anyone about these issues. Officers may be scared to seek any type of professional assistance. This can be detrimental to a police officer in many ways. In the officer's mind, it is a Catch-22 situation. When an officer is psychologically unfit for duty, he may be asked to relinquish their weapon and ID, and cannot perform the job as a police officer. Requesting psychological help can leak out to just one person, rumors spread, and there is no telling the reaction by fellow officers. Just the stigma and being labeled by comrades, superiors, or police management as possibly unstable or having psychological issues may cause other officers to shun or not want to work with the officer. Other officers may view him or her as a liability on the street. The stigma is there and it will never go away. Also, the officer may not be able to work side jobs that are security based, because he cannot carry a weapon, causing a financial burden as well. It may take the officer a considerable amount of time to go through the process and attain help for his problems. One problem now has escalated and has created many additional issues that the officer must embrace.

Superintendent Terry Hillard said that seeking help due to stress- and job-related issues is recommended. Asking for emotional help in a time of crisis is not weakness. It should not be held against an officer if he wishes to discuss issues that are bothering him. Emotional issues should not be bottled up and kept a secret. Officers need to let someone know they are in crisis. Anderson (2014) said that more than any other occupation, law enforcement is an emotionally and physically dangerous job. Police officers continually face the effects of murder, violence, accidents, and disasters. Rotating shifts, long hours, and exposure to life's tragedies exact a heavy toll on police officers and their families. The results are alarming: high divorce rates, suicide, domestic violence, heart attacks, cancer, depression, and alcoholism. Law enforcement, the media, and the public foster the myth that police officers can experience trauma and violence without suffering any ill effects. Research has shown just the opposite: when stressors are prolonged and overwhelming, an individual's ability to cope becomes difficult.

Paul's Story

Officer Paul stated that "many officers feel that suicide is something the department just sweeps under the table, like it just doesn't exist. It is rarely talked about, but you know it's there. There is a lot of stress being a cop. I relieve stress by working out, and that makes me feel better. Some officers that I have worked with are struggling to make ends meet. I know they are burning the candle at both ends. They go to work, then to a side job; by the time they get home, they clean up and barely get enough sleep before they report for duty the next day. The officers are sleepy, tired, and crabby. Their routine turns into months then years. They are running on "empty" for most of their police careers. Eventually has to take its toll. It is not good for their bodies, their family life, or the citizens that they are protecting; I am always worried who is going to assist me if I ever need back up...it's scary. The other day I heard about a Sgt. killing himself. I heard he was a pretty decent guy and an understanding supervisor. It's a shame; I heard that he was having money issues with his ex-wife; she was taking him to court again for additional child support. He supposedly gave his little girl everything. Depression and stress takes a toll on you both mentally and physically."

The Starfish Story, Adapted from the *Star Thrower* by Loren Eiseley (1907–1977)

Once upon a time, there was a wise man who used to go to the ocean to do his writing. He had a habit of walking on the beach before he began his work. One day, as he was walking along the shore, he looked down the beach and saw a human figure moving like a dancer. He smiled to himself at the thought of someone who would dance to the day, and so, he walked faster to catch up.

As he got closer, he noticed that the figure was a young man and that what he was doing was not dancing at all. The young man was reaching down to the shore, picking up small objects, and throwing them into the ocean. He came closer still as I called out, "Good morning! May I ask what it is that you are doing?" The young man paused, looked up, and replied "Throwing starfish into the ocean."

"I must ask, then, why are you throwing starfish into the ocean?" asked the somewhat startled wise man. To this the young man replied, "The sun is up and the tide is going out. If I don't throw them in, they'll die." Upon hearing this, the wise man commented, "But young man, do you realize that there are miles and miles of beach and there are starfish all along every mile? You can't possibly make a difference!"

At this the young man bent down, picked up another starfish, and threw it into the ocean. As it met the water, he said, "It made a difference to that one."

Making a Difference

In Chicago in 2013, the Chicago Police Department thankfully did not lose any officers in the line of duty, but regretfully the Chicago Police Department lost six of its police officers to suicide. This National Study of Police Suicides (NSOPS) noted that police suicides continue at a rate much higher than the number of police officers killed by felons. Recent studies indicate that police suicide is seven times the national norm and it is the ninth leading cause of death in the United States. In 2012, the average age for suicides among police officers was 42 years old, with 16 years on the job.

Most, if not all, police officers have joined this profession because they want to help people. We have a tendency to store up our emotions and not share the fear, frustration, anger, and rage that we see every day. As officers, there is some sort of emotional attachment on every job. We often bottle up our emotions on the ills associated with law enforcement. We are human; we should be allowed to cry, but when was the last time that you saw an officer cry in public? We are taught skills to keep us alive on the streets, but our training in emotional survival needs to be incorporated as well. How nice it would be for you to walk up to a police officer today and thank him or her for doing the job that they do and keeping society safe!

As a police officer with over 20 years of experience and service with the Chicago Police Department, I have a genuine understanding of what a police officer encounters and endures on a daily basis. Law enforcement is a difficult and dangerous profession and officers need to unleash their emotional fears and struggles that have mounted over the course of time. I have seen my share of traumatic incidents that have been etched in my memory forever. I have personally witnessed stabbings, shootings, suicides, homicides, and countless people severely injured or killed in car accidents. Every critical incident is an emotional weight that accumulates over time, slowly but surely, until the officer becomes depressed, psychologically overloaded, and stressed out. As officers before me and after me, we have all been affected by our career vocation.

Suicide is the leading cause of death for police. An officer takes his own life every 18–20 hours. There is no question that there are more officers who die from suicide than those killed in the line of duty. One question that many officers may ask silently is what is the department doing to prevent this silent killer? Police departments from day one of the academy are preparing officers to be ready and prepared for the street. For whatever reason, there are many police agencies that do not directly address suicide. They do little, if anything, to prepare the officer for the emotional roller coaster ride that many police officers will experience in their career. Physical fitness and police tactics are paramount for an officer to stay alive on the streets, but emotional well-being and the officer's psychological fitness are just as important. A few larger police departments have programs that address an officer's emotional stability, but many smaller agencies fall short in this category. Police administrators should ensure that they are just as dedicated to officer survival tactically, but be able to provide emotional reinforcement as well.

I decided that if this book saves just one police officer's life (just like the starfish story—if I can make a difference in just one officer's life, I still made a difference), all of my effort in writing it was well worth my time. I would also like this book to assist any family member to seek counseling and speak with someone in EAP. It is a free service and one that should be taken advantage of. Communication is imperative in any relationship but especially to a relationship where your significant other is a police officer. I would also like to share this book with law enforcement and the general public so they understand the mind-set of police officers and what we encounter and experience every day, on or off the job. Thanks for reading this book, I hope you enjoy it.

References

Anderson, B., Police suicide: Understanding grief and loss, Metropolitan Police EAP, www.giftfrom within.org.

O'Neill, B. (2014). *The Tacoma News Tribune*. Blue Byline.

O'Neill, B. *Tacoma News Tribune*, a former South Sound police officer, is a former reader columnist, September 8, 2014. Ferguson: It's Too Early to Demonize or Canonize.

Welcome to the Police Academy

1

RON RUFO

Contents

Bravery is not the absence of fear, but the mastery of it.

—**John Berridge**

Welcome to the Police Academy

The police academy was what I expected, a paramilitary environment that commanded the respect and discipline needed to do the job as a police officer.

I loved the classroom environment, military-like instructions, and formalities. A large book of rules and regulations, followed by policies and procedures, was handed out the first day of class. This book is the virtual bible for every police officer, from the first day at the police academy to the last day on the job. The police recruits are instructed to sign a release form stating that they have received his copy of the general orders. In signing their names, they are acknowledging that they will read, understand, and do what is expected of them at all times, on and off duty. Signing the release form protects the police department from liability. Just like the law, ignorance of what is required by the officer is not an excuse. When new orders are written, they either incorporate police formalities that have not been dealt with before or update outdated orders to reflect what police are experiencing today. Any and all infractions that involve police misconduct are specifically addressed, from minor infractions that can be handled with verbal and/or written warnings to more serious infractions involving escalating levels of discipline or from verbal and/or written warnings to time off, suspension, or possible firing.

Police officers do not live normal lives. What would be considered normal by most people in society would most likely no longer be considered normal to those in law enforcement. From the first day of class, the police recruit begins a transformational change in behavior, and it will not take long for the recruit to change his way of thinking, and a definite change in his identity will occur. The instructors in the police academy will teach each new recruit to abandon everything that he has learned and that was considered normal throughout his life. Now, the recruits are in the business of speculation, deceit, and deception. Dr. Alaimo* said, "Step back and look from the perspective of day one at the Police Academy training. Police recruits are overwhelmed with the image of almost a super person. The reality of day-to-day life in law enforcement is not conveyed in terms of the need for self-care. Going back to the basics, we talk about the need for balance in the initial days of training."

Police recruits do not realize what lies in store for them in the next 25 weeks of training. The training and tactics that are presented to the new recruits are meant to reinforce survival skills that are instrumental in keeping the officer alive. New recruits are placed into a variety of scenarios that will guide them into being safe as they are handling and *controlling* the situation. This type of training, "not trusting anyone and always being in control," that is drilled into officers may be considered dysfunctional in relation to how most citizens live. Most children are encouraged at a young age to basically trust one another as they are growing up. Parents do not necessarily teach their children to be suspicious of everyone they encounter. This way

---

* Alaimo, Sr. Carl, PsyD., Personal interview.

of thinking, to trust no one and always be in control, is considered dysfunctional by many psychologists and myself. Yes, I said it, *dysfunctional*.

These same skills will eventually cause emotional scarring if this is the only training that he receives. The officer may be able to survive the streets, but will not be able to survive his own emotions, causing havoc with his personal well-being. What happens when an officer goes home after his shift? He has to do a complete 180° turn and act like a normal person. Again, who is minding the officer's *well-being*? The Chicago Police Department did not lose any officers in the line of duty so far this year (and I am grateful for that), but it saddens me that we lost six active duty officers to suicide in 2013, and two active duty officers in 2014 as of this writing.

Phil Cline* is considered a policeman's policeman by many in the Chicago Police Department. He compares the career of a police officer to that of a marathon athlete. From the first day in the police academy to the first day of retirement, it is a race to stay healthy physically and emotionally. He loved his job, even though it was stressful and sad at times. From the first day at the Police Academy, new recruits begin the journey of incorporating their own distorted perceptions regarding everyone and everything they encounter. Terry Hillard† revealed that, in the police academy, he strongly recommends that new recruits bring in their immediate families, for them to see what the new officers will be experiencing in their career. There needs to be communication, and the recruits need to be open and candid about the problems and issues they will eventually encounter as officers.

Recruits will soon realize that

- They are now the warrior
- They must stay focused and in charge
- They must be strong, never showing that they are weak
- They should never show emotion or fear
- It is now them (police) against them (society)
- They will serve and protect
- They will have, above all else, integrity

Dr. John Violanti‡ noted that the process of change from civilian to police officer is very strong in basic police training and continues to dominate officers' lives throughout their careers. Just ask any police officer and he will tell you that "police work gets in your blood. You become it and it becomes you." Socialization into the police role begins early in police training, which attempts to instill a sense of superhuman emotional strength in officers

---

* Cline, Phil, Personal interview.
† Hillard, Terry, Personal interview.
‡ Violanti, John, PhD, Personal interview.

(Violanti, 1996). From the very first day in the police academy, recruit officers are told that they are someone unique, far different from the average citizen and certainly beyond harm. During training, police recruits are further reinforced with skills of self-defense, "talking people down," street survival techniques, and extended firearms use. In addition, they are well armed and protected with bulletproof vests. By the time recruits leave the police academy, they are strongly ingrained into the police role. Given this research, it appears that police officers, through psychological and physiological mechanisms, become ingrained in police work and isolated from other life roles such as family, friendships, or community involvement. Subsequent psychological depression and social isolation may result. Police behavior is constrained and shaped by others in the system: judicial decisions, legislation, the media, and special interest groups. Common in police structures are military-style rank positions, specific work roles, and impersonal work relationships. The police organization is unique from others because of the intensity with which it restricts officers into their work role—intensity resulting from rather powerful combinations of militaristic and bureaucratic control methods (Violanti, 1996).

Jeff Murphy* pointed out that many officers coming into law enforcement are unaware of the stress that is actually associated with the job. He stated that a police officer's social contract states: "I am the police, you are not." Murphy recalls right out of the police academy many seasoned officers maintained that the three Bs will kill you on this job: bullets, booze, and broads. Since then, there has been a change in the training regimen, including a higher level of professionalism. From the first day at the police academy, recruits learn to be in control at all times, stay alert, and trust no one. Their safety is paramount. James Morrison, Law Enforcement Treatment Consultant for American Addiction Centers, explained, "An officer is taught from the first day he comes into the Police Academy that he has to be in control. If not it could cost him his life, but the officer has to realize he must share that control to get back to living life on life's terms." This is a dysfunctional approach because human beings are taught at a young age to basically trust one another as they are growing up. Parents do not necessarily teach their children to be suspicious of everyone they encounter. The training and tactics that are presented to the new recruits are meant to reinforce survival skills that are instrumental in keeping the officer alive but may eventually cause emotional scarring. The officer may be able to survive the streets, but will not be able to survive his own distorted emotions and crumbling sense of well-being. The Chicago Police Department did not lose any officers in the line of duty in 2013 (and I am grateful for that), but it saddens me that we did lose six officers to suicide.

---

* Murphy, Jeff, Personal interview.

These survival tactics may keep the officers alive on the streets, but they will have a caustic effect on their relationships if they are not prepared to leave the job at work. The officer's view of the world will change. An enthusiastic new recruit and young officer may gradually develop a negative outlook on life by seeing the worst in people and experiencing the hardships of the job. His life is constantly on the line; he lives in fear, leery of either a stranger or familiar face that approaches him. This cynicism eventually begins to overwhelm the seasoned officer. He does not trust anyone and complains about management and the administration, and family life can virtually become nonexistent. There is a lack of communication and the officer spends more and more time with the people who understand him—other police officers.

Rookies face a variety of social and family issues early in their careers. Relationships with friends (civilians) often begin to wane or become nonexistent. Having less in common diminishes past bonds as the rookies' relationships with their new family and friends (mostly all police officers) fall into place. Police work begins to shape and influence his behavior. Eventually, every individual will fall into one of four distinct categories for police officers: (1) police friends, (2) family, (3) victims, and (4) offenders.

To Serve and Protect

Police officers enter the police academy with high hopes and a desire to be the best police officers and serve the people in their communities. There is a lot of meaning and integrity behind the motto "to serve and protect." The motto associated with law enforcement is seen on the doors of thousands of police vehicles across America as every officer takes the pledge of office "to serve and protect." This statement clearly defines the commitment to the community, and it is the very backbone of every law enforcement agency in the nation. Being a police officer is often a thankless job that most Americans expect and take for granted on a daily basis. How many times will an officer hear "my taxes pay your salary"? Police officers are complimented and thanked from time to time, and speaking from experience, it is nice to hear appreciation for a job well done.

Hiram Grau* articulated that police officers are as dedicated today as they were when he first became a patrolman. To be a police officer is a tribute to that officer's sincere love for the job. There is still a bond between police officers today as there was in the past. That will never change. The reason is that police officers rely on one another, especially in the difficult times. There will always be a certain number of police officers who are not happy in their career choice, but then there is discontent in every profession.

* Grau, Hiram, Personal interview.

Bill Hogewood* noted that in the early days of being a police officer, "you joined the department where you lived and you joined for the job, not necessarily for the pay and benefits." He indicated that most young men (there were few female officers in 1969) who became police officers did it for the challenge and joy of working in law enforcement. "As recruits we were not sure about salary, or the perks and benefits of the job, nor did we care. As a police officer you had 6 bullets in your revolver and 12 in your belt. You were by yourself. We had no portable radios, just stationary radios in the squad cars. So when we got a call and left the squad, we had no way to communicate with anyone especially for backup, which was sometimes 30 to 40 minutes away at best. We had 450 officers on the job when I first started my career in Prince Georges County, Maryland, and now we have over 1700 officers covering the same area we did. I can honestly say the nature of the job was different than it is today." Hogewood emphasized that from the first day at the police academy, officers were encouraged to be strong, not showing weakness or displaying any emotion. The instructors told the recruits to "stuff their feelings" inside and keep their feelings to themselves. Don't show emotions. They insinuated that showing your emotions was perceived as a weakness. Lastly, instructors told the novice officers to never share any harmful or negative incidents with their families and keep them out of their work. I definitely see a difference from when I first started the job as a policeman in 1969 to today's young officer. It seems that many young people who are interested in law enforcement see working part time and having a take home car as major enticements. Many take any job offered and there are not as many *homegrown police officers*. Hogewood commented that the difference from when he first started to today's young officers is their sense of entitlement. He said, "New recruits appear to only be concerned about the money, benefits, and a take home car before they work their first shifts on the street. That was the farthest thing from our mind ... our hearts led us."

Father Dan Brandt† believes that everyone accepting the job as a police officer knows the risk involved; it is part of the equation when they apply for the job. Police officers are trained to survive, self-preservation, at all cost. They see more atrocities and crimes during a shift than most people see in a lifetime. They serve the public in the best way that they know how, often dealing with undesirable people (offenders) and unpleasant situations (homelessness and victims of crimes). Most often, police officers are looked upon with respect for the job that they are committed to, but the years working the streets take their toll. Can law enforcement become routine? The problem that most officers insist will never happen, but sometime does, is that the job

---

* Hogewood, Bill, Personal interview.
† Brandt, Father Daniel, Personal interview.

is not as exciting as it once was. Police officers deal with the extremes on a daily basis. An officer may be involved in a heroic act one day and the next day be involved in one of the worse tragedies he has ever seen. The highs are high and the lows are low.

While there are varying theories and descriptions of the police subculture, several characteristics and themes appear to be common. A socialization process takes place in the new officer's journey from ordinary citizen to sworn protector. Often, the result is a sense of isolation from the rest of society. A theme of solidarity forms as a means of coping with isolation. As behavior is controlled and inhibited by formal sources such as organizational structure, laws, and administrators, officers turn to the informal subculture for understanding and relief. Both, however, call strongly for conformity with existing guidelines. Officers learn that invisibility or *laying low* can further protect them from an increasingly critical world. These themes may provide useful insight into the prevention of police suicides in two ways. First, some of these characteristics may add to the potential for police suicides. They may increase conflicts with others, enhance levels of stress, contribute to the deterioration of relationships, and produce feelings of isolation. Second, they may hinder or prevent the timely detection and reporting of cases where police officers may be susceptible to, or even contemplating, suicide. This includes both cases of self-reporting and the reporting of others.

Retired Police Officer Augie Battaglia* claims that he feels sorry for the young officers today because of the seniority bid process implemented in most police departments. Today, because of seniority, many of the older officers are working days or in districts that are less dangerous. Battaglia said that inexperienced officers are working with police officers who only have a few years on the job. He believes that that is a huge mistake. Battaglia feels that young officers need the insight and knowledge that only a seasoned veteran can teach them. Battaglia stated, "Back when I was a police officer, people respected you and you were able to do your job as policemen. When I was a young officer you were acknowledged for a job well done, not only by your fellow officers but by your supervisors and the command staff. An officer may have been promoted because of his efforts. Today many officers see no benefit in going above and beyond the call of duty, due to politics within the department and especially in regard to being promoted. Another factor that concerns many officers today is the likelihood of being sued, both personally and professionally, especially with everyone using camera phones, taking videos of officers just doing their job."

* Battaglia, Augie, Personal interview.

Police Culture: Training to Survive the Streets

Police departments across the United States pride themselves on preparing their officers to face physical and verbal situations out on the street. The tactical preparation increases and intensifies as the weeks go by in the police academy. The use-of-force control model emphasizes how to handle a passive or active resistor, or an offender who displays a weapon. The physical training is intense and demanding.

The major focus of any officer's life is survival to see another day, and it is instilled in every aspect of police training. Police officers are taught to survive on the streets at all cost and that training is reinforced throughout their career. They live every day with the threat of something happening to them, leading to threat-based thoughts and perceptions and heightened sensitivity to situations. Police officers deal with many unknown factors and variables in their attempts to carry out their job, handle a situation, or investigate an incident. Every situation, no matter how innocent it may seem, is potentially dangerous and can become deadly in an instant. Officers can suffer a serious injury or even death during what began as a routine encounter.

It may not take long after leaving the police academy to realize that the job of being a law enforcement officer can wear even the most prepared officer down. According to the U.S. Department of Justice (2007), in a study conducted by Hughes and Andre (2007), there are five personality characteristics that enable a police officer to perform well. A police candidate may possess all five of these traits, but if he cannot handle stress, he is not considered a good match and may not make the best police officer:

1. Extrovert, being outgoing
2. Emotional stability
3. Agreeable
4. Conscientious
5. Open to experience

The study found there are other factors or variables that may be of importance in the selection process of new officers. The police agency should also look for individuals who are willing to work in high-crime areas and accept the police agency's administrative philosophy and structure. Henry (2004) specified that the process of *becoming* a police officer—of both acquiring a police self-identity and being recognized and accepted by others as a police officer—involves the interplay of social and psychological factors, and the social context should not be ignored. The social conflicts and pressures the rookie faces have multiple dimensions that involve the rookie's relationships with family and friends as well as relationships with other officers and the civilian clientele encountered in his work. The conflicts and pressures alter his social relationships with all these people, and in terms of his internal psychological life, they shape and influence his evolving sense of a professional or occupational self. In this chapter, my goal is to delineate the social settings and contexts that shape the images and experiences involved in the rookie's overall identity change.

A police officer's job is literally compared to visiting an amusement park every day and riding a new roller coaster—never knowing what to expect or what is behind the next turn. From the highest highs to the lowest lows, every day the constant feeling of not knowing of what lays ahead is often exhilarating.

The highs: These include the adrenaline rush of a call in progress and the excitement of what police work entails. Police officers must always be on their game, emotionally prepared, and aware of their surroundings and the situation they may ride up to or that develops. They must always be emotionally charged and always be *on the job*. Most often, the officer will only share what happens with other officers. They will understand because they can relate to each other. The officer has two families, his police family (who understands him) and his family at home (from whom he often keeps most information).

The lows: These include the sinking feeling of a fatality being pulled out of a vehicle that was totaled in an accident. When officers go home, they often are drained both physically and emotionally. One problem that may occur is a communication breakdown. The officer does not want to share what he has experienced throughout the day. The lack of communication and/or not sharing what they have experienced with their significant other or families becomes apparent. Days turn into weeks, weeks into months, and months into years. All the officer wants to do is be left alone, not make any decisions, and watch TV. An apparent pattern soon develops as many officers all too often become emotionally drained at the end of the shift. It is not unusual for them to become lethargic off-duty.

Seven "Cs" of Street Survival

Remsberg (2008) has put together a number of words that will assist an officer in having the winning mindset in order for him to survive on the street. He distinguished seven words that begin with the letter "C" that highlight street survival:

1. *Courage*: Valor, heroism
2. *Confidence*: Assurance, conviction, loyalty, assertion
3. *Cognitive*: Intellectual, perceptive, rational

4. *Control*: Direction, influence, constraint
5. *Concentration*: Attentiveness, focus
6. *Cohesion*: Structure, consistency, organization
7. *Commitment*: Loyalty, dedication, responsibility

Imminence of Violence: Responding to Internal and External Stimuli

Every officer on the street relies on his training, but in essence, he relies on his autonomic nervous system (ANS), which supports his perception of the potential threats and dangers he encounters. The ANS consists of the sympathetic nervous system (SNS) and the parasympathetic nervous system (PNS). The ANS offers coordinated effort to keep the body ready when needed in a dangerous situation (SNS) and more relaxed in a nonconfrontational or normal state (PNS).

The SNS is responsible for the quick responses police officers have to make. It induces a sympathetic response, an immediate and unconscious response that prepares the police officer for imminent and likely danger and/or threatening behavior. This part of the nervous system activates what is known as the *fight or flight* response. In response to a dangerous situation, the SNS releases adrenaline into the body. Adrenaline increases the heart rate, increases blood pressure, and allows the officer to become more energetic and challenging in his response to the danger at hand.

The PNS is the direct opposite of the SNS. It promotes a balance in the body that regulates blood pressure and heart rate. This is the part of the nervous system that helps the police officer return to a normal state after he has experienced a stressful, difficult, or painful situation or encounter.

Gut Feeling (the Sixth Sense)

Gut feeling is what most people call the *sixth* sense. In my opinion, within the first 10 seconds after encountering someone, you automatically judge that person. Everyone has the gift of intuition and perception. Police officers are constantly in tune with their gut feelings. In every encounter with the public, they will use their five senses to assess the situation for any suspicious behavior or visual irregularities. Our five senses also assist in allowing us to *tune in* to our intuition. Police officers use this instinctive and emotional ability to dissect the situation that is evolving in front of them. They have a tendency to always be on alert, and they rarely let their guard down, especially in situations that indicate there may be even a slight hint of danger.

Intuition is the process of synthesizing and deducing from all of our accumulated unconscious experiences. Therefore, we know more than we realize. According to the Peaceful Mind website, intuition can be defined as "the ability to sense or know immediately without reasoning." Cholle (2011) described gut feeling—or a hunch—as a sensation that appears quickly in one's consciousness (noticeable enough to be acted on if one chooses) without being fully aware of the underlying reasons for its occurrence. Cholle acknowledged that intuition is a process that gives us the ability to know something directly without analytic reasoning, bridging the gap between the conscious and unconscious parts of our mind and also between instinct and reason.

What may be considered normal by most people in society may not be considered normal by law enforcement personnel. Law enforcement officers incorporate negative thinking and distrust in almost every situation they encounter. They deal with many people who call the police mostly for service with problems that they have encountered. Police also encounter criminal offenders and the destructive aftermath of their behavior. This persistent negative viewpoint is reinforced on a daily basis. This negativity and lack of trust are seen as a distorted sense of perception.

To prove my point, I tried an experiment with two distinct and different criminal justice classes that I was teaching. I asked each group to take out a sheet of paper. I told them that I was going to give them a word or occupation and they were to write down the first thing that came to their mind, whatever they thought or conceptualized in their mind. One class was at Westwood College in Chicago. This class consisted of young college students pursuing their bachelor's degree in a variety of fields in the criminal justice profession. They were in class to become juvenile and adult probation officers and to be in corrections positions or jail guards, and a few students were interested in becoming police officers. The other criminal justice class was at Calumet College. This entire class consisted of police officers returning to school to attain their bachelor's degree, most of whom were in class because of the tuition reimbursement program or because they were interested in being promoted or for their own personal accomplishments.

I asked each class what the first thing that came to their mind was when I mentioned *Boy Scout leader*. The comments from the students at Westwood College were 95% positive regarding their feelings toward Boy Scout leaders. Some of the comments were that Boy Scout leaders were good with kids, dedicated, committed, and basically giving their time and energy to help young men become better members of the society. When I asked the class that was made up of all police officers, I was really not surprised by their response. Their comments were completely opposite from the Westwood College class. The entire class, 100% of the officers, said or strongly implied that *all* Boy Scout leaders were sexual predators, pedophiles, and sexual deviates, who could never be trusted with anyone.

Police Chief Kent Williams

I attended a suicide prevention seminar for law enforcement and peer support personnel in the early part of February 2013. The police chief of Bartlett, Illinois, Kent Williams*, shared his experience with police culture and the trauma surrounding police suicide. He shared his informative and personal insight on how police handle his daily routine of working on the street, dealing with management, and trying to maintain a normal life at home. Williams compared society to a picture of a sheepherder looking over the flock of sheep, sheepdogs, and wolves. Here are Williams's depiction and symbols relating to the picture:

- *Flock of sheep*: The flock of sheep represents the good and decent people in our society. Statistics show that most people in society are law abiding and respect the police. He noted that 93%–95% of civilians would be considered law abiding.
- *The sheepdog*: The sheepdogs in the picture represent the police officers. These sheepdogs are keeping an eye on the flock. A few of them are seen nipping at the heels of some of the sheep in the flock. The nipping of the heels may indicate how the police have to keep citizens in line possibly by writing tickets and keeping law and order.
- *The wolves*: The wolves represent the true criminals in our society. Chief Williams explained that the job of the police officer often focuses on the worst, dealing with the bad or evil element of society on a daily basis. About 5%–7% of Americans would be considered corrupt and immoral and are often repeat offenders. Their intent is to hurt, kill, rob, or commit any act of violence with wanton disregard. These crimes include battery, burglary, fraud, domestic violence, and homicide. The intent is there and could be either premeditated or spontaneous.
- *The sheepherder*: The sheepherder represents the police administration, keeping a watchful eye on the police.

Time Increments on the Job

One to Four Years on the Job in Law Enforcement (4-Year Time Frame)

After graduating from the police academy, almost every rookie police officer is enthusiastic about his new career and eager to prove and demonstrate

---

* Williams, Kent, Personal interview.

he is worthy of serving his community. The first 4 years are a true learning experience for the young officer. He wants to be a law enforcement officer and is most likely fulfilling a dream or a passion that has finally come true. He may have just finished his probationary period and is in the inquisitive and learning stage of his career. He is excited to be at work and often arrives early, prepared to work, and does not mind staying late if needed. He is acceptant of his role and wants to make law enforcement his career.

These officers have a tendency to be younger and do not have issues taking or following orders given to them by their superiors or even by older officers on the job. These young officers rarely complain, do not want to cause a commotion, and are often more tolerant of the general public. They listen, take notes, and try to follow closely what they have learned in the police academy. Older, more experienced officers admire their enthusiasm and will comment under their breath how things will evolve. It is not uncommon to hear, "Just wait, kid, that will change."

Five to Ten Years on the Job in Law Enforcement (5-Year Time Frame)

These officers are past the newness stage in their careers. They have been on the streets; they have experienced good and bad behaviors from citizens, victims, and offenders. They begin to see their job more as routine, answering calls and dealing with the same types of people (either victims or offenders). It has become a little less fun than when they first started, and they are not as enthusiastic as they once were about coming to work. They have experienced changes at work that they were not expecting. They are now aware of some of the little idiosyncrasies that go on within the police department, how the system works and what they need to do to stay out of trouble. These officers may have put in several years on the job, but still may not have enough seniority to get their desired watch, shift, day off, or vacation. At this stage of their career, they may have the best chance of being promoted. Retirement is still too far away even to think about.

Dr. Nancy Zarse* noted that young men and women who enter the police academy are often naïve and idealistic in their views about their profession. The first 5–7 years are thrilling and exhilarating for the officer. After the newness of the job wears off, the same officers who were once excited to come to work have become bitter and disillusioned about the job, and that same attitude continues as the years pass.

---

* Zarse, Nancy, PsyD, Personal interview.

Eleven to Seventeen Years on the Job in Law Enforcement (6-Year Time Frame)

These officers have most likely experienced a few acts of kindness that have been overshadowed by many negative acts or transgressions. Their time on the job has made them more of an authority and they are often looked up to by younger officers for advice and assistance, especially in report writing. These officers have an established working schedule, watch, or vacation. Depending on the district or precinct, watch or vacation, they have a fairly good chance of getting the bid selection they would like to have. They have experienced the criminal justice system firsthand, the wheeling and dealing of the court system. These officers have done their time, and the experience has made them stronger and better police officers or has caused them not to be so aggressive. In general, these police officers may have become more opinionated and more cynical than most people about society overall. They may begin to feel police burnout and/or may have been the victim of a few administrative transgressions. In the locker room or before or after roll call is where they may vent their anger and frustration, especially when they have a captive audience.

Seventeen to Twenty-Five Years on the Job in Law Enforcement (7-Year Time Frame)

For the most part, this group identifies with the term of being "salty" (a term for being on the job a while where the officer often has a negative attitude about everything). The officers with this much experience can relate to every incident that they were involved in, taking what they encountered and learning from the good and bad in the incident. At a party, in union meetings, or in the presence of a few officers, the officer with this much time on the job would probably start and end every conversation with a war story (some incident that happened to them that either ended well for them or bad for the offender). When I first came on the job, I heard an officer say that he was officially in the KMA club. I asked my field training officer what club that was? He said, "Kid, most of us will hopefully be in that club one day, you have a long way to go." The *KMA* club stands for "kiss my ass." This club is for police officers who have more than 20 years on the job and can retire. If they do not like something, they can submit their retirement papers and leave the department. That is the day when the officer can say goodbye to management and the department. In order to qualify for full pension, most police departments require the officer to stay on for a certain number of years (often 20 years) and be of a certain age (often 50 or older). If a police officer leaves sooner than the required time, his pension will be affected. For some, being in law enforcement is all they know and they want to stay on the job as long as they can; for others, they may be counting the days until they can turn in their star. These officers are likely thinking of retirement or are making plans to do so soon.

A few officers in every district count not only the days until they can retire or are off the job but also the time they will be off the job down to hours and minutes. An older officer, who I worked with for years, would always relate to me how many days he had left on the job. "Hi Charlie, how is it going, how much time left?" He would reply with enthusiasm, "84 days, 3 hours and 10 minutes, with my days off and holidays." He would often play the number of days left on the police department for his numbers in the lottery. This reminds me of offenders who are in prison, just waiting to get out. It is like his job as a policeman is compared to that of a prisoner in the penitentiary. They are just waiting to get released from their own personal hell. I had another police friend who retired when he was only 50 years old. He would count the number of checks before retirement. When I speak to him, he often tells me how bored he is and how he is working a few side jobs to keep busy. I know in my heart he misses the police department, even though he will not admit it.

Twenty-Six to Thirty-Three Years on the Job (8-Year Time Frame)

These officers should have prepared for retirement or will be forced to do so depending on the officer's age. They can retire at any time. Some cannot because of financial obligations, others because this is the only job that they know and retirement is not an option. Many of these officers have refused to accept the fact that their time in law enforcement is nearing the end. They have made their work experience a crusade more than a career. This group is usually the most cynical and least understanding and accepting of any changes, including directives or orders that are handed down by their superiors or by the administration. Often because of their age, this group of officers is not as patient and rarely accepts change without complaining about the new technological upsurge in law enforcement. They may have been used to writing out reports, and new computer programs pose a threat because the officers may not be as technologically savvy as the younger officer who has grown up in the computer age. It is not uncommon to hear in the locker room or before or after roll call that "this is bullshit! This is how we used to do it; management must have forgotten what it is like to be an officer and to be on the street."

Technology

Phil Cline explained that today's police are more technologically savvy and have to be smarter because the criminals are better equipped now than ever.

Another advantage of technology is implementing computer-based training. Cline stated, "Officers today have computer skills, are very knowledgeable with computers, what better way to facilitate important information and additional training to them? On the downside, social media and social networks have made it easy for officers to vent their frustrations through police blogs, remaining anonymous in their often hurtful opinions of the department or their supervisors." Bill Hogewood commented that "technology today has made the officer safer, but officers are scrutinized because of technology. Officers are now held liable and accountable for their actions because of street cameras, building surveillance and more citizens than ever that have camera phones. Reports are now streamlined on the computer, GPS is in the squad cars and radios are with the officer. This technology has changed law enforcement and sometimes may interfere with human connection."

Hiram Grau spoke of how police officers are much more advanced today, especially through technology and computers. In this profession change is constant. Today, officers have the advantage of cameras and microphones on their uniforms. He mentioned that social networking sites such as Facebook and Twitter also have been a factor in how police officers gather intelligence and are able to gather information and criminal history in their attempt to build a case surrounding an offender. Grau stated, "We have come a long way in every facet of policing. When I first started on the job, we did not have all the technology that is available to us today." Grau indicated that today's officer is under a microscope in whatever he does, especially with everyone having the capability of videotaping on their cell phones. Today, cameras are everywhere.

Camaraderie: "All for One–One for All, Officers Bond When They Share Risk"

The definition of camaraderie is the mutual trust and friendship among cohorts who spend a lot of time together. Camaraderie is often associated with law enforcement and frontline personnel. Phil Cline believed there was a special camaraderie that was associated with being a police officer, which continues today. It was fun being with the guys. They had your back on the streets and after work. Anyone who wears a badge in law enforcement circles is always considered a *brother* or *sister*. The officer could be in the same district or precinct or thousands of miles away; the term still applies. Not only does an officer have his immediate family but once he takes that oath of office, his police family will always be a part of his life. This all-inclusive police family is evident when an officer is killed *in the line of duty.*

Police officers from nearby states and beyond can be seen representing their police jurisdiction for the fallen officer. Every officer is aware of the danger he faces on a daily basis, knowing fully well that the stricken officer could easily be him. It is an officer's extended family that comes together in good times and bad.

Camaraderie is often to put to the test when an officer's actions have come into question, especially if an officer is obviously having emotional and behavioral issues. How far does an officer go to protect his brother or sister if he notices profound and unusual behavior? Will he report what he has seen to a supervisor or will he look the other way? Police expect his partners to have his back in any situation. Having an officer's back on the street is quite different than having his back when it comes to emotional problems and conflicts his partner may be experiencing. For whatever reason, most officers are leery about getting involved in his partner's *personal business*. It may be difficult for troubled officers to share what they are feeling, especially if they are hurting emotionally. An officer may hesitate to expose the problems he may be having for fear of rumors being spread. Officers oftentimes feel it is best to never admit anything that will show they are weak or vulnerable. The fear of the "word getting out" that they are emotionally unstable or the fact they are seeking counseling may cause them more grief and anguish.

Dr. Olivia Johnson (2013), founder of the Blue Wall Institute and Illinois State representative for the National Police Suicide foundation, noted that while officers display a united front, many are dealing with multiple levels of internal strife. Day in and day out, police officers spend the beginning of their shifts maneuvering through a blue sea of bureaucratic BS, personality conflicts, hidden agendas, micromanaging bosses—all before hitting the street. It seems easy enough to see how such strife could contribute to officer stress and disappointment with leadership and police work. For a culture that prides itself on shared values and cultural norms, there is certainly a lot of strife and departmental discontentment among the rank and file. So much so that many are left asking, "Are we on the same team?" Johnson believes that time and again officers are trained for what happens on the street, but not for what happens in the department. They expect the belligerent drunk and the angry driver ticketed for speeding. They even expect the occasional foot chase, bar brawl, and resisting subject. But what they are not prepared for, what they are not trained to deal with, are often the things that contribute to some of the greatest stress. So, not surprisingly, one of the greatest stressors for law enforcement personnel remains leadership. That's probably why many officers avoid the department like the plague, believing if they are out of sight, they are out of mind. Avoidance may work for a while, but who can maintain this cat and mouse game for an entire career? And better yet, who should have to?

Supervisors

> When you have a good boss, you want to do your best.—Anonymous P.O.
>
> Everyone wants that occasional pat on the back, knowing that you have done a good job.—Anonymous P.O.
>
> All bosses have their favorites; you can only hope to be one of them.—Anonymous P.O.
>
> Funny I had a supervisor who went bankrupt twice, 2 divorces, his kids hated him, his personal life was a total mess, and here he is running the ship, unbelievable.—Anonymous P.O.

An immediate supervisor or the command staff can have a dramatic effect on the stress an officer must deal with on a day-to-day basis. The officer may experience the supervisor's wrath when personalities clash. The officer may feel that he needs to deal with the anxiety instead of complaining, which may cause more problems. Another obstacle that many law enforcement officers face on a daily basis is making their immediate supervisors happy, especially if that supervisor is inflexible and demanding.

Robert Douglas Jr.* said that police officers struggle with the supervisors they encounter on a daily basis; their perception is validated that no one values them. They are looking for completeness in their life, instead of family fragmentation and alcoholism. Being appreciated and respected are components that many police officers look for in a leader, and these are what they need to be fulfilled in their line of work. It is the same mindset of a sheepherder leading his flock. The sheep follow the good shepherd, not the other way around. The perception of good leaders soon becomes reality. For leaders to be successful, they need to change their perceptions by continuing to lead in an effective manner. Leading by example is very important, but that is often not the case. How many supervisors will give an order, "I'll tell you what to do and you'll do it"? In certain situations and circumstances, this could be the best alternative, but regarding day-to-day management skills, this type of mentality is not effective. Leaders with this attitude are careless about the feelings of their subordinates. Police deal with negativity (seldom positive) on a day-to-day basis, and this reflects negativity in everything that we do. After a while, negativity ultimately takes its toll and will eventually have an impact on the officer.

Bill Hogewood stated that management was often approachable back when he was a young officer. Supervisors actually took the time to sit down with an officer who was experiencing difficulty handling a traumatic or emotionally tense event. Management was more social and supportive than today. It did not mean that we respected them any less; the respect was always there.

* Douglas, Jr., Robert, Personal interview.

An officer still respected the hierarchy and the chain of command of the department, but it was not unusual to go for a beer with the district commander after your shift. Today, I just don't see that happening. Supervisors and upper layer management seem reluctant to socialize with their subordinates. Achieving rank and holding on to an assignment often are the greater ambition than the actual job. And there are just too many managerial layers in law enforcement and too few line supervisors, affecting the span of control.

Every officer has some concerns about his immediate supervisor, likes, dislikes, and quirks, especially a new supervisor assigned to the officers' beat, district, area, or city. Whether it is a new superintendent, chief of police, or the officer's immediate supervisor, there is always some apprehension and worry. A few questions that may come up, especially at roll calls, are as follows:

- Has anyone heard anything about the new boss coming in?
- I wonder how long they have been a supervisor.
- I am wondering what they are going to change.
- Will I be able to keep the same hours (watch), beat, car, partner, or privileges that I have now?

Oftentimes, officers are forced to accept assignments or shifts they do not want. Most often, better *spots or assignments* are given to officers who have more time or are politically connected. There should be no room for politics in the police department, but I would be naïve to say that it doesn't exist. Politics has been and will always be a problem in law enforcement agencies, from promotions, preferable treatment, special assignments, preferable watches or shifts, partners, to how someone is disciplined. This is something that will never change and is just accepted.

Police Management and Administration

It is rare for an officer to escape the wrath of the "dreaded administration" at some point in his career. The police administration section is a separate entity unto itself. As many officers soon realize, it is something that they cannot control. (Remember, police are taught to be in control; our doctrine really preys upon our total being.) As much as it is needed by the department, it is often despised as well.

Management controls and hands out

- Unwanted reassignment
- Hours or shifts that need to be changed
- Days off or vacations that must be cancelled
- Compensatory time, vacation day, personal day, or day off refused

- Pending manpower issues
- Disciplinary concerns
- Policy and procedures
- Discontent regarding promotional fairness

On a lighter note, Father Brandt has been involved in the police graduation for the last years on an average of four times a year. I always have a captive audience. The command staff always sits to my right when I am up on stage. I usually give a passage from scripture when I say the invocation. The benediction is often on the lighter side, and I often joke with the young recruits telling them not to become callous, bitter, and jaded like those white shirts to my right. The crowd laughs as the command staff looks out into the crowd, not knowing how to respond.

Acknowledgment

I acknowledge that both men and women are actively involved in law enforcement, but for ease of reading, I will address everyone as the male gender.

References

Cholle, F. P. (2011). What is intuition, and how do we use it? *Psychology Today*, Published on August 31, 2011, Intuitive Compass.

Henry, V. E. (2004). *Death Work: Police, Trauma, and the Psychology of Survival.* Oxford, U.K.: Oxford University Press.

Johnson, O. (2013). Founder of the Blue Wall Institute and Illinois State representative for the National Police Suicide Foundation, Brass Versus Officers; Distrust Gets Us Nowhere.

Morrison, J. Law Enforcement Treatment Consultant for American Addiction Centers.

Peaceful Minds, Andrew Pacholyk @ www.peacefulmind.com, 917-843-3623.

Remsberg, C. (June 1995). *Tactics for Criminal Patrol: Vehicle Stops, Drug Discovery and Officer Survival; Blood Lessons: What Cops Learn From Life-or-Death Encounters,* 2008?

U.S. Department of Justice, Hughes, F. and Andre, L. B. (2007). Problem officer variables and early warning system, *The Police Chief,* 74(10), October 2007. Washington, DC: Office of Community Oriented Policing Services.

Violanti, J. M. (1996). *Police Suicide: Epidemic in Blue.* Springfield, IL: Charles C. Thomas, pp. 10–86.

Violanti, J. M., Vena, J. E., and Marshall, J. R. (1996). Suicide, homicides, and accidental death: A comparative risk assessment of police officers and municipal workers. *American Journal of Industrial Medicine,* 30, 99–104.

Police and the Three Arenas of Social Interaction

2

KENT WILLIAMS

In God we trust.
All others get your hands against the wall!

Author unknown

Every billionaire businessman who has written a book about his success will brag about the moment he realized the secret to business success. *Empower your employees!* Trust your employees and turn them loose. Put policies and systems in place that reflects this belief system. Soon the employees will predictably respond to this positive environment by behaving as if they have a vested interest in the success of the business and those who work within it. Predictably empowered and trusted employees will behave like they in fact own the business themselves, because in very spiritual and real ways, they do. If police departments were businesses, we'd all be bankrupt!

Police officers represent a rare and legitimate occupation endeavor where the better you are at what you do at work, the more likely you are to struggle or fail in all your significant relationships. Police work operates in three concurrent arenas of social interaction that is so unique to police officers. Each arena can be compared to walking three dogs, on three separate leashes, and all three pulling in different directions. Those being

1. The street
2. The police department
3. Their family and personal life

The better operator the officer is on the street (maybe even officer of the year), the more likely this same officer will struggle in the other two arenas. Can we teach our law enforcement staff to master this unique and predictable transition from an optimistic, highly trusting, and noncontrolling civilian who is highly flexible into a pessimistic, nontrusting, control freak who fights change everywhere it occurs? If this predictable transition is not mastered, it will predictably manipulate the officer, leading to what I have termed the caustic consequences of performing well in law enforcement.

Law enforcement leadership is significantly challenged. How do we explain away a body of research that attests that for every officer who dies in the line of duty, at least three officers take their own lives? Ask many senior law enforcement officials what they're urgently doing about this problem and they'll either say "I wasn't aware the problem existed" or "Sorry not my issue." The level of unintended ignorance exhibited by leadership pertaining to the wellness of their own personnel is at levels that can be described as uninformed at best, unethical at its worst.

One might understand why this dilemma could be described as uninformed, but unethical? Yes unethical. Law enforcement has a distinctly different culture than any other profession in a free society. This culture is based upon a fundamental philosophy that is trained early and often: *trust less/control more*. This mantra, although given many other names such as survival skills, defensive tactics, and weapons training, is very important to an officer. They also indoctrinate an officer into a culture where individuals are rewarded for trusting others less and controlling others more. When an officer becomes distrustful of others, he looks at them with a pessimistic perspective. This distrustful perceptual stance keeps the officer safe. It also occasionally builds a case that a deviant act against society has been or is about to be committed. However, when this personality is fully developed, usually within the first 5 years, the officer's ability to turn off his suspicions and to not control others, if left unaddressed, begins to decline.

This is where leadership should be more involved with this predictable dilemma. If law enforcement is going to continue to proactively recruit successful and socially integrated individuals (trusting/noncontrolling) into a profession, which in turn immediately teaches them that to trust and be noncontrolling is professionally unacceptable, then the ramifications of such a transformational shift in both culture and personality should be fully understood and addressed with the individuals and their significant others. To do otherwise is simply to shame young healthy people into adopting a culture that is all together foreign to them, for reasons they wrongfully believe to be in everyone's best interest.

When young officers are told to embrace an articulated vision or program that teaches them how to behave and why, without educating them regarding the possible ramifications, disaster may strike in the form of poor professional performance, unsuccessful personal relationships, and sadly occasional suicides. The vision is clear: serve and protect. If not properly and ethically addressed, how officers learn to serve and protect can destroy fundamentally important relationships and support systems. Therefore, in order to ask a team to follow you in processes and purposes that leadership articulates as important and essential, then as an industry we must first assure these processes are thoughtfully designed and implemented in the best interest of all involved. Without deeper insight into the important aspects of the police culture and personality, officers are readily encouraged and rewarded by becoming *socially dysfunctional*. Distrustful + overcontrolling = dysfunction.

Ralph Waldo Emerson said, "Our distrust is very expensive." Try to imagine any productive relationship in the absence of trust. In fact, the lack of trust is thought of first as a primary cause in any unproductive relationship. Left unchecked, this dysfunction leads to *controlling contempt*. Controlling contempt for others breeds *cynicism*, which leads to a *personal belief that everyone has a price*. Once the officer reaches this point, he is living in a very dark world, which can be described as dangerously helpless and hopeless.

Police officers are a very strong group emotionally and psychologically. After years of consistent exposures to violent untrustworthy offenders, abusive and lying spouses, battered and betrayed children, and a whole host of hoodwinked victims, their spiritual recovery from these examples of breached trust is a little slower. Officers spend most of their time alone, highly self-sufficient, wondering when the next significant crisis will come and what will it look like. Officers begin to project the behavior of the worst-case suspects upon society in general in order to be crisis ready at all times. For many officers the world begins to grow shady. Officers are paying for this filtered perspective dearly. The problem with police department culture is they are often replete with nontrusting/controlling personalities throughout all ranks, because those attributes are rewarded early and often in policing. Therefore, police departments often consist of nontrusting/controlling executives leading to nontrusting/controlling command staff, who are in charge of their nontrusting/controlling sergeants and supervisors who are in turn responsible for the actions of their nontrusting/controlling police officers and support staff. Sounds great doesn't it?

A wise and trusted mentor of mine once advised me, "Too much of a good thing is still too much." At first glance, that statement could appear overly simple. Of course I know if I eat too much ice cream (a good thing), I'll get sick (too much). You can distrust too much. You can control too much. However, upon closer observation, this statement is quite profound as it describes a very complex set of social traps insidiously set for every man and woman serving faithfully in law enforcement. I've also heard it put this way: any virtue taken to its extreme quickly becomes the vice. In short, law enforcement is replete with virtues becoming vices.

Attributes exhibited by an officer on the street may be deemed totally essential and effective, yet when interacting within a departmental setting or within his own home life, these same virtues may quickly become excessive vices, for example, when a police officer tells an upset and unpredictably intoxicated subject during a domestic dispute to "Sit down! Do it now!" This behavior would describe a competent and confident officer doing his best to keep a volatile incident under control to the best of his professional abilities. This same officer 3 h later shouting at his own children at bed time to "Brush your teeth! Do it now!" could potentially be considered verbally hostile and abusive. An officer's virtues quickly becoming vices is so common in law enforcement, I'm of the belief it serves as the foundation of most angst in the industry.

The paramount importance of demeanor transitioning is paradoxically so taken for granted that it is in fact completely misunderstood and unmastered. Can an officer drive his squad car through the various streets of his assigned beat for 8, 10, or 12 h with the personality traits he must have and never apologize for his actions? When he pulls that squad into the department parking lot and turns the squad's engine off, can he also shut down those good and necessary traits (virtues when he flips through his key ring and find the key that opens the back door to the police station, and he puts that key in the lock and open that door)? Can he in effect have a *breach point* as he crosses the threshold of the doorway, as a different person with a different set of world views and perspectives? It's difficult at best to make that transition from officer on the beat to that officer going home.

Let's take a look at a few more examples of typical police "virtues becoming vices."

Virtues		Vices
Collecting intelligence on street gangs	vs.	Partaking in gossip concerning coworkers
Controlling suspects on the street	vs.	Micromanaging your subordinates
Demanding a suspect shows their hands	vs.	Demanding your spouse cleans the house
Command bearing during bar fights	vs.	Always having to be right when at home

Too often his squad car engine gets turned off, but his perspectives do not. His good and necessary perspectives on the street follow him around both on and off duty, which are all good and necessary qualities when exhibited by a police officer *on the street*. However, when working with his colleagues in the department, or most importantly when interacting with those who care and count on him the most, which is his family at home, these same qualities become too much, often leading to frustrations, disappointments, and resentments, if not long-term damage to his most important relationships.

Let's take this analogy to its logical conclusion. An officer would not consider getting into his personnel car after his shift and driving home with those same virtues he has been using all evening. I certainly hope not. If he is fumbling through his keys to find the one that matches the lock to the rear door of his home, with the same virtuous perspectives he has been utilizing while on the street, he is set up for trouble. In fact, he must have a profound breach point when crossing the threshold of his family doorway or he will suffer immensely.

It is my personal and professional belief that most stressors experienced by police personnel can be attributed to the subtle and misunderstood nuances of various police personality traits being so important and virtuous in one-third of their lives (the street), and becoming too much of a good thing in two-thirds of their lives (the department and the personal life).

Tell Me That I Am Wrong
Who We Are versus Who We Ought to Be

3

THOMAS CLINE

Contents

> Happiness consists in fulfilling the purpose of our being.
>
> **Fulton J. Sheen**

Foundations

Reread the earlier quote by Sheen. How many people in law enforcement consider the purpose of law enforcement and their purpose within it? Have you, and if so, what is your purpose? These are tough and necessary questions if one is to have a satisfying career.

The following is the first paragraph from a Jack London short story entitled *In a Far Country*.

When a man journeys into a far country, he must be prepared to forget many of the things he has learned, and to acquire such customs as are inherent with existence in the new land; he must abandon the old ideals and the old gods, and oftentimes he must reverse the very codes by which his conduct has hitherto been shaped. To those who have the protean faculty of adaptability, the novelty of such change may even be a source of pleasure; but to those who happen to be hardened to the ruts in which they were created, the pressure of the altered environment is unbearable, and they chafe in body and in spirit under the new restrictions which they do not understand. This chafing is bound to act and react, producing divers' evils and leading to various misfortunes. It were better for the man who cannot fit himself to the new groove to return to his own country; if he delays too long, he will surely die.

London's description is an analogy for law enforcers in that entrance and acceptance in the law enforcement culture requires an examination of one's own ideals and beliefs versus the ideals and beliefs of the law enforcement culture. I do not mean the stated ideals found in codes of ethics or missions statements touted by organizations. I refer to the unwritten codes and paradigms that reward or punish behaviors of members.

If you wish to discover what the image on the next page says, look at it while holding the book parallel to your desk at eye level. A thing that at first appears confusing becomes clear. That is what this chapter attempts to do. A case is being made that a community-serving attitude is a healthier and more productive paradigm than the prevalent self-serving attitude found in organizations. The purpose of this piece is to make you think and reflect on the law enforcement culture and use logic and practical experience to draw conclusions about your place in that culture and your purpose for existing. Further, if you find this thesis makes sense, then you *ought* to discuss the ideas with peers so they may have a better career experience. The foundation of this supposition is that the laws that govern human behavior are as rigid as those governing the physical universe. These laws are discovered, mostly through human suffering. They are objective, consistent, and applicable to all people at all times. Nature bats last! Men may change laws in their legislatures, but laws governing how humans ought to treat each other do not change. It is never right to hate, murder, steal, or commit adultery. These wrongs may be declared legal but are still wrong.

Their violation results in suffering and confusion that, for individuals, are likely related to the legion of mental maladies that fostered the use of brain-altering drugs. These discovered laws, once a standard part of a liberal education, are now absent from curriculums. During the Nuremburg trials of the Nazi war criminals in 1946, the mass murderers defended their crimes by saying they were following the laws of their land, those on Germany's books. These were laws made up by the power holders, based on feelings, opinions, and the flawed part of human nature. The judges of the international court conducting the trials said, "The fact that the defendant acted pursuant to order of his government or of a superior shall not free him from responsibility." In other words, there are laws that must be obeyed that are higher than those made up by men. People that hold power have greater opportunity and temptation to violate these laws.

In Dr. Stephen Covey's course, *7 Habits of Highly Effective People* for law enforcement, there is a model called see–do–get. It influences everything in a person's life. The model says that the way we see something, our point of view or perspective on a person, place, or thing, determines what we do or how we treat the thing in question. What we do determines results, consequences, or what we get.

EINSTEIN ON INSANITY

"Insanity: doing the same thing over and over again and expecting different results"

The results people get in life depend on what they do. What people do depends on how they see their world and the people in it. The way they see, understand, and interpret the world is the mental map followed in what they do. Consequently, if a person wants to change results or what he gets in a situation, the way it is seen must be changed. The see-do-get model might be considered a principle related to the governance of human behavior. Does this make sense?

What Law Do You Follow?

In today's culture few people use a set of standards to guide their behavior. Most base their decisions on how they feel about a situation, absent consideration of objective, transcendent morality, or again, those laws that govern human behavior. The problem with using feelings to guide behavior is that they are arbitrary, easily changed, and unrelated to a person's moral compass or conscience. In law enforcement, this presents major problems because it leads to the justification of poor means to reach good ends. The officer who is angry with what he sees as an unfair circuit court judge is tempted to commit perjury in order to give victims justice and offenders their just due. Have you ever felt excessive force justified because of the vicious nature of an offender's crime, or, worse, because a person's words or behavior offended you? Perhaps the question should be, "How often?" If you just took umbrage, why? Officers who use a set of standards, reviewed daily, to govern professional and personal life tend to make better decisions. Feelings may sometimes be appropriate in matters of the heart, but rarely in those of duty.

Each of Us Is Two People

In the United States, between 125 and 150 law enforcement officers die in the line of duty yearly. Murder accounts for about 60 of the deaths; the rest are classified accidents in the performance of duty, many from vehicle crashes. Sources disagree on the number of yearly police suicides; however, all agree that more officers are killed by their own hand than murdered by felons. Suicide rates for retired officers are unreliable too. Many believe they are significantly higher than that of the working officer. Depression is the number one cause, but why? Many mental health professionals cite chemical imbalances in the brain, their answer being a pill to restore balance. They don't know which chemical restores balance, if it does. Here is an alternate opinion. Each of us is two people. The first is "Who I am," the person with flaws and secrets that cause shame. I don't want anyone to find out about this person who picks his nose and passes gas too often. The other is "Who I ought to be."

The person *I ought to be* requires a daily *Inner Inspection* to stay on the right life course. The most basic *Inner Inspection* is simply the following three questions asked daily and applied to personal and professional life. These are the same questions teams use in mission debriefs:

1. What did I do well today?
2. What did I do poorly or wrong?
3. How will I correct mistakes or do better tomorrow?

The greater the distance between "Who I am" and "Who I ought to be," the more tension enters my life. This is painful, unless one is a sociopath. Stress is cited by doctors as causing 95% of their patients' maladies. Officers must understand who they *ought to be* and how to move closer to that person. Failure to do so causes painful disharmony as behavior conflicts with core beliefs.

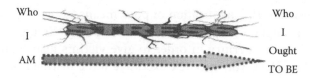

The idea of *ought to be* is ridiculed in a hedonist, pleasure-seeking culture. Anger, greed, sloth, pride, lust, envy, and gluttony dominate many. Those vices, once viewed as harmful, are tolerated now, sometimes rewarded and affirmed. Additionally, there is less enforced morality, social stigma, and legal punishment from sources that once demanded order. Abraham Lincoln said, "When I do good, I feel good. When I do bad, I feel bad. That is my religion." He understood that when his behavior was consistent with who he *ought to be*, he felt good and had less stress. This is not surprising if one believes in the laws governing human behavior. One of the central ones is, "You cannot help another without helping yourself." Do you agree with that law?

Why Did You Become a Cop?

Think back to what motivated you to choose law enforcement as a vocation. Most people say they became a cop because they wanted to make a difference, help people. In week 1 I ask each recruit class at the Chicago Police Academy why they want to become a cop. Their answers are the same as yours were. They want to help people. If that is true and the law "you can't help another without helping yourself" is valid, then theoretically, cops should be pretty happy campers, shouldn't they? Is that a sarcastic laugh I hear?

In week 22 of our program I ask the now probationary patrol officers what their focus will be when they hit the street in a few days. They first say, "Go home safe." That being a given, I press and ask for further definition of their focus. They tap dance around the answer saying things like "Work hard," or "Learn as much as I can." Finally, I have to ask that someone tell me what they really mean and one will say, almost sheepishly, "Lock up bad guys." The next question asked is, "How many of you want to go to a specialized unit, i.e., tact team, gangs, narcotics, etc.?" Eighty percent of their hands go up. And, "What must one do to get selected for the specialized units?" Somebody always responds, "Have a phone call." Remember, this is Chicago. I explain that may help, but most do not have phone calls. They respond by saying once again, "Make arrests!" When asked, "What kind of arrests?" they excitedly say, "Gangs, drugs, guns, felonies!" They are chomping at the bit to get out and arrest someone, sometimes anyone.

After they are reminded that 80% of their calls will be service calls that require help with minor, often mundane, things, this question arises, "If your personal agenda is to lock up bad guys, how is helping people viewed?" There is usually a stunned silence. After about 20–30 s, the silence creates such discomfort that someone must answer. Honesty gushes forth in the routine answers, "It's bullshit," "Unimportant," "An intrusion on what I want to do." So there it is. They see arresting people as their primary purpose. Do you see what is coming? A similar line of questions is used in promotional classes and in-service classes. They chuckle at this progression. I ask them to tell me I am wrong; they do not.

The next question for veterans is this, "Who has had a family member that had contact with the police and was treated rudely until the officer discovered your loved one was from a law enforcement family?" Why does a law enforcer's family member get treated differently than an unrelated citizen? The answer is simple; it is see–do–get in motion. The Law Enforcement Officer (LEO) saw your loved one as one of "them" (not the police), one from the unwashed masses, not worthy of the respect due to police and their families. Usually about 50% of officers in classes admit to having a family member who has had the experience. Is that how we *ought* to behave?

Let's return to (the view of) probationary police officers, who on entering the academy wanted to help people, but now are focused on arresting or, perhaps a better word, hunting. The benefits of hunting over helping are strong. Hunters get accolades and awards. Their peers buy them beers and tell heroic stories about them. Less experienced officers idolize them. Bosses give them slack and perks because they bring in numbers and notoriety that make higher-ups shine and boast of the agency's efficiency. Do not misinterpret this. Hunting is a necessary part of law enforcement. *What is important for the individual officer is how he views his purpose. Is he focused on helping someone, applying to help others/help self-law, or is his focus on hunting because it is fun and exciting, garners recognition and awards, and moves one up the agency's ladder?* If they view themselves as a helper first, what they *ought to do*, it is likely that arrests will naturally come in abundance. However, if they focus solely on hunting, selfishness is the motivating factor rather than generosity. What do you think? Think about your first 5 years on the job. Did you ever say this, "I can't believe they pay me to do this #%&*!!!" "I've been off on furlough for 2 weeks. I can't wait to get back!" What makes us view this job as so great? The possible answer to that is deferred.

First, think about officers who are between 5 and 10 years into their career. How many say, "This job sucks!"? Whoa, what happened? They go from, "I can't believe they pay me to do this #%&*!!!" to "This job sucks!" Has the job changed? Blame for the change in point of view is placed on jerk bosses, betrayal by leadership, citizens that lack respect, unfair portrayal in the media, etc. The job does not change: same circus, different clowns. Put this reason on your mental scales and mull it. They have broken the law of "you can't help another without helping yourself" for several years; selfishness, rather than generosity, has become the default in responding to those they serve and protect. "This job sucks!" translated is, "I do not like the way I am behaving, but refuse to change." We become disgusted with ourselves as we move further away from who we ought to be. This does not happen to everyone; however, far too many of us identify with this paradigm. Tell me I am wrong.

Let's return to the statement, "I can't believe they pay me to do this #%&*!!!" Why do so many of us say that? Based on the nature of human preference for that which is pleasurable, the answer lies in this question: Which is more fun, helping or hunting? Most of us like hunting more, but why? Well, what does your agency reward members for doing, helping, or hunting?

I spoke with a sergeant who put an officer in for an award because on a parade detail, the officer went out of his way to position a woman pushing a wheelchair with her handicapped child on the parade route so the excited child could see the festivities. Several higher-ups thought it foolish to be rewarded for this. Describing the sergeant or the subordinate as wussified would be a grave error. Courage was necessary to engage in both actions. Sadly, in our culture most recognition and reward are given to hunters. Helpers help at their peril, sometimes being the brunt of jokes from peers or the bane of supervision. What are you rewarded for in your unit?

Here is a civilian writer's thought on being helped by a police officer.

GOOD COP: IS HELPFULNESS A RARITY?

Their credo is "Protect and serve," so why are helpful police officers an anomaly?

Posted March 12, 2013, in the New Jersey Monthly by Michael Aaron Rockland

Recently, driving home from New Brunswick, where I work, to Morristown, where I live, I heard the sudden flap, flap, flap of a flat tire. I pulled to the side of Route 287. Anxiously, I got the jack out of my trunk and was trying to figure out how it worked when a state police cruiser pulled behind me, lights flashing. This made me even more anxious.

But the officer got out of his car and said, "Can I help you, sir?" I was surprised. I had never heard this question from a policeman before.

I have had a somewhat uneasy relationship with policemen ever since, at age 15, crossing a small, dark park; someone stepped out of the shadows and stuck a gun in my ribs. I was returning home from a Saturday afternoon movie. "Hands up," he barked. Terrified, I complied, though a more natural response might have been to run for my life; I hadn't yet made out that he was a policeman. Would he have shot me if I ran? Apparently a neighborhood jewelry store had been robbed, and the police had fanned out through the area accosting "suspicious-looking" passersby like myself. The cop patted me down, asked me what I was doing there, and then said, "You can go now, kid." He didn't apologize, and my ribs hurt for a week.

Ever afterward, I have felt that there is something wrong with the relationship between citizens and the police in America. Police are public servants; they work for us. They should be unfailingly courteous and helpful. And we citizens should be exactly the same with them. Too often, however, there is an adversarial relationship: us versus them. And it cuts both ways. Should cars approaching you from the other direction flash their lights to warn you that there is a policeman up the road giving out speeding tickets? Without being a goody two-shoes about it, would it not be better for society, assuming one is speeding, that a ticket be issued?

That day, on the shoulder of Route 287, the state policeman and I worked together to jack up my car and replace the damaged tire with the donut.

"Anything else I can do for you, sir?" he asked.

In fact, there was. I explained that I didn't have my cell phone. I had a very important appointment at home, and now I was late. "No problem," the policeman said. He dialed the Morristown police and asked them to call my house and tell my wife that I was running 20 minutes late. She should tell my guest to wait.

I thanked him effusively. "That's okay," the officer said. "Just part of the job."

I wondered whether it was; he seemed exceptionally nice and helpful. A few days later I phoned state police headquarters in Trenton and was told by the duty sergeant that what the officer had done was "normal protocol." Perhaps, but I had never seen a policeman help a citizen in such a fashion. In fact, when the officer was about to drive off, I had leaned into his window and requested his name and badge number.

"Why do you want to know?" he asked, eyeing me warily.

"Because I'd like to write a letter of commendation," I said, thinking he would be pleased. "Where would I send it?"

"If you don't mind," he replied, "I'd rather you didn't."

"Why?" I asked. "It's the least I can do."

He thanked me but said, "The guys at the barracks already think I'm a wimp. A letter from you would make things worse." And with that he pulled onto the highway and was gone.

I don't know which startled me more, his assistance or his unwillingness to let me acknowledge that help. He had demonstrated that there definitely are kindhearted cops and that the relationship between citizens and police need not be adversarial. But if the officers at the barracks think helping a citizen makes a cop a wimp, the problem isn't going away any time soon. As for me, if trying to be kind and helpful makes you a wimp, sign me up.

Michael Aaron Rockland is professor of American Studies at Rutgers University. His latest book is a memoir, *An American Diplomat in Franco Spain*.

Economics 101 and Psych 101 teach a common truth. Behavior rewarded increases; behavior punished decreases. Most law enforcement organizations reward hunting more than helping, and in too many units and agencies, helping is punished. Is that consistent with your experience? There is another factor that makes hunting more attractive that may be more dominant depending on the competency, confidence, disposition, and character of the individual. The most fun and exciting thing a human can do is use power over another. History is nothing more than stories of the struggle for and abuse of power: one strong group of people exercising and abusing their power over another. Often, abuses were legal in the law books of the abusers.

At one time the sun never set on the British Empire and the reason was that the British armies went into countries and murdered until the population agreed to be the king's subjects. An armed outpost was installed to remind new subjects that murder was always an option in the maintenance of order, or rather the imbalance of power. How about our government and the Native Americans or the racial hatred still present because of the abuse of power, all in the name of truth, justice, and the American way?

Lord Acton's famous quote "Power corrupts; absolute power corrupts absolutely" is dead on. The truth is humans do not handle power well. In a police/citizen contact, the officer has the power to do whatever he wants. The default setting for most of us is "Who I am," not "Who I ought to be." What do you think? Maybe we need to spend time talking about "Who we ought to be." Remember, stress and tension enter our life as "Who I am" and "Who I ought to be" move further apart. Can anyone say that intoxication of power is not related to the statement, "This job sucks!"

Supervisors, Take This Test

Do you encourage your officers to help others? Write an explanation of why.

_____

_____

If your charges view their role as helpers rather than hunters, will you benefit? How?

_____

Which do you prefer: helping your charges become happy and satisfied or sad and discouraged?

_____

_____

Within your span of control, decide upon three things you will do to encourage your charges to focus on helping people.

_____

_____

If you want to make a difference, transform the perspective of those in your charge.

The Other Side of the Story

The last section focused on the individual's purpose for being, their role in the law enforcement organization, and temptations that can lead one to adapt the point of view that this job sucks! Now let's look at the bigger picture and law enforcement's purpose and its relation to progress or regression. What do you think? Are we progressing or regressing as a society? Yes, progress has been made: in medicine, race relations, and technology. We have more information available, yet more high school graduates cannot read, write, add, or subtract. One in four of our youth have an STD. Man-made law says we can kill the most defenseless of society up till they pass through six inches of birth canal. Is this progress or regression? Maybury

(1993) said, "Until the 1970s, each generation of Americans was expected to do better than any who came before. No more. Statistics confirm that our children are the first Americans ever to have little chance of living as well as their parents."

Examine the following table. Tell me it is not so.

1960s	2012
1 income supported a family	2 incomes necessary for family basics
• Avg. car cost, $2000	• Avg. car cost, $31,252
• Home prices, about 70% of yearly wage	• Home prices, 300 to 400% of yearly wage
	• Job requirements = min. 2 yrs college
• Job requirements = HS diploma	• Avg. student college loan debt nears $29,400 in 2013
• Few had college debt	• (Ref: http://money.cnn.com/2013/12/04/pf/college/student-loan-debt/)

Do you remember the proud day you graduated from the Police Academy? In front of your family, your agency's leadership, and your God, you raised your right hand and took an oath promising to act justly and impartially, to defend the Constitution. The Founding Fathers drew conclusions, *based on history*, about how people ought to treat one another. They recognized that when people acted as they ought to, all in the society benefited. They were the first to set up a system that made man more important than the state creating government the way it ought to be.

The Shortest Story of Human History

To understand the role of law enforcement, historical perspective is necessary.

Most people believe that the quality of life for humans has, more or less, been uptrending since humans appeared on earth; that is myth. The quality of life for most of time was rotten. There has been minimal food, clothing, and shelter; disease, filth, and hardship have been the norm. Violence was the lot of people. Life span was about 30 years of age; infant mortality was high. Royalty, through most of history, lived worse than the poor of the United States today! Most of the third world still lives this existence. Few people in the United States know the hardship present in the rest of the world. Today, what many call poverty in the United States is not poverty. Food, housing, and education are available to all. What many consider poverty, mostly in inner cities, is really squalor caused by neglect, not lack of resources.

In the short span of about 250 years, quality of life for humans exploded. The drastic upward trend started in 1776 with the Declaration of Independence. It was the first time in history that a group of leaders attempted to start a government that said, "All men are created equal." This meant those governing were on par with those governed. Few understood this, even then. Thomas Jefferson wrote to James Madison, "My God, how little do my countrymen know what precious blessings they are in possession of, and which no other people on earth enjoy!" The idea that all are created equal in dignity, not wealth, skills, or intelligence, changed the world, improving life for people everywhere. For the first time in history, a government was established that outlined specific rights of individuals that applied to rulers and the ruled. Once people believed they had rights to protect them from encroaching government, creativity and industriousness exploded. They felt free to create out of self-interest and keep the fruits of their labors.

Test This Idea

What in your life that makes its quality better was invented and available to the masses before 1776?

Medicine? Plumbing? Transportation? Refrigeration? Communications? Roads? Garbage pickup? Mail?

Things like books, tools, and creature comforts may have been around, but not available to the masses.

Law enforcement is the most visible and available part of government. Not only do we protect life and property; we *ought* to protect the liberty of the people *from* the government that employs us, *liberty that raised man from disease, filth, sickness, poverty and misery*. Regress we will; unless we protect it. Again, our system is unique because the founders were the first in human history to declare that all men are equal in dignity and *attempt* to make leadership live by the same rules as citizens. Cops, guardians of fairness, *ought* to ensure liberty. Absent liberty, we devolve to the pitiful human condition that is present in most countries on this planet. We are guardians of a treasure, not occupiers. What perception of you is held by the people you serve and protect: guardian or occupier? If the answer is occupier, you are seen as the indigenous peoples viewed the British and Roman occupying armies. How *ought* we be viewed?

It was stated that you cannot help another without helping yourself and that is one of the laws that governs humans. In the law enforcement version of Covey's class *7 Habits of Highly Effective People*, there is an exercise that asks participants to write about one of their most satisfying days on the job.

In the 20 or more classes I facilitated, nobody cited an arrest situation. All told stories of helping citizens. One from a commander, not known for his kind nature, was of the return of a grandmother with Alzheimer's to her family living in the projects. Here are two other discovered laws that govern us: one tells us what to do and the other what not to do. They are universal, the foundation of our legal system, and wherever applied, life gets better for everyone. They are as follows:

- Do all you have agreed to do (*contract law*).
- Do not encroach on other persons or their property (*tort and criminal law*).

These laws are written in our hearts. We may not be able to recite them but we clearly recognize when they have been violated. They concern justice. If you think this is not true, try this test. Next time you go to a family party ask if you can be in charge of the dessert at the children's table. After dinner bring the goodies, a cake, and cookies, whatever. If it is a cake, cut it up unevenly. It will be the last time you'll be given that job. Kids may not know the two laws, but they know when they have been treated unfairly. That is at the root of all of this. Today, in places where these principles are most closely followed, the masses have clean food and water, cars, refrigeration, air conditioning, computers, cell phones, etc. In places where the principles are most rejected, abject poverty and misery are the norm for the masses of inhabitants. People simply want to be treated with respect and fairness. This is a universal truth. The point is clearly made by Jack Hoban and Bruce J. Gourlie in a hunting story retold in a piece entitled *The Ethical Warrior*, which originally appeared on PoliceOne.com.

The Hunting Story

The Ethical Warrior: The Hunting Story

By Jack E. Hoban and Bruce J. Gourlie

Physical and ethical training used by USMC may help officers confront, survive, and live with the realities of modern law enforcement.

Robert L. Humphrey, an Iwo Jima Marine rifle platoon commander who worked for the State Department during the Cold War, had to resolve a conflict between the United States and an allied country in Asia Minor. The local people wanted the Americans to go home, while the Americans had a strategic interest in keeping the Cold War missile base. Humphrey discovered that many of the U.S. servicemen considered the locals to be "stupid, dumb, dirty, dishonest, untrustworthy, disloyal, cowardly, lazy, unsanitary, immoral, cruel, crazy, and downright subhuman."

Understandably, the local people's perception was that the Americans did not view them as equal human beings. Their opposition to the presence of the U.S. installation was based on the fact that they simply wanted to be treated with respect and dignity.

One day, as a diversion from his job, Humphrey decided to go hunting for wild boar with some personnel from the American embassy. They took a truck from the motor pool and headed out to the boondocks, stopping at a village to hire some local men to beat the brush and act as guides. This village was very poor. The huts were made of mud and there was no electricity or running water. The streets were unpaved dirt and the whole village smelled. The men looked surly and wore dirty clothes. The women covered their faces, and the children had runny noses and were dressed in rags.

One American in the truck said, "This place stinks."

Another said, "These people live just like animals."

Finally, a young air force man said, "Yeah, they got nothing to live for; they may as well be dead."

Then, an old sergeant in the truck spoke up. He was the quiet type who never said much. In fact, except for his uniform, he kind of reminded you of one of the tough men in the village. He looked at the young airman and said, "You think they got nothing to live for, do you? Well, if you are so sure, why don't you just take my knife, jump down off the back of this truck, and go try to kill one of them?"

Dead silence. Humphrey was amazed.

It was the first time that anyone had said anything that had actually silenced the negative talk about these local people. The sergeant went on to say, "I don't know either why they value their lives so much. Maybe it's those snotty nosed kids, or the women in the pantaloons. But whatever it is, they care about their lives and the lives of their loved ones, same as we Americans do. And if we don't stop talking bad about them, they will kick us out of this country!"

Humphrey asked him what we Americans, with all our wealth, could do to prove our belief in the peasants' equality despite their destitution. The sergeant answered, "You got to be brave enough to jump off the back of this truck, knee deep in the mud and sheep dung. You got to have the courage to walk through this village with a smile on your face. And when you see the smelliest, scariest looking peasant, you got to be able to look him in the face and let him know, just with your eyes, that you know he is a man who hurts like you do, and hopes like you do, and wants for his kids just like we all do. It is that way, or we lose."

The hunting story has immediate and strong emotional impact. We sympathize with those poor villagers, perhaps because most people naturally root for the "underdog."

Almost everyone understands the pain and anger that arise from disrespect. The people in that village weren't speaking out, but in their hearts each of them was saying: "Don't look down on me. You are my equal—my life and the lives of my loved ones are as important to me as yours are to you." Everyone in the truck suddenly understood two things. First, despite how worthless the villager's life might appear, no one would actually try to kill him because taking innocent human life is anathema to all moral people. Second, if attacked, the villager would have defended himself with all his might because he loved his life and the lives of his loved ones just as much as everyone else. At last, here was Humphrey's way to make the truth that "all men are created equal" truly self-evident.

Humphrey had great success relating this insight he called the *Life Value* to other military personnel at the U.S. base in formal presentations. However, he realized that he needed a way to sustain the idea of equality while reinforcing the important physical aspect of the moral lesson. Drawing on his own experience and relying on the universal impulse for young servicemen to prove their manhood, Humphrey offered free boxing lessons to anyone interested. He found that moral lessons were easier to teach when the students bonded through the combination of physical danger and fortitude necessary to excel at boxing.

Valuing one's own life is only half of the equation. When we talk about the Life Value, whose life are we exactly talking about? The Life Value is a dual value—self and others. Ethical people have a good sense of how to keep that balance. There is no more important factor at any level of law enforcement than the duty to protect the community being served. A focus on this *Dual Life Value* of self and others may be an excellent moral basis upon which to build a sense of duty to *protect and serve* as a law enforcement officer.

Ethics are moral values in action. A person who knows the difference between right and wrong—and prefers the right—is moral. A person whose morality is reflected in their willingness to do the right thing— even if it is hard or dangerous—is ethical. It starts in the school yard.

Almost everybody knows that the bully is wrong—that's morality. But only a few will speak up to protect the one getting bullied by calling for a teacher—that's ethics. Even fewer will step in physically to actually protect the child being bullied—that's the behavior of an Ethical Warrior.

Law enforcement officers serve daily in a jungle full of "experts" in criminal behavior and moral gray areas. But life is the "true north" of the moral compass that can keep officers on track. When we possess a calibrated compass, we can more reliably navigate that jungle. Without trying to gloss over the very real fact that Ethical Warriors like Marines and law enforcement officers may need to use force, we can articulate clearly that force is only to be used to protect life. The Dual Life Value is the guiding bedrock principle that can inspire us to protect and serve.

Why Martial Arts?

As the hunting story illustrates, ethics are ultimately moral–physical. Moral people may want to step up and do the right thing, but they often lack the physical courage and ability. Martial arts give them the necessary skills and confidence. And that is why Ethical Warrior training includes—and must include—martial arts, especially for professionals like Marines or law enforcement officers.

It is also important that the training be ongoing. An interesting challenge with Ethical Warriorship is that the lessons tend to *wear off* without sustainment. The warrior ethic must be sustained by continuous physical–moral training. For the Marines, that means at least a few hours a week of the physical MCMAP training with the moral tie-ins. For law enforcement, that would mean a deliberate effort to integrate appropriate warrior ethics tie-ins into some type of tactical training.

In Summary

So how do we apply the Marine Ethical Warrior approach to the law enforcement profession? The answer may lie in determining the value of a proposed description of the desired end state. A law enforcement Ethical Warrior would view everyone foremost as a life to be valued, protected, and defended, regardless of race, nationality, economic, or legal status. When called upon to deal with someone engaging in criminal behavior, the law enforcement Ethical Warrior would be motivated first by protecting those he or she serves and ultimately even protecting the criminal if possible.

This vision may be appropriate to community policing. Involving the community in policing has worked. The success of this approach depends on developing relationships with community leaders and organizations and developing trust and respect between officers and the community. One obstacle to developing trust is for the police and the community served to each view their counterpart as the *other*. Police in Salinas, Calif., recently started incorporating military counterinsurgency theory into their policing strategy as a way to win the hearts and minds of gang members. Commitment to the Dual Life Value could be a way for the law enforcement side to bridge this divide. It could also support departmental morale by giving officers a renewed sense of being a protector.

If we conclude that the Ethical Warrior approach could be useful, we must address how the training can be adapted to law enforcement. The demands of patrol, investigation, and other functions occupy most law enforcement time and resources. Yet adaptation and innovation could devise an effective approach.

All law enforcement agencies have defensive tactics program. These programs possess what could be integrated with values to teach the warrior ethic.

Dr. Humphrey's stories resonate with most people, but other appropriate law enforcement stories could convey the same lessons of valuing and protecting life. The training sessions could be short, scheduled regularly to accomplish sustainment.

Law enforcement officers should live the best values of the societies they serve. Physical–moral training and a sustainment regimen activate nobility in our officers and perhaps help them avoid PTSD (or burnout). The result will be more motivated officers, greater respect for the law enforcement profession, and more effective policing for our communities.

Jack E. Hoban (is president of Resolution Group International and a subject matter expert for the U.S. Marine Corps Martial Arts Program)

Bruce J. Gourlie (is a special agent of the FBI and a former U.S. Army infantry officer.)

Correspondence can be sent to authors by e-mailing jhoban@resgroupintl.com.

It does not matter if people are living in a third-world jungle or a Western city ghetto; people want to be treated with respect and fairness. Jack Hoban makes the point that a universal thought is, "My life and my loved ones are worth as much to me as yours are to you." Referring to the see–do–get model, how do the men and women of your agency see or perceive the people in the communities they serve? How do you see them? Here is a way to reveal this perception. Listen to the words officers use to describe those they serve in stationhouse banter. I have done the following exercise in classes 50–100 times. The results are consistent.

Class Exercise

Ask everyone to write two words used between officers on patrol that describe the people on their beat. Amid chuckles and sarcastic comments, I ask they read what they wrote.

The run-of-the-mill answers are scumbags, assholes, animals, dirtbags, shitheads, etc. Usually, a class of 25 participants will net 46 or 47 negative answers and 3 or 4 neutral or positive answers like *civilians*, though those are often reported sarcastically.

The words a person uses to describe things are how he sees them. If we see those we serve in negative ways, does that affect how we treat them, what we do? The logic is inescapable. Further, there are consequences to the individual who views people as such. The most immediate consequence comes from what we get from those we view in derogatory terms. Professional language may be used, but disdain or negative view leeches into facial expression, body language, and tone of voice. In the Hunting Story, the indigenous population did not understand English but clearly understood what was being said about them was disrespectful and dehumanizing. Is it different for law enforcement? Is this how we *ought* to act, and does it move us closer to, or further away from, who we *ought* to be? Recall that moving away brings more tension into a person's life.

There are other consequences, far worse, for the person who constantly sees people negatively. Dr. Jonathan Shay, doctor and clinical psychiatrist, worked for the U.S. Department of Veterans Affairs specializing in counseling Vietnam veterans with PTSD. He wrote two books on the nature and treatment of PTSD, *Achilles in Vietnam* and *Odysseus in America*. In *Achilles in Vietnam*, he says the three main causes of PTSD are exposure to trauma, betrayal by leadership, and dehumanizing people, typically those seen as the enemy.

Dr. Jonathan Shay's Three Causes of PTSD

#1 Cause: Exposure to Trauma

People in law enforcement certainly are exposed to their share of trauma. In Lt. Colonel Dave Grossman's work *On Killing*, he cites interpersonal violence as the thing humans fear most.

On Killing by Lt. Colonel Dave Grossman, p. 76

The *Diagnostic and Statistical Manual of Mental Disorders* (DSM), the bible of psychology, states that in post-traumatic stress disorders "the disorder may be especially severe or longer lasting when the stressor is of human design." We want desperately to be liked, loved, and in control of our lives; and intentional, overt, *human* hostility and aggression—more than anything else in life—assaults our self-image, our sense of control, and our sense of the world as a meaningful and comprehensible place—ultimately, our mental and physical health.

The ultimate fear and horror in most modern lives is to be raped or beaten, to be physically degraded in front of our loved ones, to have our family harmed and the sanctity of our homes invaded by aggressive and hateful intruders. Death and debilitation by disease and accidents are far more likely to occur than death or debilitation by malicious action, but the statistics do not calm our basically irrational fears. It is not fear of death or injury by disease or accident but rather acts of personal depredation and domination by our fellow human beings that strike terror and loathing in our hearts.

On February 1, 2013 *USA TODAY* staff writer Gregg Zoroya writes that today's soldiers are exposed to this trauma daily for 9-12 months in a single tour in a hostile environment. Its threat is constant, 24 hours per day, in combat zones. On average, 22 veterans per day are committing suicide after returning home according to a Veterans Affairs study. People in law enforcement may not be exposed to such intense trauma as combat soldiers, but the threat of it is present during their tours of duty, and it occurs over a 20–30-year span of a career.

#2 Cause: Betrayal by Leadership

Do people in law enforcement feel betrayed by leadership? In his book *Emotional Survival for Law Enforcement*, Dr. Kevin Gilmartin says that police report that more stress comes from inside their agency than outside. It is manifest in the statement, "I can handle the assholes on the street. I just can't handle the assholes running this agency." It really means, "I feel more threatened by the people in management." Officers are saying that they feel disrespected and treated unfairly by those in authority, the same complaint citizens have against police officers. Leaders can and *ought* to change this.

#3 Cause: Dehumanizing People

Soldiers are trained to see the enemy as less than human. An enemy perceived as not human is easier to kill, though for the soldiers, it seems harder to reconcile with conscience. Samuel Lyman Atwood Marshall was a chief U.S. Army combat historian during World War II. He concluded that the average and healthy individual has such an inner and usually unrealized resistance toward killing a fellow man that he will not of his own volition take a life if it is possible to turn away from that responsibility. Marshall noted that the soldier "becomes a conscientious objector and that soldiers must dehumanize in order to kill." Must cops dehumanize to do their job? I believe the answer is *no*; however, I think it becomes easier to disrespect people because of the dehumanization by law enforcement. Earlier I asked these two questions:

- Who has had a family member that had contact with the police and was treated rudely until the officer discovered your loved one was from a law enforcement family?
- Why does a law enforcer's family member get treated different than an unrelated citizen?

I believe the answer to the second is we condition ourselves to view all but ourselves and our families as less than human. We tend to see citizens as *arrests* or *numbers* that earn us recognition, respect, and accolades from bosses and peers. The person's "being equal in dignity" is lost on us. It becomes harder to abuse one's power when we see the abused as human. It is a law we cannot escape. Those that say "This job sucks!" are not criticizing the job (it doesn't change) but expressing the disgust they feel after years of dehumanizing those they swore to serve and protect. What does your gut tell you?

Dehumanization moves us farther from who we *ought* to be, engaging the animal, reptilian part of the brain rather than the rational, human part. The human part concludes all human life is to be respected. The reptilian part does not. The following quote is from a New York cop, though it could easily be from one anywhere: "Sometimes I feel like a garbage man, because I deal with human trash all day long." This is not the way one *ought* to feel in a job that gives the opportunity to help people daily.

Solutions

Remember, we enter law enforcement intending to help people, which is what we *ought* to do.

A short list of the things in law enforcement that change officers worldview includes the following:

- Most organizations, units, and peers reward hunting. Helping is tolerated, sometimes punished, seldom rewarded. Do you disagree?

- Other parts of the system, state attorneys, for example, are rewarded for numbers too; some may suggest and sanction perjury to garner the rewards their system offers.
- The most fun and exciting thing humans do is exercise power over others. In a one-on-one contact, law enforcers have more power over a person than anyone else in the society. The temptation to abuse is overwhelming.

Understand this. The system you are in is not likely to change. Peers and bosses are not likely to start acting as they *ought* to in an effort to reduce tension in their lives. The good news is you can! The broad solution is to work on yourself harder than on the job. Here are specific suggestions: What standards do you use to make decisions? If specific standards are not guiding behavior, then it is likely feelings do. Bad move. Feelings often move us closer to *who we are* and further from *who we ought to be*. Select a set of standards; review them daily. Unsure which to use? Did your parents raise you in a faith? Examine the standards set forth by the faith you were taught. Most religions have similar standards. Christians are reminded that Jesus came to *serve*. If that is not your cup of tea, try these from a *Guide for Peacekeepers*, written by Erasmus in 1503. Living by standards or a moral code moves us closer to *who we ought to be*, diminishing stress.

A GUIDE FOR THE PEACEKEEPER, BY ERASMUS, 1503

How To Be Strong While Remaining Virtuous In A Dangerous World

First Rule: INCREASE YOUR FAITH. *Even if the entire world appears mad.*

Second Rule: ACT UPON YOUR FAITH. *Even if you must undergo the loss of everything.*

Third Rule: ANALYZE YOUR FEARS. *You will find that things are not as bad as they appear.*

Fourth Rule: MAKE VIRTUE THE ONLY GOAL OF YOUR LIFE. *Dedicate all your enthusiasm, all your effort, your leisure as well as your business.*

Fifth Rule: TURN AWAY FROM MATERIAL THINGS. *If you are greatly concerned with money you will be weak of spirit.*

Sixth Rule: TRAIN YOUR MIND TO DISTINGUISH GOOD AND EVIL. *Let your rule of government be determined by the common good.*

Seventh Rule: NEVER LET ANY SETBACK STOP YOU IN YOUR QUEST. *We are not perfect - this only means we should try harder.*

Eighth Rule: IF YOU HAVE FREQUENT TEMPTATIONS, DO NOT WORRY.

Begin to worry when you do not have temptation, because that is a sure sign that you cannot distinguish good from evil.

Ninth Rule: ALWAYS BE PREPARED FOR AN ATTACK. *Careful generals set guards even in times of peace.*

Tenth Rule: SPIT, AS IT WERE, IN THE FACE OF DANGER. *Keep a stirring quotation with you for encouragement.*

Eleventh Rule: THERE ARE TWO DANGERS: ONE IS GIVING UP, THE OTHER IS PRIDE. *After you have performed some worthy task, give all the credit to someone else.*

Twelfth Rule: TURN YOUR WEAKNESS INTO VIRTUE. *If you are inclined to be selfish, make a deliberate effort to be giving.*

Thirteenth Rule: TREAT EACH BATTLE AS THOUGH IT WERE YOUR LAST. *And you will finish, in the end, victorious!*

Fourteenth Rule: DON'T ASSUME THAT DOING GOOD ALLOWS YOU TO KEEP A FEW VICES. *The enemy you ignore the most is the one who conquers you.*

Fifteenth Rule: WEIGH YOUR ALTERNATIVES CAREFULLY. *The wrong way will often seem easier than the right way.*

Sixteenth Rule: NEVER ADMIT DEFEAT EVEN IF YOU HAVE BEEN WOUNDED. *The good soldier's painful wounds spur him to gather his strength.*

Seventeenth Rule: ALWAYS HAVE A PLAN OF ACTION. *So when the time comes for battle, you will know what to do.*

Eighteenth Rule: CALM YOUR PASSIONS BY SEEING HOW LITTLE THERE IS TO GAIN. *We often worry and scheme about trifling matters of no real importance.*

Nineteenth Rule: SPEAK WITH YOURSELF THIS WAY. *If I do what I am considering, would I want my family to know about it?*

Twentieth Rule: VIRTUE HAS ITS OWN REWARD. *Once a person has it, they would not exchange it for anything.*

Twenty-first Rule: LIFE CAN BE SAD, DIFFICULT, AND QUICK: MAKE IT COUNT FOR SOMETHING. *Since we do not know when death will come, act honorably every day.*

Twenty-second Rule: REPENT YOUR WRONGS. *Those who do not admit their faults have the most to fear.*

Once a set of standards or moral code is decided upon, they must be checked daily. Rockets sent to outer space have a computer that checks their course many times per second. On a rocket headed to the moon, an error of 1/100 of a degree might cause the rocket to miss the moon. The small error of 1/100 of a degree multiplied by the distance of the journey, 238,856 miles, will cause the rocket to miss its mark. Things not checked regularly go off course. Are we different? Our progress is measured in time not distance. A small flaw multiplied over 10 years often ruins a person. We must check things daily or we get careless. This is the reason for daily inspection in military and semi-military organizations. Dr. Stephen Covey said we must "sharpen the saw."

Previously a most basic *Inner Inspection* was suggested. The three questions were as follows:

1. What did I do well today?
2. What did I do poorly or wrong?
3. How will I correct mistakes or do better tomorrow?

Next is a more thorough *Inner Inspection*. Use it as a reminder to be who you *ought* to be and stay on course.

Inner Inspection
- Does my life have the depth and serenity to discern important issues faced in my duties or is my life being drained by activities that are frivolous and superficial?
- Do I guard my sight and imagination from things that are tempting, crude, pornographic, and negative for pleasure's sake?
- Am I helping or hunting?
- When I feel discouraged from the many obstacles and *rewards* that tempt me to act unjustly, do I reject the discouragement and focus on doing right?
- Do I have a plan for my life?
- Do I try to make good use of my time daily with a specific plan to improve my skills, particularly those involving relationships with others?
- Are there obstacles in my life that prevent me from being an example for those I influence? If so, do I have a plan to diminish or remove them?
- Are my conversations manly/womanly? Do I find myself talking about myself to others? Do I realize that gossip is not for real men and women and that it can severely damage others unjustly?
- Do I regularly give some thought to my purpose for being where I am and who I am with at this time in my life?

- Do I major in minors? Do I review my day, examining how I responded to the major events of the day?
- Do I try to learn all I can from my experiences with others, both positive and negative? Can I make use of past negative experiences so as to act positively, constructively, now?

Because the job is fun (remember, "I can't believe they pay me to do this #%&*!!!"), some law enforcement officers develop a disordered dedication that leads to neglect of more important things, family, and appropriate stress management. Face it, what is more fun, chasing a bad guy, using skills and power to subdue him in the name of truth, justice and the American way, or changing diapers, reading *Cat in the Hat* for the six-hundredth time, and listening to a spouse's mundane, daily story? As fun as the job is, cops on their deathbeds do not wish they would have made another felony, gun, or narcotics arrest; they regret not giving proper attention to loved ones and wish they would have helped more. The lure of the job is strong; overcome it, or it will overwhelm you.

Balance in life means that a person's priorities are in order. Are yours? Take the test to find out.

Write five things to which you assign high value in your personal value system and one sentence explaining why you see each as valuable.

1. _____
2. _____
3. _____
4. _____
5. _____

What are the five things that consume the most time and/or effort in your life? Measure the hours spent in each activity, exercise, social with family, reading, internet, videogames, TV, etc. *The job* will be first on this list because, including travel, it is likely that 60 hours per week are used. Write the other four.

1. The Job 40 to hours per week
2. _____
3. _____
4. _____
5. _____

Now, the big question, Do the lists match? They *ought* to, with the job being the outlier. There are negative consequences for inconsistencies in the lists. Are the things you claim to highly value given high effort and/or time? If the lists do not match, you won't need a crystal ball to see your future, just honesty with self.

Who Am I Around?

A person trying to discover how he *ought* to act usually needs help. We are not objective about areas where we need improvement. There is an ancient saying, "One ignoring other's advice consults only a fool." If you want to know about those areas, ask your siblings or your spouse. If you are a supervisor, ask your charges. Those are difficult and humbling things to do and few can muster the courage, so here is another option: get around people better than you. Ask them how they became who they are, what books did they read, classes they took, etc. Sometimes we get lucky, and somebody better will take us under their wing, mentor us. Also, find someone you can mentor. It can be a peer, or you can find an organization like Big Brothers/Sisters. This is particularly helpful for those who have no children. Helping another act as they *ought* pressures the mentor to act as he *ought*.

Barfield Method

Supervisors, I offer you the *Barfield method*, named for police trainer/Chief Timothy J. Barfield of Wellington, Ohio Police Department. He has trained his officers in this technique. When a peer sees an officer becoming intoxicated with power and emotion, in other words, under stress-induced adrenaline overload, the officer more in control taps the other on the shoulder and says, "I got this." As it may take more than one attempt to interrupt the focus of tunnel vision, the shoulder tap and "I got this" are done as many times as necessary to make the out-of-control officer relinquish his overreach. Lt. Barfield, admitting his human nature, says it has saved him more than once and other officers have used the method successfully. He believes it saves careers, diminishes occasions for disciplinary action, and saves the department from scandal and the taxpayers from lawsuits. If we care for our brother and sister officers, we *ought* to be trained in this type of intervention rather than relying on the "code of silence" and/or creative writing after the fact. Several roll call role plays could make this a default response in officers in your charge.

Final Thoughts

There is a story about an old Indian Chief teaching his grandson about life. "A fight is going on inside of me," he said to his grandson. "It is a terrible fight between two wolves," he continued. "One is evil-or-angry, envious, sorrowful, regretful, greedy, arrogant, self-pitying, guilt-ridden, resentful, lying, full of false pride, and ego driven" (who I am) and "The other wolf is good, joyful, peaceful, loving, hopeful, serene, humble, kind, empathetic, generous, truthful, compassionate, and faithful" (who I ought to be). "The same fight is going on inside of you, grandson, and in every person," said the Chief. The grandson thought about this for a moment, turned to the Chief, and said, "But, grandfather, which wolf will win?" The old Chief replied, "The one that you feed."

The Chief was explaining an incontrovertible law that governs humans. In science, the law is, for every action, there is an equal and opposite reaction. In computer terms, it is GIGO, Garbage In, Garbage out; in physical health, you are what you eat. It is the law of sowing and reaping. Plant corn, you get corn. Why do so many people ignore this law when it comes to the seeds we plant in our minds and hearts? Those words, sounds, and images are seeds of our thoughts that turn into words, deeds, and reports. Our culture fills us with things that are valueless, pornographic, violent, and negative. Tell me I am wrong. If the law of sowing and reaping is incontrovertible, then we must, in our off time, plant seeds that are good, pure, clean, powerful, and positive, lest we absorb the negative cultural values.

Answer these questions:

- What kind of books and magazines do I choose to read?
- What movies do I view?
- What kind of music do I listen to?
- What Internet sites do I visit?
- What kinds of links do my friends send me?

Do those things I allow in myself generate thoughts that lead me to act as *I ought*? Friedrich Nietzsche said, "Beware that, when fighting monsters, you yourself do not become a monster, for when you gaze long into the abyss, the abyss gazes also into you." Law enforcers gaze into the abyss daily and see, hear, smell, taste, and touch things that change how we see life and people. Dr. Kevin Gilmartin explains that the cynical view we develop is not realistic because the sampling from which we take it is only a small part of human behavior. (A polluted river is the exception, not the norm.) Since we spend so much time dealing with toxic behavior, care must be taken to prevent our seeing it as the norm. Cleaning our minds and hearts with things that are good, pure, clean, powerful, and positive is an effort in this culture.

Writing this chapter has been a privilege. These ideas may be controversial, but I believe they need to be discussed if we are to protect the system that gave us, in the words of Thomas Jefferson, "My God, how little do my countrymen know what precious blessings they are in possession of, and which no other people on earth enjoy!" This system lifted the whole world because it embodied the principles that teach people how they *ought* to treat one another.

Happy helping!

References

Covey, S.R., *7 Habits of Highly Effective People*, Simon & Schuster Sound Ideas, New York, 1989.

Gilmartin, K., *Emotional Survival for Law Enforcement*, p. 29, E-S Press, Tucson, AZ, 2002.

Hoban, L., *The Ethical Warrior, Values, Morals and Ethics for Life, Work and Service*, RGI Media and Publications, Spring Lake, NJ, 2012.

Humphrey, R.L., *Values for a New Millennium*, Life Values Press, Maynardville, TN, 1992.

ITunes, U., Constitution 101 course, Hillsdale College, Hillsdale, MI, https://online. hillsdale.edu/

Kelsen, H., *Principles of International Law*, 136pp., The Lawbook Exchange, Ltd., Clark, NJ.

Maybury, R., *Whatever Happened to Justice?*, pp. 15, 30–35, Bluestocking Press, Placerville, CA, 1993.

Rockland, M.A., *An American Diplomat in Franco Spain*, Hansen Publishing Group, East Brunswick, NJ, 2012.

Shusko, J.C., Lt. Col. (USMC) Tie-ins for life, RGI Medial and Publications, Spring Lake, NJ.

Skousen, C., *5000 Year Leap*, National Center for Constitutional Studies, Washington, DC, 2007.

Willis, B. and R. Scheidt, *Am I that Man?* Warrior Spirit Books, Calgary, Alberta, Canada, 2013.

YouTube, *The Ox Bow Incident* with Henry Fonda and Harry Morgan.

Zoroya, G., VA study: 22 vets commit suicide every day, *USA TODAY*, February 1, 2013.

Police Stress and Burnout

4

RON RUFO

Contents

Too often we enjoy the comfort of opinion without the discomfort of thought.

John F. Kennedy

Police Stress and Burnout

Like a combat soldier in the military, police are never off duty. Most combat or military tours of duty last from 2 to 4 years unless the soldier reenlists. Imagine a police career only lasting that long, reenlisting if the need arises. Yet a typical police career that can secure a pension can last a minimum of 20 years and is oftentimes longer. A police career depends on whether the officer maintains his good health and if he feels he can still be productive in the law enforcement field. In Chicago, it is not unusual to have an officer work 37 years and a day in order to secure 75% of his pension. Most officers will leave the job if they are financially secure and are in good health so they can enjoy retirement while they are still young. A few officers make law enforcement their personal crusade, staying until they are forced out, mainly due to age requirements. In Chicago, it is mandatory for an officer to retire once he turns 63 years of age, no matter if he is the best officer in the city or the most decorated. Many officers will work as long as they are physically capable, productive, and still in good health.

Everyone handles stress in their own way. Stress is relative and it is often an internal warning that something is wrong.

Robert Douglas Jr.* noted that police deal with three different stressors:

1. The stress of working on the street, never knowing what they will encounter.
2. Stress from management, bosses on the job, and politics of the job. Dealing with their agency is the greatest stress they will experience.
3. The last stress they encounter is at home, the family fragmentation.

* Douglas Jr., Robert, Personal interview.

Dr. John Mayer* confirmed that being a police officer is an extremely difficult profession, especially for beat cops, who deal with an enormous amount of stress and tension on a daily basis. Officers can become jaded because they deal with pessimism; their job becomes caustic and they become cynical because of what they see. Officers are not equipped to deal with it, eventually taking it home with them.

Dr. Dean C. Angelo†, Sr., stated that being a police officer is not an easy line of work; there is a lot of stress in the lives of officers. Police are generally risk takers by career choice and many times they are in need of an adrenaline rush. Generally speaking, no one likes the police. Police officers take people to jail, write tickets, and do the work that the rest of society either fails at or wants someone else to do for them. Each and every day, officers do what they need to do to get the job done. A lot of the time, we are perceived as being the bad guy. Officers just don't get that attitude from the public. They call us, we respond and then do what is required of us; and we are the bad guy? If a person [officer] wanted to be liked, they should have become a fireman. Everyone loves the firefighters. Over time, we can get swept up in the job. Few people get to see the good side of an officer. It is to allow oneself to get caught up in all of the negativity; therefore, it can become easy to become miserable. Police officers are constantly surrounded by misery, heartache, frustration, and disrespect. Misery loves company; it is like a cancer. Police work is a thankless job. Angelo compared the police culture regularly taking hits to that of a quote from General George Patton of the U.S. Military, "It is not how hard you fall that counts; it is how high you bounce."

Dr. John Violanti‡ explained that being ingrained in the police role can reduce one's ability to deal with stress inside and outside of police work. Inflexible styles associated with the police role hinder effective coping with stress and heighten risk factors associated with the potential for suicide. Thus, as a consequence of the police culture, officers may deal with most life situations, good or bad, from the standpoint of their police role. This raises the question of the impact of the police role on life relationships that may precipitate psychological stress and societal relationships.

According to Jeremy Travis of the U.S. Department of Justice (1996), law enforcement has always been a stressful occupation. However, there appear to be new and more severe sources of stress for law enforcement officers than ever before. Some of these stresses are related to increased scrutiny and criticism from the media and the public and anxiety and loss of morale as a result of layoffs and reduced salary increases. Even positive changes in law enforcement have increased stress for some officers: while community policing can increase

---

* Mayer, John, PhD, Personal interview.
† Angelo, Sr., Dean C., EdD, Personal interview.
‡ Violanti, John PhD, Personal interview.

officer job satisfaction and overall departmental efficiency and morale, the transition to this approach can cause apprehension. Furthermore, in recent years, there has been increased recognition of long-standing sources of stress, including those that some police organizations themselves may inadvertently create for officers because of their rigid hierarchical structures, a culture of machismo, minimal opportunities for advancement, and paperwork requirements. It is also becoming increasingly clear that law enforcement frequently exacts a severe toll on the family of the officer. We should be concerned about the stress that law enforcement work creates for family members for its own sake, and we also need to recognize that a stressful home environment can impair an officer's ability to perform his job in a safe and effective manner.

Symptoms of Stress

Lisa Wimberger* pointed out a few different ways police officers can recognize certain stressors they encounter in their profession. Officers are trained to identify different stressors that are associated with traumatic incidents. Wimberger explained that the brain's physiology is altered when an officer experiences a disturbing incident. The brain and nervous system ultimately store this picture in the mind. Dealing with stressors is physiological. The brain communicates messages to the body as does the body to the brain. The nervous system has two states: active, ready, and mobile (sympathetic) and relaxed or restorative (parasympathetic).

Robert Douglas Jr. states that stress, frustration, and dissatisfaction are the main components of police burnout. A police officer experiencing burnout is one who displays extreme symptoms of stress. Police are under more stress than the average citizen:

- Stress of being hurt or killed
- Stress of the job, dealing with the unknown
- Stress of the department
- Stress of not trusting anyone
- Stress of always being in control, not letting your guard down
- Stress of family life, emotional let down

Five Phases of Elevated Risk (Separate Levels of Intensities associated with Distress)

Law enforcement officers are frequently placed into dangerous situations, some because they were at the wrong place at the wrong time.

* Wimberger, Lisa, Personal interview.

A police officer is likely to experience dangerous or devastating situations throughout his career. There is no set time period to go from one phase to the next.

Cautious/Apprehension Phase

This is the initial stage of an officer approaching a situation that he encounters in his daily routine or beat. Anything can happen; an ordinary situation can turn into the unexpected or dangerous ordeal. The officer's blood pressure begins to rise, a heightened feeling of awareness takes place, and an element of caution becomes the overwhelming option. This is where *gut feeling* becomes a component in how the officer reacts to the external stimuli that he has encountered. His *gut* feeling indicates that something is wrong. He is confronted with danger, often beyond his control. There is an indication that something bad will happen. The initial threat will often cause a release of adrenaline into the blood stream. This release of adrenaline is a natural defense mechanism that will prepare the officer both mentally and physically for the possible *fight* or *flight* circumstance.

In the police academy, I remember a particular training called *Psych Workshop* that was run by off-duty Chicago police supervisors and officers. It involved various nonconfrontational scenarios that could easily turn into dangerous situations where police officers could be hurt or killed. Each police recruit was placed into a situation by themselves to see what they would do if/when something went wrong. The scenario that is entrenched in my memory started out simple enough. I was asked to pick up lunch for the watch commander at a local pub down the street. That was all of the information given. I was by myself and was sent down to the specific classroom (mock pub). I was in uniform, a duty belt with a police radio (in contact with the instructors overseeing the scenario) and a fake weapon.

The door of the classroom had a 6 in. by 2 ft glass enclosure in it where I could see into the *pub*. One of the first things I noticed looking through the window was that the *pub* was very dark, but lit enough to see about 10 guys, 5 on each side of the table facing each other, all standing with both hands on the table. I was apprehensive to walk in. My gut feeling was that something was not right. I looked in again and reluctantly went against my gut feeling, saying to myself, I am the police. The moment that I walked in and closed the door, I heard the distinct sound of the forestock (fore end) of the shotgun being cocked and the trigger being pulled, as I heard one of the training officers yell, "You're dead officer." I learned a valuable lesson that I have not forgotten to this day. Any situation can be deadly, trust your *gut* feeling, and if a situation does not seem right, take a step back, call for backup. The life you may save may be your own.

Conflict/Altercation Phase

This phase incorporates the potential for danger. The officer can be dispatched to this situation, or the officer can happen to come upon this type of incident, being either verbal or physical in nature. The officer may have to not only rely on his police training but his instinct regarding the situation as well. Does the situation call for additional manpower and backup or can the officer handle this particular incident alone? This is a decision that must be made and acted upon quickly. Nothing can be considered routine in this type of situation. Anything can happen. An adage that most of us have heard growing up is called Murphy's law: "If something can go wrong, it will go wrong."

Pinnacle Phase

This is the ultimate phase that a police officer does not want to encounter. Going from the conflict/altercation phase to the pinnacle phase may only take a matter of seconds. The officer may not be in the position to call for backup, or backup may be on the way but not there yet. The officer is in an all-out battle to survive. It is the pinnacle stage or *fight* stage that the officer does what he can to take control of the entire situation. At one point the officer may even experience a feeling of being overwhelmed by the offender(s) or by the situation itself. The *flight* stage may be considered an option if outside help or resources do not arrive soon or the situation cannot be controlled or handled without the possibility of getting seriously hurt or killed.

Relief Phase

This phase occurs when the officer physically takes control of the situation or other officers arrive on the scene and the offender(s) are taken into custody. It is the reassurance that the officer is no longer in danger and feeling a sense of relief that the incident is over and that he survived. After the encounter, the officer may be in a physical and mental state of exhaustion.

Reflection Phase

The officer will often look back calmly and rationally, thinking what he could have done to be more prepared in that type of situation next time should it occur again. They may reenact what they did correctly or wrong before the incident occurred, during the confrontation, and how the episode ended. Human nature is such that the officer will always question his actions especially if there were tragic or negative results because of his intervention. Police officers rarely get the proper amount of recovery time before the next job or a stress-related incident starts the process all over again. The duration of stress-related incidents eventually take its toll on officers. The more stress that an officer encounters, the longer it will take the officer to relax and recover.

Distress (Bad Stress) vs. Eustress (Good Stress)

There are a few different types of stress that are common in society and may be typical of what police officers experience. Minor incidents of stress can often lead to monumental problems for the officer. Stress is the way the human body responds to changing internal and external stimuli. There are two distinct and different forms of stress that an officer may experience on a daily basis, bad stress (often referred to as distress) and good stress (often referred to as eustress).

Distress

Everyone handles stress in their own way. Some officers can handle the rigors of the *streets*, while others have difficulty accepting the career path they have chosen as a law enforcement officer. Minor stress can build to what can be compared to a snowball rolling down a snow-covered mountain, becoming larger and larger and soon out of control. Soon many minor issues will develop into major issues for the officer. When police work becomes overwhelming for the officer, he may show signs of both emotional breakdown and physical issues.

Emotional Breakdown	Physical Issues
Panic attack	Fatigue
Symptoms of depression	Headaches/backaches
Relationship problems	Weight gain/loss

Eustress

Eustress is often associated with a positive, short-term euphoria often experienced in the workplace or in a motivational challenge or setting. A few examples of eustress are as follows:

- Given a new or challenging assignment
- Anticipation of being on the promotional list that may come out that day
- Receiving an award at the awards ceremony that the officer was invited to

Job-Related Factors of Stress

On-the-job stress can have a negative and detrimental effect on most police officers, and it can be a factor in health problems and family issues. Dr. Carl Alaimo* said that extreme stress on the job and the lack of ongoing self-evaluation is prevalent in law enforcement. Instructors briefly educate regarding stress and mental health issues in our training academies, but what does not exist across the board is annual training in stress management relief, substance use and dependency, and mental illness–related issues. The challenge for today's law enforcement agencies is to take responsibility in terms of an educational approach, focusing on personnel and the conflicts of stress.

Dr. Jack Digliani† has conceptualized an idea about primary and secondary dangers that officers face. He notes that the *primary danger* of policing is the actual risk of the job, including confronting dangerous and violent offenders, exposure to critical incidents, and traffic accidents. The *secondary danger* of policing, supported by much of the police culture, is the idea that asking for help is expressing personal and professional weakness. He emphasized that the secondary danger is truly the number one killer of police officers. How serious is secondary danger? It is so serious that some officers will choose suicide over asking for help. Digliani stated that there are three *seconds* in law enforcement: secondary danger; *secondary* injury, the harm that can be caused to officers when they are poorly treated following the involvement in a critical incident; and *secondary* trauma, also known as vicarious trauma, the indirect traumatization that can occur when a person is exposed to others who have been directly traumatized (often a concern for police peer support team members, police spouses, and family members).

Father Dan Brandt‡ noted that cops share stories with other cops, sometimes at work, at a bar, or at a party. It is one way to ease the pain and suffering they see while patrolling the streets. Father Brandt said that no one calls the police when things are fine. Police often become desensitized after dealing with problems on a daily basis. Officers do not want to appear vulnerable and keep their emotions inside and intact, rarely sharing anything with family or friends outside of the job. Bob, an officer on the job over 20 years, told Father Brandt that his wife asked him every day how his day went, and every day, the officer would say one word, "fine." He would never say another word about what he encountered on the job. His wife, after years of accepting the same answer said, "I saw on the news today that there was a lot going on in your district, but you never share what happens to you. I am your life's

---

* Alaimo Sr., Carl, PsyD, Personal interview.
† Digliani, Jack, PhD, EdD, Personal interview.
‡ Brandt, Father Daniel, Personal interview.

partner, your support system, your soul mate; you can tell me how your day was." The very next day, his wife said "how was your day today?" Bob replied, "Well my first call out of the box was a dead baby stuffed into a microwave oven." Bob's wife said, "Remember that I insisted you tell me how your day went. I do not need to know any more, just forget about it!!!"

Criminals: Us against Them Mentality

Even though a small segment of the population is responsible for the majority of crimes committed, it is dealing with the same negative elements of crime such as homicides, robbery victims, burglary, gangs, guns, drugs, and prostitution, as well as the homeless and destitute, day in and day out, that will take its toll on the officer. The repetition of despair and grief will often cause many officers to be cynical. It is sad when officers develop a pessimistic view of society, interacting and not trusting anyone they come in contact with.

Hiram Grau* stated that in police work, officers will often view the worst in people and the ugly side of society. He stated that he cannot get over "man's capacity for hatred and violence. In today's society, there are many individuals, especially gang members, who have no respect and definitely no fear of the police. They do not respect themselves, how can they respect the police?"

High Energy: All of the Time

The human body was not meant to constantly and continuously run in high intensity, but an officer's entire tour of duty is often on high alert and awareness. That is why many police officers shut down when they get home. Their body and mind needs and wants to relax. That is when they are able to just go home. Many officers have side jobs, court, late arrests, etc., where the continuous demand on their emotions and body continues. They are not able to relax, not yet. When they get home, they are drained and exhausted but must continue to be ready and available for their family. Many officers have responded that their family is what is most important to them, but many are quiet and will not share their day with their wife/husband or significant other. Sometimes police officers need to vent and let out what they are feeling or how their day has gone, good or bad, but that may not occur very often.

The stress of the job, along with the stress of not bringing the *job* home with them, eventually adds up. In the academy, it was revealed to the entire

---

* Grau, Hiram, Personal interview.

incoming class that 80% of all police officers that are married in the academy will be divorced as their career progresses. What changes in the marriage, is it the officer or is it the spouse? The officer will often blame the department, society, and the continuous stress that he goes through. It is often the police officer breaking down the needed lines of communication that keeps any marriage alive.

Always Be in Control

Officers are taught from the first day in the academy to always be in control, show no emotion, be strong, and survive. The officer is always there to be the one with the answers, handle what he has to do, taking care of the situation. The stress of doing this day in and day out will eventually take its toll on officers. The erosion of emotional health will be taxing on the officer's physical health. It is not unusual to see many police officers experience high blood pressure, diabetes, heart problems, weight gain, headaches, and other physical problems because of the constant and continuous need to be the dominant enforcer in this demanding job.

Captain Barry Thomas* stated that society expects law enforcement officers to be in complete control at all times and when they struggle with their own emotions. Many a times officers don't know how to cope in a healthy manner with the lack of control. This leads to alcohol abuse, substance abuse, sex addiction, and other means of self-medication. Thomas feels this has contributed to a suicide rate in law enforcement, which he views as staggering.

Anxiety due to Lack of Trust

The continual speculation of individuals they encounter can eventually be detrimental to even the most well-grounded officer. Officer safety is important and the officer must keep a close eye on anyone that he approaches or who approaches him. Traffic stops are routine for police officers because of the motorist that may have committed a traffic violation or because there might be genuine suspicion about the driver and/or passengers. Traffic stops are the number one incident that causes harm or death to an officer. Trust issues may also arise in domestic violence situations. These are among the most dangerous calls that an officer will go on. This unknown and volatile situation could become dangerous and turn deadly in a matter of seconds. Officers start to see everyone as the criminals they deal with daily. What is the motive of someone they encounter, always being leery and suspicious?

* Thomas, Barry, Captain, Personal interview.

Broken-Down Equipment

In larger police departments, the biggest problem many officers often encounter is the amount of neglected and misused equipment they are forced to use. An officer's safety often depends on the quality of his equipment. Squad cars are being used 24 h a day, 7 days a week. Broken-down equipment can be a legitimate and significant source of frustration and aggravation.

Making an Arrest: Preliminary Investigator

The power to place any individual under arrest or deny a person their freedom or civil liberties is a powerful tool that an officer can enforce at his discretion. Stopping someone and questioning them relies on probable cause. An officer making an arrest has many points that must be considered. The decision to make an arrest can be determined by the facts (evidence) provided or it can be a judgment call that relies on circumstantial evidence (hearsay). Gathering and interviewing witnesses also is an important component in the decision to arrest the individual or set them free. The process of subduing an individual, either cooperative or defiant, is the first step in making the arrest.

After searching an offender for weapons, handcuffing the individual, and inventorying their property, they are transported into the station for processing. If an arrest is made, it can take up most of the officer's tour of duty, which can keep the officer off of the street for 2–3 h at a time, or it can mean the officer must work overtime, where he may be rewarded with compensatory time or can chose additional money added to his check. It is extremely important that the ensuring paperwork be done correctly. The officer needs to clearly state the probable cause for the arrest and that the time frames are accurately recorded.

Writing Reports

Most departments now use computer-generated reports. It was not too long ago that police officers were writing reports by hand; now, officers transmit their reports by computer. For the older officers, they may not be as computer literate as their younger counterparts and are more likely to complain about how reports are generated. The biggest complaint now is not the excessive amount of paperwork previously needed to be filed, but the many computer screens that need to be completed. One older officer remarked, "We can do the reports on paper in half the time that it takes us to input the pertinent information on the computer, especially when I do not type as fast on the computer."

Going to Court

Frustration, aggravation, and disappointment are often associated to how police officers view the judicial system in the United States. The judicial system is seriously flawed. Many of the criminals arrested may be released because of a minor detail the police officer may have left out in his report. High-priced attorneys question the intentions and integrity of an officer. Officers have to take time out of their schedule knowing that many court cases they are involved with will end up continued or dismissed. Officers are often questioned about the probable cause that was exercised in the course of the arrest. All of this can have a continuous, detrimental, and cumulative effect on the officer's stress level.

If an officer is summoned to criminal court because of a previous arrest or to traffic court over a person wanting to appeal his ticket, he will have to go either when he is working or off duty. If the officer works days, there is a good possibility that he will go to court while he is on duty. An officer who works afternoons or midnights can count on overtime because most court dates have morning or afternoon calls. Midnight officers, especially those who worked the night before, may have to travel to court as soon as they check off. They may have to wait a few hours before court actually begins and may catnap in their car, as their daily routine has now been changed. In court, it is not uncommon for the officer to take the witness stand and state what happened. A defense attorney attempting to clear his client may question the integrity of the officer and how he initiated the arrest or determined the violation. In most courtroom settings, a law enforcement officer may become disheartened because the offender may accept a plea deal. Basically, a plea deal benefits the offender, as he will often accept a lesser charge and will receive a substantially less harsh punishment and not the penalty that the offender deserves. All of the officer's hard work and effort may end up being dismissed by the judge.

Cannot Control the Department, Policies, or Procedures

Working in an ever-changing environment can be stressful for any law enforcement officer. Between the bureaucratic *red* tape and the politics within the department, an officer may often feel that he is personally expendable. Does management do all that it can to minimize stress in a police officer's life? There are many rules, regulations, and policies that an officer must follow. Often, officers view these guidelines as unreasonable and impertinent. At one point or another in a police officer's career, he will be treated unfairly by management or the police administration. It is just the nature of the beast. An officer may get turned down for a day off, the watch he wants to be on, the vacation he asked for, or a promotion he was hoping to receive. For an officer always being in control, that is quite a different scenario, where the officer has no control of a particular situation and may be at the mercy of a superior in charge of his fate.

Working Off Duty (Side Job)

If a person asks an officer what he is doing after work or for the weekend, the average police officer is working a side job on his day off. Working a side job may benefit the family financially, but it will have a gradual effect on the relaxation time away from the job. Some departments do not allow their officers to work more than 20 h a week off duty. This was instrumental in keeping officers from overworking themselves. It was done for officer safety. Management believed that officers would get the needed rest they required and not fall asleep and/or be tired on the job, especially on the midnight shift. Officers who are tired are more likely to get into verbal altercations and will not fully concentrate on the task at hand when they are on duty. Many officers complained to no avail. They did not want to be controlled or told what to do; they felt pressured by the administration, especially when it came to making less money.

About 95% of police officers will say that they have to work a side job. Many officers will make attending court on a regular basis a way to make extra money. A few officers have been known to work every day of their entire vacations. Some departments offer *special employment* where officers can work for their department in another capacity. The work can include working in public transportation, movie details, working housing projects that have gang and drug problems, or working a beat car that targets a specific high-crime area of the city.

There is often very little time for any type of recreation or family time. In many instances, the officer has good intentions to relax as he purchases expensive cars, boats, jet skis, vacation homes, and other expensive toys and items. To pay for these simple pleasures, he often works additional jobs, so there will not be a financial burden to his family. It is a true Catch-22, getting expensive things to relax and then working additional hours, often seeing these expensive items just sitting there, not being used.

Dr. Gilmartin (2002), in his book *Emotional Survival*, mentions this as well. Gilmartin noted that the men and women who began their police careers as bright, well-rounded, ethical officers begin experiencing major behavioral deficits in their personal lives. Because of the "I usta" syndrome, officers can begin distancing themselves from core aspects of their sense of self. The officer's identity becomes tied only to the police role.

It is not uncommon for officers to not do things they would always do before for relaxation and exercise.

I used to bowl...	"I do not have time anymore."
I used to play tennis...	"but I have to work my part-time job instead."
I have a new boat...	"It has been sitting for years, can't afford the payments, gas, and insurance. I need to find another part-time job; I should sell it, but I will be taking a big financial loss. I will use it someday, maybe when I retire...."
What vacation?...	"I worked every day during my entire vacation; I really couldn't afford to go anywhere anyway. This extra money will help pay tuition, even though I really needed a break from police work...."

Dr. John Mayer noted that one example of a police officer's coping mechanisms is an officer who wants to buy an expensive boat to relax and have fun. The officer works two side jobs, extra court, whatever he can do to pay for his new toy and be able to relax. After 6 years of working part-time jobs, rarely enjoying the boat, the officer realizes that the boat is not being used as much as he would like. He winds up selling it, loses money. The 2 happiest days are when the officer buys the boat and the day he sells it.

Weight Gain: Where Are the Donuts?

Police and donuts are often synonymous with each other. Many officers need that jolt of caffeine during their shift to help them stay alert. Often the temptation of a donut along with the coffee is hard to resist. Weight gain can become a problem for the officer after the academy, especially if the law enforcement agency does not have a provision in their contract that staying physically fit is mandatory. The Illinois State Police have such a program, where the Illinois state trooper must pass a physical fitness test once a year in order to stay on the job. The Chicago Police Department does not require its officers to remain physically fit as a requirement to stay on the job, but they do offer an incentive of $300 if the officers pass the physical fitness test once a year.

Police officers often have a half hour to relax and enjoy lunch. To be able to eat lunch in this amount of time, officers often have to visit fast-food restaurants. Most fast-food restaurant menus are laden with higher-caloric food. This and the fact that most officers ride in a squad car most of their shift accounts for many officers gaining weight by the time they have a few years on the job. The combination of weight gain along with stress can cause officers to die of a stroke or heart attack at an earlier age.

Low Morale

"Deny me one day…and I will go on the medical and I will hurt you for three."

Disgruntled P.O.

Hiram Grau indicated that just a few officers are truly unhappy. "Take the police blogs" that are so prevalent today. He remarked, "Officers who post to those blogs will often post 3 or 4 complaints under the name anonymous." The officers who vent on the police blogs often display hatred in their writing, and these cynical officers may be discouraged because they may have been skipped over for a promotion, may have recently been disciplined, or may be going through a divorce or personal problems. Whatever the case, these same disgruntled officers would most likely go in the other direction if a fellow officer were in immediate danger or placed an immediate call for help. Robert Douglas Jr. said that police officers often complain and are angry because they feel that the organization does not care about them. They experience a lot of stress because the job describes who they are and not what they do. Happiness on the job comes from someone that feels good about themselves and others.

Dr. Ellen Scrivner* noted that in the beginning of a police officer's career, there is a lot of early exuberance but the excitement often starts to get snuffed out by different things that happen within the culture of the department, generally more than just being out on the street. Being out on the street, the officer tends to grow and respond to different kinds of incidents. After a while, all of that can become routine, but while that is happening, police officers may begin to feel there are experiences within the department that are not too pleasant. For instance, officers did not get an assignment that they thought was promised to them, they lose out on a promotion, they are the brunt of a supervisor's continual criticism, or they begin to feel betrayed at times by peers. Naturally, anger starts to develop but it can't be expressed openly because it will only make the situation worse and the officer could be labeled as a recalcitrant.

If a person would venture into a police blog, they would most likely find police officers who are on the job complaining anonymously about something. These police blogs give the officer a chance to vent their frustration while remaining anonymous. Most often, the officer on the blog is complaining about a supervisor, a fellow officer, or the administration. Many occupations have disgruntled employees, but when a police officer is unhappy, it could have a drastic effect on everyone the officer comes in contact with. A resentful officer will have an audience in the locker room,

---

* Scrivner, Ellen, PhD, Personal interview.

right before or after roll call. The argumentative officer preaches about how he was unjustly treated. Some officers will listen and give the complainer their complete attention, and even chime in, trading stories of how they too were victimized. The complaint could be from a day off denied to the working conditions the officer has to put up with. Whatever the controversy, the officer is sure to explain how the department has cheated him in some way. The officer may proudly boast that he will not write as many tickets as he used to write: "I will get even with them. I won't write any parkers or movers this week."

Police officers, like everyone else, enjoy an occasional pat on the back for a job well done. Some departments honor a good job by presenting officers with an honorable mention stating they did their job above and beyond the call of duty. Often, departments may have a formal awards ceremony where the officer is presented an award that can be displayed on the outer garment or vest that indicates that the officer did an outstanding job in the line of duty. Some officers feel that the recognition for a job well done does not come often enough and many acts of kindness or heroism go unnoticed by their superiors. Officers may not give 100% especially if their supervisors are quick to criticize their behavior, or write them up because of errors made in the field. The main complaint many officers have expressed is the backing of their supervisor in questionable situations. The biggest complaint many older officers have expressed is that supervisors took care of and stood by their subordinates, but that is often not the case any longer. If an officer had a mishap in the field, he is more than likely going to be reprimanded for his actions.

Lack of Career Opportunities (Promotions)

From large police departments to smaller police agencies, the lack of career opportunities becomes a concern and major source of stress for officers who would like to take advantage of the promotional process. To advance in the law enforcement field, especially in larger departments, often requires testing well on a promotional exam. Many officers take the exam for a few positions that may become available due to attrition and other openings. Many agencies do not rely on the promotional exam alone, but promote meritoriously from within. An officer may be promoted because of his performance in the line of duty or because he may be a friend or relative of the person in charge of promotions. This is frustrating to some officers because of the limited and unfair (often political influence and possible nepotism) merit process.

Dr. Dean C. Angelo, Sr., said there's a lot of competition and even some jealousy within the police departments. Everyone wants to succeed and mostly everyone wants to be promoted. Some officers merely want to work in plain clothes (out of uniform) and others want to work in special assignments. Many times police officers feel that the other girl or guy has it better. No matter what your position, or what your unit of assignment or rank is, everyone deals with the same garbage at their individual levels. Some deal with the internal trash, while others deal with the external trash.

Angelo feels that many people in larger urban department wind up getting promoted because of having family members on the job, and not because they have been the best police officers. He truly believes that supervisors and command staff should be elevated because they are good at policing and good at supervising people, and not just because they were related to someone that was promoted at an earlier time. This is a very frustrating condition of employment that many officers deal with on an all-too-often basis; and it can lead to problems with morale as well.

Cynicism

Working the streets as a police officer can be either exciting and fulfilling or pessimistic and exhausting. I believe it is how the officer perceives life itself. If the person is happy with himself, then most likely he will be happy in his law enforcement career. The reciprocal of that is also true; if the officer is miserable and not happy with himself, it definitely shows in his career in law enforcement. I remember the saying that when you wake up, you have a choice to be either happy or sad. Some people wake up happy and accept what comes their way; others wake up miserable and everything they do or say reflects their pessimistic attitude, even if they encounter something happy or positive.

I guess like everything else, a person will get complacent (and often bored) in his careers and relationships, especially with longevity. Young officers are not as attached to the agency, and they often love coming to work seeking the thrill and excitement of the job. They are more resilient and accepting of change. Older police officers often become cynical and are eager to leave the job and most likely see the world as a terrible place. "Just wait until you get to be my age kid, you will feel the same way, and you will see how this department really is. It is not a crusade kid, it is only a career, it is only a career, you'll see. Don't ask questions, stay under the radar, and just do it." The element of risk cannot be taken lightly or without due caution. There are many instances that a police officer cannot control, but he is emotionally and physically trapped and involved in that moment.

Cynicism causes negative consequences that lead to increased blood pressure, greater chance of heart attack, stroke, sugar diabetes, and long-term health problems. I am often amazed how many *old timers* have lost the enthusiasm they once had for their job as a police officer. Once jubilant and vibrant officers, they have become cynical in their thinking. Now, these officers are always looking at the negative instead of the positive. Listening to one officer, you often get a chorus of other officers repeating the same sentiment. Getting a room filled with disgruntled officers reminds me of the saying "misery loves company" and "birds of a feather flock together." With cynicism comes distrust for the department. The older officer will show the administration who really is the boss:

- So they denied me time for a few days off, how will they like it when I take extra time on lunch and a personal. They can forget about any traffic tickets for a while.
- There is no justice in this department, I will show them, and I will just slow down going to jobs, take longer writing reports, and coming clear.
- This department is not what I remember, it is not fun anymore. Now they want us to be the warm and fuzzy police. Why reach out to that gangbanger, he is only going to be in prison soon or dead.

Robert Douglas Jr. said that cumulative career trauma stress is a buildup of continuous negativity and cynicism. It accounts for 70% of law enforcement issues. Officers really never learn how to extract their emotions and share their thoughts. By keeping these toxic sentiments intact, police officers experience more physical illnesses, family problems, and death at a younger age. Gilmartin (2002) stated that "Some individuals in law enforcement, once they become self-perceived victims, can cease investing in the work role many years before they retire or leave. Once officers see themselves as being victimized, it can be hard to let it go and return to enthusiastic and committed work, particularly if the offending commander is still present in the organization. Without assistance or insight into the dynamics of malcontentism and overinvestment, these officers potentially begin a predictable system of thinking that can start guiding their judgment and behavior. When officers begin seeing themselves as victims, they begin to process many clearly identifiable attributes:

- Merging of personal and professional roles.
- Hypersensitivity to change.
- Rigidity and inflexibility.
- Ever-present feeling of threat from the organization.
- Belief one is being controlled or persecuted by the agency.
- Need to retaliate against management hierarchy for perceived wrongs.

- Social isolation from others in the organization except a "few true believers."
- Grandiose sense of self-importance: "I'm one of the best cops in this department."
- Exaggerated perception of past accomplishments.
- Internalized sense of entitlement.

Father Dan Brandt said that it does not take long for officers to become callous, unsympathetic, and cynical. Once they get home, they have a difficult time relaxing, it is hard to turn this off. Basically that is what keeps them alive on the street, but it can have equally damaging effects emotionally. It is imperative for officers to keep balance in their lives. Just like anything else, some officers are good at it and others are not. He said that police can make light of a situation, not showing any disrespect, but just a way to deflect the gruesome incidents officers experience on a daily basis. Father Brandt gave this example: One of his first calls from Operations Command was about a retiree who hung himself in a park on the south side of Chicago. Father Brandt wanted to get as much information as possible, but the officer on the other end of the phone said, "it was a bad kite accident."

Dr. John Mayer said that the cynicism officers have about life eventually leads to paranoia. An officer whose life revolves around cynicism after a while believes that is reality. Life is bad and it is not just a hunch. Officers feel like they are dealing with assholes, with the exclusion of the officer's police family. It's a fraternity, hence the name Fraternal Order of Police. There is a minority of officers who can actually disengage their job from the rest of their life.

Bullshit and Assholes

"This is bullshit and they're assholes." If a police officer has been on the job long enough, there is a strong likelihood that he will not only hear this throughout the locker room or roll call room, he has said this phrase himself. The longer an officer is on the job, the more *bullshit* and *assholes* he will encounter. After a while, everyone is an *asshole* and whatever happens is *bullshit*. Any officer who has been on the job for a significant amount of time is fiercely unaccepting of change. I can almost guarantee that the next few phrases are uttered in most locker rooms, roll call rooms, or squad cars on a daily basis:

- "I had this asshole on a traffic stop; he gave me a bunch of bullshit about his license."
- "This is how it has always been done for years; why are these assholes changing it again; this is bullshit."

- "The bosses are assholes (and they were promoted for who they know); they forgot what it is like to work on the street; this is bullshit."
- "I don't know how much more bullshit I can take."
- "That asshole refused my comp time request; when they need the time off they get it; this is bullshit."
- "It is us against them, another day dealing with assholes!"

Dr John Mayer acknowledged that the negativity is constant in a police officer's job. No one calls the police about good news or a happy event; the public calls police because they are having a problem, they are involved in an accident, or they want a report regarding an issue that directly affects them. Someone is always having a problem. Officers who are involved in specialized units such as gangs, homicide, and vice have additional trauma and stress in their career that is long-lasting. Mayer said that he sees the added stress from the job in many police officers and their families that he encounters in his practice. There is no training that is in place to cope with negativity. Cops use the terms *asshole and bullshit*. This is their way to cope with issues they encounter; it helps them deal with the negativity.

Only Police Friends

When an officer begins his police career, a transformation occurs. Officers begin to make excuses as to why they cannot be with their old friends. The officer's friends before he was on the job soon become a distant memory. A new phase begins in the officer's life, where the only friends the officer has are his fellow officers who *understand* his role as an officer and what he encounters on a day-to-day basis. Many officers have stated that "their old friends just do not understand the nature of the job and just want to hear horror stories." The police officer may soon begin to experience a unique bond with other officers in that they begin to socialize with each other more and more.

Some of the reasons that law enforcement officers find comfort with other law enforcement officers are as follows:

- They understand what we go through; it is now camaraderie (us against them).
- They go to bars and sporting events with other officers, not only to be accepted but to unwind by having a few cocktails to *wind down*, a pattern that may soon develop into a daily or weekly ritual.
- They deal with the same *bullshit* from management and supervisors on a daily basis.
- They deal with the same *assholes* on the street.

- They begin to share the same war stories with each other.
- They begin to socialize with other officers at 10-1 parties (in Chicago Police Department code, 10-1 is used when an officer is in trouble in the field; other departments may use a different call sign, but the meaning is the same):
  - If an officer is being suspended or punished by the department
  - If the officer may be in the process of being terminated
  - If the officer is experiencing a prolonged illness or injury that is putting a financial burden on his immediate family
  - If there is an illness of one of the officer's immediate family members

Police Chief Mike Holub* stated that police officers need a support base outside the department. Officers need other friends besides police officers. It is important that they have a circle of friends with different perceptions, with different points of view.

Shift Change

> "I anticipated the anxiety of change day, I felt anxious, heart pounding, and I would have panic attacks the closer change day approached….I hated my life as an officer then."

Anonymous female officer.

The Chicago Police Department ended shift change in January of 1994. Shift change lasted 28 days, which was called a police period (for the purpose of scheduling, it works out to 13 police periods for the year). Basically it was for all things considered backward. If the rotating shifts started on days (2nd watch, 7 a.m. and ended at 3 p.m.). The next 28 days, the officer would work midnights (1st watch 11 p.m.–7 a.m.) and then on to afternoons (3rd watch, 3 p.m.–11 p.m.).

The problem that many officers experience with changing shifts is adjusting to a continuous change. Adjusting to a new work environment every 28 days was their way of life, and not an easy one. According to many officers who have worked at some time in their career changing shifts, their only positive remarks were that there seemed to be camaraderie and respect for the officers on their shift. In Chicago, they rotated with the same officers; they experienced those same incidents on their watch together. Everyone shared the same experience. They socialized together, shared being tired together, and partied together, especially watch parties.

* Holub, Michael, Personal interview.

Police relied on each other more. Working a new shift every 28 days gave the officers a chance to experience all phases of how the district and the neighborhoods operated. They saw and mingled with different people at different times of the day. The police were able to be the police. The officers did not fear repercussions from management and supervisors, who often stood by them, even if the supervisor had his doubts about the officer's sincerity. Anyone who was promoted was often promoted based on the work that they did. Politics within the police department will always be evident, but at least a hard working police officer without any political clout may have been recommended for promotion because of his effort. In law enforcement today, many officers are leery about becoming too aggressive for a variety of reasons. Police officers fear being fired and/or sued because their behavior can be misconstrued or considered overly aggressive, especially because many citizens now have camera phones that not only take pictures but can record an incident that an officer cannot deny. Jim Padar explained that shift changes wreaked havoc on his home life. It was insane by today's standards. Looking back, he said that he missed many special occasions. School functions, baseball games, family get-togethers, and holidays were fractured because of his schedule. Padar mentioned that he has four sons, and the first three got cheated by not seeing their father very often.

Augie Battaglia*, who worked as a police officer in the late 1960s, mentioned that shift change had quite an effect on the body. He said, "Everything was affected, from your sleeping and eating habits to raising your family. I was always tired because I could not get a good night's sleep. None of the guys got the amount of sleep that we should have." The camaraderie was apparent during these earlier times in the police department that shift change strengthened this bonding. Officers congratulated and acknowledged fellow officers for a good arrest, their additional effort, and on a job well done. Older officers almost always offered advice to the younger, less experienced officers. There was always someone on the watch that knew what they were doing, knew what to do, and knew who to notify regarding the incident. Battaglia joked that after roll call on the first day working as a police officer, he was carrying all of his books out to the squad car. The veteran officer that was assigned to help him turned and said, "What do you have in your hands, kid?" Battaglia enthusiastically said, "The Police Academy instructors told us to make sure we bring our books with us on patrol." The old-timer told the young Battaglia, "Kid put those books back in your trunk, keep them there, you won't need them anymore. What you are going to learn is how it is done on the street. I am going to show you how to survive." Rarely did an officer seek advice from his sergeant (who often had his own agenda), because it was almost an unwritten rule to seek help from the more experienced officers.

* Battaglia, Augie, Personal interview.

The older officers were often glad to help so that a young officer would not mess up an arrest. During that time, reports were handwritten and younger officers could take the time and read a report in order to learn the best way to write a report. It was not uncommon for younger officers to have actual copies of reports with them to refer back to if the need arose. Battaglia noted that there was a review officer in the station who would put all of the hand-written reports into a category by report numbers (called RD numbers) and keep statistics on crimes for the district commander. Many of the young officers would look over the reports to see how the report was written, to gather information, or to see if a pattern of crime was evident. With technology today, most police reports are generated by computer. The sergeant is often the only person reviewing the reports because they must approve them. New officers do not have the luxury to pull up a report on the computer to see how it is done. One older officer commented that "some officers, who had a few drinks, were better than some of the sober officers today."

Kevin McNulty*, a Chicago Police officer for the last 34 years, remembers that most of his career as an officer was spent working shift change. He explained that changing shifts was not very easy and that he was tired most of the time. McNulty noted, "when I worked midnights, I was always physically tired and mentally exhausted; I napped when I could and never felt fully rested." He mentioned that after 2 weeks on the midnight shift, his wife would often ignore him, because he was so crabby and irritable. He said that he felt irritable most of the time. Officers who went from midnights to afternoons would often celebrate with a watch party. Watch parties were something many officers looked forward to. After work, the midnight officers whose next shift would be afternoons would have time to congregate with the other officers that they worked with. Usually in the winter months, everyone would meet at a local bar; oftentimes in the summer months, the watch parties would be held in a nearby park. It was not uncommon for 75% of the officers to attend the watch parties. Many officers said the watch parties had more talking (war stories) and camaraderie, good food, and alcoholic beverages if one cared to indulge. It was not uncommon for officers to start playing cards or start shooting dice (craps) for money. Every once in a while, a watch party would have a few officers disagreeing or arguing with each other, ending in a fight. It was a good way to interact and hang out.

Sleep Deprivation and Fatigue

Sleep deprivation is hazardous and dangerous to many in law enforcement. It is a common denominator that most police officers share. It is not

* McNulty, Kevin, Personal interview.

uncommon for officers to work long shifts, go to court, and work a side job all in a 24-h period. An officer suffering from continual sleep deprivation always feels tired during his tour of duty. A sign of this occurring is when the officer continually nods off or is tired most of the day.

Police officers who experience sleep deprivation may often experience mood swings and be irritable and short tempered. A sleep-deprived officer is not only physically tired but emotionally strapped when dealing with the public, especially the nature of people he encounters. Being continuously tired and exhausted can also cause the officer to become less tolerant when handling a situation or altercation on the street. With a lower tolerance level, the likelihood of more physical and verbal complaints when dealing with the public becomes more apparent. A simple situation that can be handled by speaking rationally to an individual (suspicious or not) may end up in a verbal or physical altercation. It is not uncommon for the police department to receive more complaints of verbal abuse and excessive force because of tired officers. Sleep deprivation is a major factor in many car accidents and injuries at work.

Vila (2006) said that fatigue is one of the most common health and safety hazards faced by police officers. Police officers in the United States often are overly fatigued because of long and erratic work hours, shift work, and insufficient sleep. These factors contribute to elevated levels of morbidity and mortality, psychological disorders, and family dysfunction observed among police. Vila acknowledged that sleep-loss-related fatigue degrades performance, productivity, and safety as well as health and well-being. It also degrades cognitive performance, differentially impairing the parts of the brain that are most important for making sound judgments, deciding on appropriate courses of action, and exercising restraint in the face of threat and provocation.

Causes of Police Fatigue

Vila (2006) said that in shift workers such as police officers, fatigue and its effects are rooted in four different variables.

Time of Day

Police work is a 24/7 activity, but the biochemical, physiological, and behavioral systems of human bodies are synchronized by circadian rhythms that strongly favor working during the day and sleeping at night. Police officers, like all humans, tend to be much more vulnerable to fatigue from 11 p.m. to 6 a.m.

Quantity of Sleep

Our sleep reservoirs fill up when we sleep for 7.5–8 h and then are drained during each waking hour. This means an officer who gets a full quota of sleep, rises at 7 a.m., and then starts a 12-h shift at 11 a.m. is likely to be very impaired by 11 p.m.—roughly the equivalent of a blood alcohol concentration of 0.05%. If the officer starts his shift with less than a full quota of sleep, he is likely to be even more impaired by the end of his shift. Moreover, sleep debt is cumulative and, if not repaid, will likely cause the officer to become increasingly impaired over time.

Quality of Sleep

Many police officers have serious sleep disorders that disrupt sleep or make it difficult to fall asleep and stay asleep. A sleep-disordered officer who spends 8 h in bed each night (or day) may not be getting enough quality sleep to make it through a work shift safely. Currently, the only way to manage this problem is to have officers screened periodically by a qualified sleep physician.

Number of Sequential Workdays

Police officers, like all people, get progressively more tired with each day of work. This effect is especially pronounced if the successive shifts require officers to sleep during the day rather than during the night, since night sleep is much more natural and tends to be more restorative. While many people try to catch up on lost sleep during their days off, this may be impossible for an officer whose sleep debt is too large to be repaid.

Managing Police Fatigue

Tim J. Freesmeyer* said, "I have had the good fortune of working with many police agencies across the country over the last 10 years ranging in size from 13 officers to 1300 officers. Even with the technology, communications, and increased availability of knowledge via the Internet, many police agencies are still using legacy work schedules that have been in place for decades. I routinely come across agencies employing schedules that are in absolute conflict with current research on fatigue, shift work, circadian disruptions, and officer health and wellness. Common scheduling mistakes include

* Freesmeyer, Tim, Personal interview.

long shift lengths over the midnight shift hours for four or more consecutive nights, split shifts where officer start times vary across the 7 days of the week, poor start times that increase the risk of fatigue-related accidents while officers are driving home, backward shift rotations where officers are *short shifted* with less than 12 h off between shifts, and continual rotation between day and night shifts. Scientific research tells us clearly that such scheduling practices lead to increased fatigue, long-term medical issues, and an increase in the risk of injury to the officers and the citizens they serve. However, I have come to the conclusion that these issues are a self-perpetuating source of stress in law enforcement primarily due to the reluctance to embrace change by the officers. Time and time again, I have pointed out schedule changes for agencies that would increase agency efficiencies and improve the health and welfare of their officers, yet the officers within the agency will defend their current schedule with all of its flaws to the point of grievances and arbitration. Law enforcement officers are taught from the first day in the academy to gain as much knowledge about a situation or circumstance as they can and then to control their environment. In a profession where they confront unknown circumstances behind every door, the drawbacks and fallacies of a known and familiar schedule is favored over the unknown results of something new and different. Therefore, they will stay with the "devil they know" rather than openly invite an unknown change regardless of the improvements such change can bring. Before we can manage stress through schedule improvements, we must first master the ability to manage change within the agency.

Vila (2008) mentioned that managing police fatigue requires balancing the biological and social needs of police officers against those of the organizations that employ them and the communities they serve. Police work is one of the most critical and expensive government activities. Communities must have sufficient officers on duty at any moment to respond to emergencies, prevent crime, and arrest offenders, but not so many that public resources are wasted. To complicate matters, the need for police services fluctuates across the day, week, and season. This scheduling problem is compounded by the complexities of managing fatigue and work hours. If officers are impaired by fatigue, they become less alert, their cognitive and physical abilities decline, their moods worsen, and they become less able to deal with stress. This reduces both public and officer safety because risks of job-related accidents, injuries, errors, and misconduct increase. Over the long term, chronic sleep loss makes officers more vulnerable to illness, chronic disorders, and certain kinds of cancers. Fatigue also corrodes the quality of family and social interactions that help ground officers and buffer the impact of repeated exposure to a toxic work environment over the course of a decades-long career. Preventive measures and treatment require consideration of these systematic processes that cause sleep loss and interfere with recuperation as well as the internal systems associated with patients in distress.

Shift Change

A female officer who was in her early twenties when she began her law enforcement career hated shift change. It ultimately affected her health, as she was always tired and depressed. Officer Dee said that she would have panic attacks and heart palpitations when she had to work the midnight rotation. She indicated that she would stress out just anticipating the adjustment that she had to make all over again at the beginning of the new period. To work a shift change, an officer needed to initiate a different mindset every 28 days. She articulated that an officer had to be flexible, and it was apparent that many officers who came to work needed more rest, often driving sleepy to and from work. Everyone on her watch had a difficult time sleeping during the day. Because of her schedule, Officer Dee missed parties, weddings, and many social events. She explained that she would not work a split shift ever again and would quit if it was forced upon her. Officer Dee stressed that working straight shifts are much better because an officer can establish a needed pattern in his life. She now works days on a straight shift schedule.

Lt. Colonel Dave Grossman* stated that sleep management is crucial to handling incident stress, day-to-day problems, and stress from life. Officers need time to shut down and relax. If a person has a medical problem, they see a doctor. The same should hold true if a person has problems sleeping. They should go to a sleep clinic that can implement a solution. Everyone sleeps a third of their life and it is important for police officers to get a good, solid night's sleep. There are many police officers who are sleep deprived because of their schedule, work load, and other activities. Lack of sleep, along with stress, is a key factor in depression that can lead to suicide. Police suicide occurs when you mix stress and sleep deprivation together. It is a toxic cocktail. Jeff Murphy acknowledged that officers' deal with stress associated with shift change and other related job issues that eventually cause problems at home. Years ago, officers worked 28 days to get used to midnights. When that officer and their family got used to the schedule, they had to start all over. They shifted backward; it was the worst way possible. It affected the officer's sleep and physical health.

Dr. Alexis Artwohl disclosed that sleep deprivation can cause an officer to be cranky and more emotional. There are many professions that are 24/7;

* Grossman, Dave. Lt Colonel, Personal interview.

anyone in this type of job needs to be able to cope. Police administrations need to optimize shift configurations that are the least damaging to their officers. How does an officer cope working a midnight shift? Some people can adapt better than others. Working midnights requires a particular skill. It is definitely a behavioral change in that person's life. There is a lot of pressure on an officer who works the midnight shift. They try to have a normal life; there is a lot of stress for the officers as they often play catch-up, as they try to interact normally with their family members. There should be additional training for officers who work midnights, but their family members should also receive some guidance regarding their schedule.

Hiram Grau stated that an officer's behavior also affects his family life as well. When Grau was a patrolman, he mentioned that the changing shifts often took a toll on the marriages of many police officers. When the officer returns home from a midnight shift, his spouse may have had a difficult time keeping the children quiet so the officer could rest. This resulted in many officers being tired and irritable most of the time because of the lack of rest. Rotating shifts every 28 days not only took a toll on an officer's physical health but it also affected his emotional health and well-being. Grau stated, "You can see why many police officers had marital and relationship problems, some officers that I knew were married 4 times. Clearly something was wrong when an officer would rather spend more time with his fellow officers than with his family." Grau mentioned there were a few officers he worked with that would head to the bar right after their shift, no matter what time of the day it was. He quipped about the old adage, "Misery loves company."

Midnight Shift

The human body is affected by the constant presence of darkness. When the officer arrives home, he experiences sunshine, hustle and bustle of a city beginning its day, and typical noises of cars, trucks, and buses, people mowing lawns, and children playing. It is difficult to get a full night of sleep. It is often that a midnight shift officer may average 4–6 h a sleep, a far cry from the average of 8 h that is recommended by most doctors. This sleep deprivation can often be blamed for higher incidences of verbal and physical abuse by people they come in contact with while they are on their shift.

Working the midnight shift can be extremely taxing on the body. Pushing the human body to perform in a normal way night in and night out can have a dramatic effect on even the most stable of individuals. The midnight shift will often win and eventually take a toll even on the most disciplined officer. Police officers working the midnight shift can expect different and radical changes in their lifestyle. This shift is often considered the most difficult shift to work as a police officer. These officers are in for a rude awakening for a variety of reasons. In most police departments, it is the recruits or officers with little time on the job that will be assigned to this shift. Most recruits and younger officers are often put on this shift because most officers with seniority prefer working during the days or the afternoon shift. Not only are they new and learning about law enforcement, but they will be forced to alter the way they eat, sleep, and routinely function. Officers assigned to the midnight shift will notice a change in their behavior, attitude, and sleep patterns. Vila (2008) stated that shift work interferes with normal sleep and forces people to work at unnatural times of the day when their bodies are programmed to sleep.

The lack of sleep and working the midnight shift often go hand in hand. A common complaint of most midnight shift officers is the lack of sleep and always feeling tired. Lack of sleep is most likely the biggest concern and inherent problem that most midnight shift officers experience. A collective response from officers who work midnights is "I am tired; this shift is killing me." Being awake when the majority of people are home in their beds sleeping can be difficult for a few reasons. It is not unusual to find most employees who work the midnight shift to be sleep deprived. Sleep deprivation is one of the most common disorders that many American workers must deal with when working the midnight or late shift. Not getting the normal 6–8 h of uninterrupted sleep that most people receive can often have various side effects that an officer who works day or afternoon shift may not experience.

Most officers who work the midnight shift have their own strategy to when they will sleep when they get home. Some officers go to sleep right away; others stay up and may take their children to school, work around the house, or whatever they have planned. Others may take short catnaps throughout the day, getting a few hours in when time allows. An officer who works midnights has to coordinate his time, especially in regard to police-related duties that may interfere with his personal life. Attending court is a priority for all officers, especially traffic court, domestic violence court, and criminal court. An officer can be reprimanded if he fails to appear at his appointed or scheduled court date and time. Attending court could be physically demanding in terms of sleep for the midnight officer, which most often starts at 9 a.m. and continues throughout the day. Officers who work this shift often get off a few hours earlier than most courts begin. The officer may try *catnap* for a few hours or stay up the best that he can, especially after a demanding night on the job.

Day and afternoon shift officers often go home and can develop a normal routine and sleep pattern in their lives. Officers who work days and afternoons for the most part receive a sufficient amount of sleep. Every situation and every officer is different. It is not unusual to have officers with 20 years or more experience choose to work days. This shift is often the most preferred by law enforcement officers because of the apparent normality of working a regular job, at a regular time like most of society. Normally, officers who work days are on a one-person car. There may be manpower issues that can disrupt scheduling and the availability of officers that may change any situation. Manpower issues must always be met. Other officers with less time on the job, 5–15 years on the job, often have enough time to bid and stay on afternoons.

Dr. Robyn Kroll (2014) noted that officers also often experience unhealthy sleep cycles due to work shift changes and rotations that regularly switch from days to nights or assignments to special units that require putting in long hours, which can contribute to stress and unhealthy lifestyles. In addition, officers are notorious for working side jobs, not only to support their families but to support their addiction habits as well, leading to further sleep deprivation and perpetuating the cycle.

Affholter (2003) said, "Studies have shown our ability to think clearly and perform sensory-motor functions are greatly diminished when we are overly tired. Since police officers who work the midnight shift are typically subjected to some of the most violent, and physically demanding, calls for service, our ability to make split-second life or death decisions should be of the utmost importance. If we are overly tired, or suffering from sleep deprivation, the physical and mental wherewithal needed to utilize the training we have received is compromised. The midnight shift worker faces special problems in trying to maintain family relationships and social and community ties. It becomes difficult to balance work, sleep, and personal time. The need to sleep during the day (or, for the evening worker, to be on the job during the dinner hour and the family-oriented part of the day) means that the midnight shift worker often misses out on family activities, entertainment, and other social interaction. Sleep loss and feeling at odds with the rest of the world can make you irritable, stressed, and depressed. These issues can add to the stresses already encountered in the day-to-day life of a police officer."

Relieving Stress

Lisa Wimberger is well known in police circles for her relaxation techniques and coping mechanisms that enhance a person's emotional well-being. Wimberger founded the Neurosculpting® Institute that is used by many law enforcement agencies throughout the country, especially for an officer's emotional survival. Neurosculpting is a model that incorporates meditative practice, nutritional guidance, and practical exercises that officers can use on a daily basis. The method that Wimberger incorporates creates a better brain state and improved health and emotional resilience that will ultimately help an officer manage his stress. Meditative and breathing techniques are used as tools to release the stress. If an officer cannot relax because of the stress from the job, he can begin deep breathing techniques. According to Wimberger, the body associates deep breathing with a parasympathetic release, which imparts the feeling of relaxation to the brain. Long, deep breaths actually stimulate artificial relaxation. When the officer focuses on a novel experience, along with this breathing technique, it will elicit a relaxation response. This is an invaluable tool that is important for the officer's emotional well-being, especially after a stressful scene such as a shooting or traumatic experience. Wimberger noted that everyone is born with this gift of intentional visualization and that the brain has the ability to remap and rewire through positive imagining.

Father Rubey* does not know if police officers have a healthy way of relieving stress and tension in their life. They definitely need an outlet to relieve anxiety and pressure. Father Rubey stated, "For me, I relieve stress by working out every day. Police officers have gyms in the newer districts; they should be used more. If an officer fits going to the gym into his daily schedule, it is a great stress reliever, keeping them mentally and physically fit. Relieving stress should be a priority for every police officer. All work and no play is not good, especially in their line of work. It is as important as eating, sleeping, and bathing. It leaves a person with a healthy outlook on life."

References

Affholter, S., Preparing for the physical and mental demands of working the midnight shift. Police Department, Wyandotte, MI, 2003.

Gilmartin, K. M. *Emotional Survival for Law Enforcement: A Guide of Officers and Their Families.* E-S Press, Tucson, AZ (2002).

Kroll, R. Managing the dark side: Treating officers with addiction. *The Police Chief Magazine,* LXXXI(9), September 2014.

Travis, J., Director of the National Institute of Justice, *Developing a Law Enforcement Stress Program for Officers and Their Families,* U.S. Department of Justice (1996).

Vila, B. Managing police fatigue: A high-wire act. *Gazette Magazine,* Vol. 70, No. 3. Washington State University (2008).

Vila, B. The impact of long work hours on police officers and the communities they serve. *American Journal of Industrial Medicine,* 49, 972–980, November 2006.

* Rubey, Father Charles, Personal interview.

Trauma, Critical Incidents, Risk Factors, Acute Stress, and PTSD

5

RON RUFO

Contents

Trauma

Our society is exposed to numerous traumatic events daily via the Internet, television, and social media. Every day news stations reveal to their viewers the violence that happened over the day before in their city and across the nation. Society has become immune to the continuous onslaught of violence and senseless killings that have occurred within our neighborhoods and communities. Our culture and humanity have become callous and accepting of the endless stream of malicious acts of violence that occur on a daily basis. Trauma is an emotional response to a terrible and dreadful event that can create a substantial and lasting effect on a person. A police officer is likely to experience many traumatic and life-altering incidents in his career.

Pam Church[*] said that dealing with traumatic incidents can take a toll on any officer, especially over a 30-year career. Traumatic incidents and stress from the job will have a cumulative effect on most officers. Bill Hogewood[†] disclosed that in 1983, "I was asked to be in a project where many of us were trained to support our sisters and brothers in the aftermath of a trauma and also in the ongoing problems of life. After all, a police officer is still a person with ongoing relationships, financial, child rearing and daily pressures of life. Add to that, death, horrific scenes, career criminals, and those that need help in a variety of ways. Compounding this are the media outlets that seem to thrive on the mistakes that officers make. Certainly more so than the attention paid to doctors, lawyers, professionals and blue collar careers."

Dr. Nancy Zarse[‡] noted that very few police officers get through their career without some exposure to trauma. The question is how does an officer handle the trauma that he has encountered? "I believe the police have a difficult time talking about their feelings and asking for help. They do not want to appear weak or vulnerable; they are conditioned to not talk about their feelings. There is a stigma attached. The last 20–30 years were spent never expressing any emotions. This leads to depression and overwhelming thoughts of suicide, a way to stop the pain and loneliness. It is not that the police department does not have a strong support system; it is that they do not use it effectively when it comes to dealing with trauma. Part of the culture is the misinformation about

[*] Church, Pam, Personal interview.
[†] Hogewood, Bill, Personal interview.
[‡] Zarse, Nancy, PsyD, Personal interview.

getting and receiving help through counseling and therapy. The police culture discourages anyone from receiving help, and most officers are afraid that their department will punish them for seeking help. Documented contemplation of suicide can lead to an officer being stripped of his FOID card, which means he cannot carry a firearm, and thus, his time as an officer may soon come to an end. The department realizes that the officer may become a liability. There needs to be a safe haven. As an officer, he should be able to say he is in bad shape emotionally and not be punished for seeking assistance. There needs to be a shift in the department's way of thinking, keeping the officer from losing his FOID card and keeping the star and job."

Lisa Wimberger* indicated that officers have put high expectations on themselves of being superhuman, and often do not want to address their own feelings, especially after a traumatic incident in their life. First responders and related professionals see more in a short span of time than the community will see in a lifetime. Officers not only have to deal with the stress from their profession, but also the stress that filters into, and enhances, the problems in their personal life. Wimberger noted that because she is not a therapist, many officers will talk with her about problems that they are experiencing. The bottom line is emotional resilience. Wimberger noted that officers need to identify cycles that happen in the body, and these need to be addressed long before the officers are overwhelmed with the feeling of hopelessness.

Rick's Story

The old adage to "walk in someone's shoes for a mile" in reality applies to the many unsuspecting people who truly do not understand what a police officer experiences on a daily basis. Law enforcement officers typically have a difficult time when they are continuously bombarded with traumatic incidents. Officer Rick explained that he wanted to quit working as a policeman for the first 7 years on the job. He mentioned that it did not say anything in the job description about recurring traumatic experiences. Officer Rick recalled seeing numerous dead bodies while working on the streets of Chicago. He noted that he had nightmares and rarely slept through the night, often waking up unexpectedly, terrified, panicked, and scared. Officer Rick said that he remembered everything on his shift because it was seared into his memory. He knew that he had to not let things affect him and gradually built a wall that helped ease the emotional pain that he was feeling. Officer Rick said that the wall was finally built when he was dispatched to a job where a person had blown his head off.

* Wimberger, Lisa, Personal interview.

Officer Rick explained that seeing this victim did not faze or affect him at all. He surmised, "I knew in my heart that I could deal with anything after that point; it was scary—my wall was complete."

Critical Incidents

Father Charles Rubey* noted that every police district in the city is different; some officers see more crime than others, but every officer has traumatic incident(s) that they distinctly remember. Police see the underside of the city, experiencing domestic violence and gangs on a daily basis.

A critical incident can be any event, episode, or outcome that would cause a person to experience a great amount of anxiety and stress, often in a short period of time. A few examples of a critical incident are

- A traffic accident that involves a serious injury, dismemberment, or death
- Walking into a home where a person has been stabbed or shot to death
- Any catastrophe a police officer encounters that will be engraved in his memory for a lifetime, something not easy to forget or erase
- Seeing countless accidents, homicides, and tragedy that can have a detrimental and devastating effect on an officer

Our entire nation has experienced numerous critical incidents. Some examples are the Columbine High School massacre on April 20, 1999; the attack on the World Trade Center on September 11, 2001; the Sandy Hook Elementary School shootings on December 14, 2012; and the Boston Marathon bombings on April 15, 2013. Each critical incident is marked by symbols of remembrance on the anniversaries of the date the disasters occurred. Recent studies have confirmed that a number of critical incidents that an officer experiences in his career can have a gradual and ever-changing effect. An officer not sharing his traumatic experiences with anyone can stockpile adverse feelings, which most likely will cause emotional problems later on in life.

I have chosen eight critical incidents that can have an adverse effect on any law enforcement officer:

1. An officer seriously injured or killed in the line of duty
2. Police shooting (justified or accidental). An officer seriously wounding or killing an offender
3. Coming onto a scene that is sudden and unexpected: car accident/homicide

---

* Rubey, Father Charles, Personal interview.

4. Devastating consequence: act of terrorism
5. Natural or intended disasters
6. Active shooter incidents
7. Detectives handling sex abuse cases
8. Traumatic events involving children

Officer Seriously Injured in the Line of Duty

Some officers feel that the uniform they are wearing is like a target for a disgruntled member of society. Officers who respond to daily service calls are unaware beforehand of the danger or intensity of the incident they are called to handle, not knowing that it could be their last. Many police officers go to work day after day, saying goodbye to their families, hoping to make it back safely at the end of their tour of duty. The thought of being hurt or killed in the line of duty is always present and always in the back of the officer's mind, but it is never discussed or spoken about.

Jimmy Mullen Story

When hearing the news of an officer seriously wounded in the line of duty, it makes any officer realize that his life can change in an instant. A good friend of mine, Chicago Police Officer Jim Mullen, was seriously wounded in the line of duty. He was shot in the neck while responding to a call in 1996, in the 24th District, on the north side of Chicago. The bullet struck Jim in the right cheek and traveled to his spinal cord, instantly paralyzing him. Jim breathes with the use of a ventilator. Because of the shooting, Mullen is a quadriplegic and permanently disabled. I remember Jim saying, "that the only difference between him and I is that he can get there faster than I can, I'm happy to be alive. I'm happy to be a father, happy to be a husband. I've got a lot of things I'm very happy for. Believe this or not, I'm still the same old guy I was before I got shot." Mullen has not let this incident dampen his spirit. He and his wife, Athena, started an applesauce business based on Jim's mom's family applesauce recipe (Mullen's Apple Sauce). Jim and Athena donate a portion of the profits to the Chicago Police Memorial Foundation. This foundation assists families of police officers who were hurt or killed in the line of duty. Jim is one of the few officers who has accepted his injury and has made the best of this sad situation.

Densey Cole Story

Densey Cole, a Chicago Police officer, is also a good friend of mine. In 2009 on routine patrol, Officer Cole activated his lights and siren responding to a call of a burglary in process. A few minutes later, he collided with another vehicle in a busy intersection. The accident left Officer Cole paralyzed. A few minutes after the traffic accident, a teenage hoodlum opened up Officer Cole's squad car door and attempted to take his weapon and wallet as he lay across the steering wheel paralyzed from a broken neck. Some doctors believe that Cole's spinal injury was made worse when the teenager pulled and pushed the disabled officer's body as he tried to get access to the gun. The teenager who tried to take his weapon was eventually convicted and sentenced to 10 years in prison. Every day, thousands of officers respond to similar calls; they never know what may happen to them in an emergency situation.

Officer Killed in the Line of Duty

On June 1, 2009, Chicago Police Officer Alejandro Valadez was killed conducting a field interview regarding a recent shooting that occurred on his beat. Officer Valadez was shot in the chest as he was questioning a witness on a warm summer night. The Englewood district is one of the most violent and crime-ridden areas in Chicago. A police officer's worst nightmare comes true when he arrives at the scene of a fellow officer killed. As TV news cameras scurried to reveal the gruesome details of the incident, Valadez's fellow officers were in disbelief that one of their own was shot and killed.

When an officer is killed in the line of duty, it is not uncommon for everyone involved in the law enforcement profession to reflect on the dangerous career they chose. Countless police officers look back on their careers to similar incidents they have experienced that could have gone bad. They too could have been the slain officer wearing the badge that now lies motionless at the county morgue. When news travels throughout the department that one of their own has been killed, many police officers realize that life is short and reflect on their own mortality. All three offenders involved in Officer Valadez's tragic death were in their twenties, and they will each serve out a life sentence. Each offender associated with the officer's murder was sentenced to over 100 years in prison. Justice was served, but a young and vibrant officer will be missed, not only by his wife and infant child but by his police family as well.

Police Shooting: Seriously Wounding or Killing an Offender, Innocent Person While on Duty

Officers are trained to protect life at any cost and will often draw their weapon many times in the course of their career. Actually, very few officers will ever fire their weapon in the line of duty. Killing an offender who is committing a crime is looked upon by other officers as what they do on the streets or as a job well done. Many officers have the mindset that they would pull the trigger to shoot an offender if the situation warrants. An offender dying on the street is often seen as one less person that the officer would have encountered again. A statement that is often heard among officers is, "I would rather be judged by 12 (typical number of jurors in a courtroom) than be carried in by 6 (typical number of pallbearers carrying in a casket at a funeral)."

Police television dramas highlight police officers taking out their weapons, shooting criminals, and then just walking away unscathed like it is an everyday occurrence. It is never an officer's intent to kill anyone without justification. Shooting and killing someone in the line of duty can instantly cause a lifetime of regret and emotional anguish. Police officers are trained extensively to be cautious and self-preserving, but the worst feeling in the world for an officer is when they may have killed someone accidentally, especially if the victim was a child.

An officer shot an eighth grade student because he thought the young man was a serious threat with a gun. The gun turned out to be a toy gun. In defense of the officer, he felt justified in his actions. Realistically, the officer may struggle personally, knowing that he killed a child. He will have to justify his actions to the police board and the department. The news media will often perpetuate the situation when an officer unnecessarily uses deadly force. The likelihood of civil lawsuits will continue to haunt the officer for years. Those problems only seem to escalate the troubles that he has faced and will endure in his future professional and personal life. In a vast majority of cases, when an officer is involved in a police shooting, an investigation that follows will show that the shooting was either justified or nonjustified. Police officers have to answer many questions after they shoot their weapon. There may be many unanswered questions of "what if," especially if the person shot was not the person involved or the intended target. Many cases that involve police shootings involve cases where the officer thought the person had a gun, but no gun was found.

Any shooting that involves death or injury can have a detrimental effect on the officer's emotional well-being. The feeling of guilt and "could I have handled that situation differently" plays on the mind of the officer. In Chicago, if an officer is involved in a shooting where the person that he shot is wounded or killed, the officer is mandated to report to the Employee Assistance Program (EAP) section of the Chicago Police Department within 72 h of the shooting. This is a police counseling unit staffed by trained psychologists who will discuss the effect of the shooting and the officer's emotional state to determine if he is capable of returning to work on the street. Officers may appear to be strong on the outside but be fearful of the unknown and uncertain of their future on the department: what may weigh heavily on the officer involved in the shooting is

- Handling the shooting emotionally, the worry, and the stress
- Personal financial loss due to impending lawsuits
- Possibility of being suspended or fired from the department
- Extended trial or court proceedings
- Negative media coverage
- Possibility of incarceration

The ongoing frustration is often too much for the officer to handle, contemplating the future and weighing the option of what he has to look forward to. He may contemplate suicide rather than deal with the emotional battle and trauma he will encounter for an extended period of time.

The police department investigating the shooting has to be thorough in their investigation. If not, it could lead to potentially damaging monetary awards against the department and the city that they serve. The officer involved in the shooting and any officers at the scene could be held accountable for their actions and be sued personally.

Every law enforcement agency handles police shootings differently. Previously in Chicago was the round table. The officer involved in the shooting and any officers who witnessed the shooting were questioned. Intense questioning is directed at the officer to reveal important facts about the shooting. It is human nature for any person in this type of situation to be defensive, as his actions regarding the incident race through his mind. Recalling small incidentals may be difficult because of the spur of the moment encounter that could have jeopardized not only the officer's life but also other citizens in the immediate vicinity. The traumatic scene is replayed over and over in the officer's mind, scrutinizing every detail as he justifies in his mind everything that occurred.

Pertinent information about the shooting was highlighted, especially, if the officers followed proper procedures, the department's use-of-force model, and the Chicago Police Departments' rules and regulations. The round table is attended by the officer that discharged the weapon and

- The officer's representative or lawyer from the Fraternal Order of Police (FOP)
- The officer's commander of the district or district supervisor
- Internal affairs
- Office of Professional Standards
- A detective assigned to the case

A police shooting often involves many conflicting reports and details of the event. Every witness may see something entirely differently as to what may have happened. A victim or witness may tell a different side of the story just to protect themselves. The passage of time may cause a person to forget key elements of the shooting. In most police departments, after a police shooting, the officer involved will most likely be questioned by his superiors, to see if he was justified in shooting the person(s) that were hurt or killed.

Did the officer do everything in his power to follow general orders and follow their department's use of force model/policy to effectively handle and control the situation? In Chicago, when an officer is involved in a shooting, if the officer has not been hurt or shot, he will explain in detail what transpired and tell his side of the story within an hour or two of the incident. The officer will tell his side of the story and how everything about the shooting situation evolved. The officer will have to explain in detail the following:

- Why they were at the scene?
- What happened before the shooting?
- Who was near the perimeter of the shooting, including other officers, witnesses, victims, and citizens before, during, and after the shooting began?
- The officer(s) will be questioned to see if the shooting was justifiable.
- Were policy, procedure, and general orders followed?
- Could there have been any viable alternatives other than discharging their weapon (pepper spray, Taser, baton, or asp)?

Not only is the police shooting and situation of a round table taxing on the officer, but his actions will be scrutinized in the media, by witnesses at the scene, and by the victim(s)'s family members. There is a strong possibility that a lawsuit will be filed against the officer and the police department that would question the officer's judgment and training. The officer may be sued civilly as well, where his personal assets may be in jeopardy.

A few stress-related and traumatic incidents that may affect the officer after a shooting are the following:

- Uncertainty about the future and the possible disciplinary action that may occur if it is determined that the shooting was the result of negligence on the part of the officer.
- A likelihood of being disciplined with the possibility of being suspended or fired. The stigma of being suspended or fired will create a financial burden on the officer because of the loss of wages. The dishonor and humiliation of being fired may ruin the chances of ever working in law enforcement again.
- Possible negative reputation among fellow officers who may decline to work with the officer. Scrutiny regarding previous police work and future confrontations.

- Long court proceedings and extended trial. Never being able to put the incident behind and rectify the past. Negative media coverage of the trial and constant pain of reliving and recreating the incident.
- The fear of lawsuits, financial restraints, and possible incarceration.
- Debriefing.

Denis Adams*, of the EAP office, declared that the Chicago Police Department provides a wide range of free and confidential counseling services to all employees and their families. Adams acknowledged, "We deliver individual, couple and family counseling. Our unit is responsible for delivering trauma debriefings as required for police officers following a critical incident (i.e., on- or off-duty shootings). A mandatory debriefing was not readily accepted after a police shooting when it was first initiated in 2001. The first year, many officers did anything possible not to attend the review of the impact of events on the officer after a shooting. It took 5 years for officers to readily accept the debriefing session. The purpose is to put meaning to something that may seem meaningless. Most officers have prepared themselves psychologically to survive danger on the streets. In a debriefing, they recognize their inner resilience and flexibility when it comes to risk."

Lt. Colonel Dave Grossman† believes that police officers need to be educated and informed about incident stress, especially if they are involved in a police shooting. Grossman said that in many debriefings, officers involved in a shooting experience gaps in memory, with 20% of officers experiencing memory distortion and tunnel vision. For some officers, it is quite normal for them not to hear the shots that were fired. It is not uncommon for officers to replay the gunfight in their mind in slow motion.

Death of an Innocent Victim

On June 4, 1999 in Chicago, two uniformed officers were on routine patrol. The female officer was driving and her male partner rode in the passenger seat. Both officers noticed a car double parked with a male driver and female passenger. As they pulled up beside the car, the officers asked the driver for his license and insurance. The driver drove off without producing either document. The officers stopped the vehicle for the second time and the driver again sped away recklessly. The officers radioed that they were pursuing the vehicle through the streets of the south side of Chicago, as the male officer in the passenger seat fired shots at the fleeing vehicle. The supervisor monitoring the radio zone called off the chase because the circumstances

---

* Adams, Denis, LSCW, Personal interview.
† Grossman, Lt. Colonel David, Personal interview.

surrounding the situation did not warrant the officers proceeding with the pursuit. The officers did not obey the direct order to stop the pursuit and continued on, and in fact, the officer riding in the passenger seat again fired his weapon at the vehicle.

A short time later, the driver of the vehicle in the chase pulled over, and the officers immediately pulled right behind the car. Another squad car that was monitoring the chase also assisted. All four officers hurriedly ran toward the car with their guns drawn, yelling at the two occupants to turn off the vehicle and exit the car. The female occupant was slow to exit the vehicle. The female officer yelled again to the female passenger to exit the vehicle. The female officer saw a shiny silver object she thought was a gun. Without hesitation, the female officer shot into the vehicle, killing the female passenger. The female officer mistook a silver object in the car for a gun. There was no gun, it was a silver lock.

Three officers were fired on 18 counts of misconduct, and a fourth officer on the scene was recommended to be suspended for a year without pay on 14 counts of misconduct. That sentence was later appealed to 4 months without pay. The three officers were fired for a variety of police procedures that were ignored during the chase. It was apparent that the officers were grossly reckless in their actions.

1. The officers ignored a sergeant's direct order to end the chase.
2. The officers also failed to summon medical help for the injured female passenger.
3. The officers fired at a vehicle without justification.
4. The officers failed to report shots fired at the beginning of the chase.
5. The use of deadly force was not warranted.

The family of the slain girl received an $18 million settlement from the Chicago Police Department.

Police Shooting Off-Duty Story of Survival: I Did What I Was Trained to Do

It was a warm night in June, and Donny, an off-duty police officer, was working a side job as a clown, a job he enjoys because it brings smiles, laughter, and joy to many children. A child day care center in a strip mall on the south side of Chicago planned a sleep over party for about 30 children. Donny was hired out that night as a clown. A night that began with fun and laughter ended with tragedy and heartbreak. Donny was just finishing his performance and, still dressed in his clown outfit, was bringing his equipment back to his car parked a few feet away from the front door of the day care center. As he was loading the trunk of his vehicle, two young men approached

Donny. "Hey," one of the young men called out, "do you have change for $100?" Donny immediately replied, "Sorry, but I do not have it." The young man shouted back "How about a solid fifty?" Donny, being suspicious of their inquiries replied back, "Sorry fellas, I do not have any cash on me." Donny diligently watched them as they turned the corner walking down the street until they were out of sight.

Donny walked back to the day care center to retrieve the rest of his props and say goodbye. Tired, yet happy, he closed the trunk of his car and soon sat behind the steering wheel, preparing to leave. As Donny was closing the door, the young man who asked for change, was blocking the door from closing. Donny, surprised at his presence, saw the 38 caliber blue-steel revolver in his hand. The would-be offender announced, "Up everything you got." Donny, still shocked and in disbelief that this was happening, realized he did not have his duty weapon on him. His thoughts were, "I am going to be with kids tonight, I do not need it, better to leave it home for their safety."

The thief had turned to see if anyone was watching him when Donny seized the opportunity to jump out of the car and grab the offender's gun. The only thought that occurred to Donny was one of survival, as his police training kicked in. They both began to tussle as Donny tried to turn the gun on his attacker. Donny continuously told the offender that he was the police and to let go of the gun. The young man intensified his attack as Donny slammed him into the plate glass window of a business next to the day care center. Off balance, Donny was able to wrestle the gun away and shot his attacker four times in the chest. Everything happened so quickly. The young attacker was killed instantly. It turned out that the offender was a 16-year-old boy from the neighborhood with an extensive arrest record. Donny immediately called 911 and explained what happened.

Many uniformed and plain clothes police officers, a field lieutenant, detectives and the commander, FOP representative, two ambulances, news reporters, and numerous TV cameras arrived on the scene. The young criminal was pronounced dead at the scene. The paramedics checked Donny and discovered his blood pressure was extremely elevated, considered at stroke level, and he was rushed to the hospital. Donny played the scene over and over in his mind, thinking that he could have arrested the offender instead of shooting him. Going over his ordeal, Donny explained, "It was a stressful situation; I did what I was trained to do, survive."

After the shooting, the stress of the ordeal began to unfold. After being treated at the local hospital, the two detectives assigned to the case were not very sympathetic to the off-duty officer's plight. He said, "They treated me as if I were the criminal, not the other way around." Donny stated, "Both detectives made me feel very uncomfortable, just their attitude and the way that they handled the questioning and the interview. It was not only frustrating but stressful, like they were blaming me for what happened. I thought to myself that they must have forgotten that I was a police officer."

According to the Chicago Police Department's General Orders, any officer involved in a shooting must see a professional therapist from the EAP. The therapist declared that Donny was cleared for duty and seemed to be doing well after the shooting. Donny was scheduled to go on vacation the next day, and he stated that his vacation could not have come at a better time. The next few weeks after the shooting, he was able to relax and recover from what had been his first police involved shooting. He was promised a lot after the shooting—an award of valor and 3 days off for the shooting. That never happened and nothing ever came to fruition. In fact, he was kicked off the detail that he was assigned to, adding to the frustration of the shooting. Donny relayed that for all that he went through after what happened, he could see how a weak-minded person would think about killing himself. Today, Donny is working on midnights in a busy district in Chicago, and he still thinks about the incident often, especially when he puts on his clown outfit for children's parties.

Coming onto a Scene That Is Sudden and Unexpected: Fatal Car Accident, Homicide(s)

An officer may encounter a sudden and unexpected catastrophe such as a horrendous and fatal car accident or a crime scene that involves multiple homicides. Either circumstance will alter his perspective about life forever.

A police officer intently listens to the radio as a call comes in about a very bad traffic accident that just occurred. Heart pounding and adrenaline rushing, the officer activates the lights and siren as he rushes to the call. The expected scene of a collision turns out to be a horrifying and fatal car accident. Bodies are strewn across the roadway, mangled steel machines crumbled by the impact of speed. After calling for an ambulance, the officer begins to unravel the tragedy and listen to witnesses' accounts of the tragedy for the traffic report only deepens the pain and heartache of the situation.

The officer has many responsibilities that he must take care of after any accident but especially after a fatality. After the accident, the officer goes back to his regular duties and routine. The officer stores the vivid picture of the accident deep in his memory, rarely sharing his inner feelings about what happened. In his mind, he may question why he received that particular call. After a few days, the tragic scene may play on his mind, being reminded every time he has to pass the intersection where the accident occurred. The officer may need to discuss how he has been affected by the crash, often speaking occasionally to his peers about it, but rarely sharing his true feelings with his family. The officer's sleep may be affected as it may be difficult to accept what happened. The officer may just accept that it is part of the job that he signed up for. Many officers that handle horrific accidents on a daily basis just have to sweep their emotions under the carpet.

Mike Holub* stated that in his village of La Grange, Illinois, there are many tragic pedestrian-train suicides that his officers have to handle. The bodies are often mangled and in pretty bad shape. Everyone suffers from this heartbreaking tragedy at the scene, the officers, the paramedics, the fire department, pedestrians who have witnessed the accident, and the train engineer. The train engineer involved in the accidental killing is often angry at the dead person for putting them into that situation. When his officers handle a horrific situation such as a person killed by a train, his department mandates that the officers at the scene report to EAP. The officers are encouraged to express their feelings with a professional counselor experienced in dealing with tragedies that occur in the performance of their duties. These officers need to address their emotions and the horror they have seen, not to internalize their feelings. Officers should feel comfortable speaking with a mental health professional, even if they do not have serious issues, and not worry about any repercussions from their department.

Devastating Consequences (Acts of Terrorism)

Domestic terrorist attacks such as the Oklahoma City bombing, September 11th attack in New York, and the Boston Marathon bombings occurred unexpectedly. Law enforcement officers must react quickly to control the situation, performing their duties with little regard for their own personal safety. The FBI defines terrorism as the unlawful use of force or violence against persons or property to intimidate or coerce government, the civilian population, or any segment thereof, in furtherance of political or social objectives. Regarding incidents that involve acts of terrorism, the entire country and the law enforcement community are affected. Random acts of terrorism are meant to intimidate and horrify the people of the United States. On September 11, 2001, terrorists flew two hijacked commercial planes into the World Trade Center in New York City. Any type of traumatic incident will invoke a fight, flight, or freeze response. News clips confirm first responders running toward the scene (fight), hundreds of hysterical people running away from the destruction to safety (flight), and onlookers shocked and immobile in disbelief (freeze). On September 11, 2001, many officers were killed trying

---

* Holub, Michael, Personal interview.

to help others as they ran into the Twin Towers of the World Trade Center to help citizens to safety. The officers that survived the destruction and the aftermath of the tragedy, along with losing their police colleagues, may be affected for the rest of their lives.

Garry McCarthy*, Superintendent of Police for the Chicago Police Department, explained that one of the worst experiences of his life was the day the Twin Towers came down on September 11, 2001. McCarthy was the deputy commissioner of operations for the New York Police Department that day. McCarthy said that he remembers being caught between both towers coming down and was worried that more terrorist attacks were going to follow. Many officers could not deal with the death and destruction, but the main goal was to get Manhattan open again. Many of his men were digging for bodies and body parts weeks after the towers fell. It was overwhelming, both physically and emotionally, but I was too busy trying to restore order.

As a leader, he did not have the time to address the emotional issues that were caused by the violence and devastation. McCarthy explained that he personally lost 13 of his dearest friends in the attack on the Twin Towers, and the aftermath of September 11th still affects him to this day. He still looks at his friend's pictures that he keeps in his desk drawer every day. He explained that his biggest regret is that he felt that he did not do enough emotionally for his men and women after the attack. "Even my family was scared and distraught and they did not want to get out of bed. Upper management was not sensitive to their officers' emotional needs at the time. The destruction affected a lot of people. I had survival guilt; looking back I feel that I could have done more," McCarthy explained.

McCarthy said that being in law enforcement is the greatest job in the world. But police officers live by a double edge sword, one side is that tough image, the other side does not want to show weakness by asking for help. In my opinion, the culture of the police department is that we, as officers, can handle everything. We handle the problems of the world on a daily basis. We need more peer recognition in order to help a fellow officer. It should not be the job of the supervisor. Who knows when something is wrong other than your own partner? The catch-22 of this is that an officer may be hesitant to speak to a supervisor about his fellow officer. Officers stick together, and no one wants to be considered a squealer or rat, especially if the officer who may be going through some emotional problems may need some help. We need more supervisor and peer recognition to help stop police suicide. Suicide is a selfish act, especially by how many people that the officer leaves behind.

* McCarthy, Garry, Personal interview.

National and Intended Disasters (Floods, Hurricanes, Tornadoes, Explosions)

Depending on the region of the country, law enforcement officers may experience many different forms of natural and intended disasters. Some law enforcement agencies across the United States may have a few days' notice to prepare for oncoming disaster, while others may only have a matter of minutes to react. A natural disaster can wreak havoc for any law enforcement agency because of the uncertainty or urgency of the situation. The first priority of the police department is preserving life and property.

The local police department symbolizes the authority of the community. They are often the first to be alerted and become involved when danger is imminent and have to adjust their duties as needed. There could be an explosion (intended disaster), a tornado, or a hurricane (natural disasters). Police often have little knowledge about the situation until they actually arrive to survey the extent of the damage. The demands of the police often exceed their capabilities, even though most law enforcement agencies have plans in place for emergency and disaster situations. Law enforcement professionals' service may be in high demand. They may be needed for several hours to several weeks or longer.

Any situation can range from low priority (few minor injuries) to high priority (missing, dead, or serious injuries) that includes the pressure and strain of having enough manpower to control the situation. Police officers may need to summon additional personnel, such as other police agencies, medical/emergency medical technician or the fire department, state police, national guard, or civil defense. Supervisors can always reduce personnel at the scene and have their fellow constituents return to their normal tasks. Destruction and damage that occur in certain areas of the country can be devastating even for the most grounded officer. Officers will often have to live with the tragedy, death, devastation and destruction, and the aftermath of the catastrophe. Officer(s) often relive the atrocities in their mind, thinking of the misfortune they endured. Living through the pain and suffering and the massive casualties and devastation can have a traumatic and lasting effect on every officer involved at the scene.

On August 29, 2005, a deadly hurricane hit the gulf coast of Louisiana and Mississippi and surrounding areas. Hurricane Katrina was one of the worst and deadliest natural disasters the southern region of the United States has experienced in the last few years. Many citizens were warned only 4 days before Hurricane Katrina hit land. Many residents of Louisiana and Mississippi did not expect the devastation and force of Katrina to be as bad as predicted. Residents of the Gulf States were reluctant to leave their homes and experienced the destruction first hand.

Thousands of citizens died as a result of the hurricane and flood that followed, and millions were ultimately affected by being displaced and left homeless in the path of destruction. There were a large number of casualties left homeless, hungry, and scared. Many police officers did not know where to focus their attention first; they were pulled in all directions. Citizens turned to their local police departments for needed assistance, ranging from warning and evacuation, medical assistance and protection of life and property (looting), search and rescue, and traffic and crowd control. Many officers had to choose between serving and protecting the community and ensuring that their own family was safe and secure.

The New Orleans Police Department not only had trouble trying to attend to the many citizens that were hurt, killed, and left homeless and stopping crime (preventing widespread looting), but they also had to deal with many of their officers who abandoned their posts and decided to attend to their own families instead. Not only did the New Orleans Police Department have to deal with the devastation of the storm, they had to deal with the allegations of abandonment and other acts of misconduct. Many officers were fired from the New Orleans Police department because they abandoned or neglected their duties. Several of the officers fired gave the excuse that they needed to make sure that their own immediate families were safe and secure. A few officers were suspended from the job amid allegations of misconduct including looting and conduct unbecoming an officer.

Active Shooter Incidents

An active shooter is a person who enters a facility, building, or area with the intention of shooting intended or random targets because of animosity, revenge, or just for the thrill of killing. Statistics have revealed that most active shooters have been white males. Active shooter offenders may take weeks or months to plan their attack, but the attack often ends in a matter of minutes. The gunman's mission is to hurt or kill as many people as possible (the intended target or not). An officer responding to or approaching an active shooter incident could be walking into a death trap. It is very possible that the shooter could be waiting for any law enforcement officer to arrive on the scene. The possibility of the police officer(s) being ambushed takes on an entirely new meaning. Most often the gunman has a vendetta against someone who hurt, abused, or bullied him.

Anything is possible, and anything can happen in an active shooter situation. Past history has revealed that many active shooters kill themselves when they are trapped or are killed by the police at the scene. The active shooter most likely knows that he will not survive the ordeal that he started.

The shooter may feel that they will die a martyr for their cause or, in their own mind, to right the wrong they have experienced and feel persecuted for. It is difficult to fathom why a person would gun down or target intended and innocent victims. Notoriety may be a factor in the gunman going on a rampage. The gunman knows that any shooting they are involved in will make local and national news; that alone may entice them to kill innocent people. Several random shootings have occurred on school grounds and campuses over the last few years. Many students attending classes were gunned down needlessly.

An officer who experiences an active shooter massacre will always remember the day when he answered the call to duty that changed the rest of their lives. The memory of the victims will not be easy to forget, especially on anniversaries of the occurrence or if the officer travels near the general vicinity of the shooting. Any officer who experienced multiple shootings and a bloodbath of carnage will be affected in some way. The officer may feel that he was in the wrong place at the wrong time. Officers that have experienced multiple shootings will bear emotional scars and the psychological baggage that will stay with them the rest of their lives.

Sandy Hook Elementary School

This author could only imagine the trauma experienced and felt by the police officers and fire personnel who were the first to see the aftermath of the killing of 20 innocent children and 6 adults in the Sandy Hook Elementary School shooting on December 14, 2012, in Newtown, Connecticut. Everyone throughout the United States and other countries across the world were devastated by these senseless killings.

On December 14, 2012, one of the worst mass shootings occurred at the Sandy Hook Elementary School in Newtown, Connecticut. Twenty young children, ages 6–9, and 6 adults were massacred by the shooter, Adam Lanza. The young gunman shot his mother in the face, a true sign of anger and frustration, before he drove 5 miles to the Sandy Hook Elementary School. The many police officers, firemen, and paramedics who rushed to the scene have ingrained in their memory that brutally savage shooting of young innocent children and other victims. Every first responder that was on the scene will ultimately be affected by what they saw and experienced. More than likely, if the first responders did not take advantage of some form of debriefing about the incident, they may suffer from recurring nightmares and emotional distress later on in their career. Undeniably, this incident will have a long-lasting, emotional effect on all of those law enforcement officers and first responders who were at the scene of the horrific and deadly shooting.

"A day everyone remembers" by Douglas Fuchs* Police Chief for the Redding, Connecticut Police Department

The morning of December 14, 2012, started out like a typical morning for Chief Douglas Fuchs of the Redding, Connecticut Police Department. Chief Fuchs was scheduled to attend a meeting in Hartford, Connecticut. While en route, Chief Fuchs heard officers from the Newtown Police Department responding to what appeared to be an active shooter in one of their schools. Chief Fuchs first thought it was an active shooter drill but soon realized that it was not a drill, but a genuine active shooter incident. Fuchs, along with two other Redding Police Officers and an ambulance, headed to the Sandy Hook Elementary School.

As Chief Fuchs drove through Sandy Hook Center, he encountered four teachers who, not having any students in their classrooms when the shots rang out, fled the school and ran until they found safety. The Chief picked up those teachers and eventually reunited them with their students in the Sandy Hook Fire House. News of the shooting traveled quickly through social media, as worried parents rushed to the scene. Many television crews were reporting the horrific details to a stunned nation. The first priority of the first responders was to locate and stop the shooter. As Newtown Police Officers arrived on scene, however, the shooter took his own life.

The Newtown Police Department is a 45-man department. When a horrific event such as this takes place, it is, "All hands on deck," a "Station dump." There is no one left to backfill as everyone is involved. At that time, there was no formal peer support in place and none of the responders from Newtown or surrounding departments knew what they did not know about the importance of EAP or mental health for first responders. For a small community, there is no dedicated EAP unit like there are in larger police departments; traditionally, these services are outsourced. Officers have to continue working—in patrol, investigations, or administration—and many officers have a difficult time accepting what they have experienced. The FBI has a behavioral analysis unit that deals with emotional issues. The Connecticut State Police has the "Stops Program." On a local level, many chiefs saw the need for wellness checks, timeless resiliency plans, and the need to develop protocols. Many years ago, area chiefs made an agreement that should anything beyond the norm take place, others would respond to be with and aid the affected chief. This "Shadow the Chiefs Program" works very well. Police chiefs from other departments come together and are with the police chief that needs assistance. It takes the burden of any major problem or incident away from just one administrator. He alone has someone else to count on who can make important decisions in times of tragedy or

---

* Fuchs, Douglas, Personal interview.

larger than the norm events. Chief Fuchs related that one of the most difficult experiences by far in his law enforcement career was being in a room with 26 families, while they were all notified that no one else was coming out of the school.

"I have spent a portion of my last year lecturing. Whether it was to tell law enforcement around the country our story in an effort to impart many lessons learned or testifying for changes that would just maybe someday keep this from happening again. But with rare exception, I limited my comments to the "what and the how." I discussed the facts and the circumstances. I never talked much about what it really did to those whose job it was—it is—to each and every day shield society both physically and emotionally from what most just should not experience. If I did—what would I say?

As I continue to speak around the country, I am always asked the question to which, heretofore, I haven't ever found just the right answer, "How are you guys doing—and what can we do?" And while I could easily answer that in a number of ways…"We're healing" or "this is our new normal (which has been the favorite response)"—my answer has been steadfast throughout—"Don't stand on the sidelines as this cannot be the new paradigm which our society recognizes. Acts of kindness should not be something you do—but who you are. I have been a police officer now for 26 years. I can honestly say that there is not much that I haven't seen or heard in that amount of time. All of us in emergency services find a place within us, not easily accessible, to store those events and experiences that are part of our world and hopefully not a part of yours. After the tragic incident at Sandy Hook, the healing needs to continue. We have to learn to live our life with that experience and grow from it. We all recognize that it is a new normal—a new normal which has made us all more compassionate, more understanding and appreciative of what we do have. The mission, now, is to pass that on."

Columbine High School

April 20, 1999, changed the entire outlook regarding safety in all the U.S. schools. After the shooting massacre at Columbine High School in Littleton, Colorado, almost every school across America soon began implementing their own safety and security plan. School administrators placed metal detectors at the front doors, checking students and backpacks and implementing a zero tolerance policy regarding any type of weapon. At Columbine High School that fateful day in April, two students initiated a massacre that had never happened in any type of educational facility before. Dylan Klebold and Eric Harris were not only good friends, they were good students. The intent of both boys was to kill as many students as possible. Both planned on killing hundreds of students at one time. The bloodbath lasted 47 min, as both boys used automatic weapons and handheld propane bombs. Klebold and Harris walked into the cafeteria of the school and shot at random. They walked through the halls shooting students at random and then ended up in the library. Thirty out of seventy-six handheld propane bombs exploded. Both Klebold and Harris committed suicide as the police came upon their location. In all, 12 students and one teacher were killed, and a total of 21 students were injured and sent to area hospitals.

Virginia Tech University

Over the years, there have been many shootings on college campuses that have taken the lives of college students and often ended in the suicide of the killer. The familiar scene occurred on the campus of Virginia Tech University in Blacksburg, Virginia, 8 years after the Columbine school shootings. The headlines in papers around the world indicated Seung-Hui Cho killed 32 innocent people and injured 17 others. The shooting rampage took place at two separate shooting locations on the Virginia Tech campus. It was one of the deadliest school shootings this country has experienced. Seung-Hui Cho was a U.S. resident alien and a senior at Virginia Tech. He had previously received help for psychological issues. Seung-Hui Cho shot himself when law enforcement officers approached.

Detectives Handling Sex Abuse Cases

Every race, nationality, and religion has its share of sexual offenders and child sexual predators who seem to act out solely to achieve their own sexual gratification. Rufo (2007) confirmed that many sexual offenders and sexual predators come from dysfunctional families. Growing up in a dysfunctional family may be a precursor to a sexual predator's need to seek love, affection, and comfort from children. A sexual predator's feelings of inadequacy may cause them to use force or threatening behavior against their victims. The same inadequacies may often show themselves in a dominant position of control and power toward their victims.

It is an extremely difficult job to deal with children who have been sexually abused on a daily basis. Handling the abnormal and emotional scarring of children being physically and sexually abused may be difficult to handle. Dealing with exploited children, grieving family members, and offenders that have committed these horrendous crimes can be a traumatic experience. Detectives handling victims who were sexually abused have to deal with the same type of offenders. These types of offenders are more likely to lie about their sadistic and abusive behavior. Sex offenders are adept at grooming their victim and blaming the child, and others, for their actions.

Like any crime scene, investigators or detectives must first try to locate evidence that was left behind by the offender. Crime scene processing is an important part of the investigation. Detectives collect any evidence associated with the crime, which may include condoms, semen samples, and any other items that were discarded, all of which is significant to the case. Detectives are often called into court to testify for the prosecution on the reports that were taken at the crime scene. These reports may include any oral or written statements made by the victim, any suspects that were near or at the scene of the crime, and especially any suspects or offenders. It is not unusual for Special Victims Unit detectives to request search warrants and arrest warrants.

Traumatic Events Involving Children

Dr. Ellen Scrivner* mentioned that officers learn early on in their career, then, to swallow their emotions, just as he learns as a recruit to swallow his emotions out on the street, as when they come upon a horrible incident such as an accident where a child is killed. The officer just can't start crying like the rest of us, even though they may want to, because the people that the officer is assisting expect him to be in control so they can help others who are out of control.

Law enforcement personnel are likely to handle many traumatic events in their career. One of the most difficult calls a law enforcement officer will have to deal with in his career is a call of a serious injury to a child, or worse, the death of a child. The child's death could be from an accident, neglect, physical abuse, or homicide. Experiencing the death of a young child while on duty will always have a lasting effect on first responders. The first thoughts are that this child was too young to die. Officers may relate to their own children as they attend to the victim, realizing how precious life is, and the guilt of not spending more time with their own family.

Remembering That Little Girl

The following true story happened to me as a young patrolman on the street. I was working a beat car on the afternoon shift with a female partner on the south side of Chicago. It was a beautiful Sunday afternoon in August, many families enjoying the day and surprisingly not many radio calls. My partner

* Scrivner, Ellen, PhD, Personal interview.

and I just refueled the squad car when a call came out of a person shot about two blocks from where we were. The dispatcher gave it to the beat car, as we rode with lights and siren to the address. We were the first to arrive on the scene.

I led the stream of officers into a wide open door. With guns drawn, we approached the screams and crying with caution. A few feet away, we discovered a petite, 4-year-old girl shot in the eye. Blood oozed from her right eye where the bullet entered. Her limp body sprawled across the floor. I told the dispatcher that the victim was a young child and asked for the ambulance to hurry. Upon investigation, we found out that the girl's 11-year-old brother had picked up a revolver from his Dad's dresser, squeezed the trigger, and accidentally shot his sister in the eye. The young boy did not know it was loaded or if it was real. It looked like a toy gun to him. I could only think of my three young daughters.

The ambulance arrived seconds later and whisked the girl to Cook County Hospital. My partner and I followed the ambulance in our squad car, lights and sirens blaring, with the girl's stepmother in the back seat. After arriving at the hospital, the doctors soon had the child on a ventilator. The doctor was looking at a large x-ray that showed the path of the bullet. The bullet penetrated her eye socket and ricocheted down her neck, lodging into the top of her spine. It was obvious from the doctor's reactions that the young girl would not survive. The hospital tried to contact the girl's father to get permission for her vital organs to be donated. The entire emergency room staff was upset and in tears. My partner and I were emotional wrecks as we left the hospital to finish our report.

The next day at roll call, the watch commander summoned us to his office. He explained that the family requested that we be there when the 4-year-old victim was taken off the ventilator and life support. Her organs were donated to save other young people. The girl died peacefully. I can envision this tormenting experience as if it were yesterday. I always wonder how the boy has been coping throughout his life knowing that he pulled the trigger that killed his sister and the pain and heartache of that fateful day. It was a seemingly uneventful day on the beat that turned into a traumatic experience that will be ingrained and entrenched in my memory forever.

From the Chapter the Encounter in the Book, *On Being a Cop*, by Jay Padar

Our encounter only lasted for a matter of seconds. It happened 14 years ago, but I think about it more often than I like to. I think about it intently every Christmastime. My stare would have, I'm sure, made him feel uncomfortable or uneasy, but I am certain he never knew I was there. If he had seen the way I was staring at him, he would have sensed my helplessness and fear. That intent stare had an adverse effect on me. It locked his in my memory for an eternity. It's an image, I fear, that won't ever go away. That image is the reason I hold my 3-year-old boy tight when crossing the street. It is the reason I carry my son's twin sister across the street when she tells me that she can walk on her own. It was an event for which the police academy did not, could not prepare me. My instructors made me faster and stronger. They made me smarter and more knowledgeable. However, there are experiences on the street for which lectures and gym exercises just can't prepare you. This was one of them.

The date was December 24, 1998. I had graduated from the police academy just 10 days prior, and I was about as green as a new police officer could be. My veteran partner for the night had been on the street for about a year and a half. Thinking back, I laugh about how highly I regarded his experience. He was, and still is, a solid police officer, but at the time, he was just a kid like me. We were working the afternoon shift on Christmas Eve, just hoping to get off on time. Right before the end of the shift, the dispatcher apologetically assigned us the call.

"Sorry, two-four-forty-four, but we have a pedestrian struck by a hit-and-run driver at Rockwell and Devon. There are no other cars available. Fire is on the way."

My partner hit the gas and proceeded to the scene. At first glance, we were relieved. No pedestrian down, no ambulance, and no commotion on the street. As we happily informed the dispatcher that we could not find any victim, she advised us that the victim was taken by cab to St. Francis Hospital. All right, he can't be in bad shape if he took a cab to the hospital. We'll race there, knock out a quick report, and be at check off on time. Our Christmas was just a few hours away.

We walked into the emergency room and let the receptionist know that we were there for the hit-and-run victim. Our cavalier demeanor changed dramatically when she informed us that he was in Trauma Room Three… and his parents were with the chaplain in the private waiting area. I walked hurriedly into the ER and pulled the curtain back at Trauma Room Three. That's when my eyes locked onto him. His naked and bloodied little body lay lifeless on the gurney. The doctors and nurses were working on him feverishly to revive him. They were pumping his chest and working on him in a manner I can only describe as controlled chaos. They were working on him the way a dying 3-year-old boy deserves to be worked on. All of the medical technology available and the intense effort by the emergency room staff would not be enough to save this little boy. His short life would end tonight.

After what seemed like an eternity, I closed the curtain and walked slowly to the private waiting area—a waiting area where no one wants to be. The boy's father sat sobbing in a chair with his head in his hands, clothes soaked with the little boy's blood. He held his son in the cab on the way to the hospital. His mother sat almost expressionless, in a state of shock, holding their new born baby as the hospital chaplain spoke softly to her. I knew I could offer no comfort or be any help to anyone. I could sense the uneasiness in my partner as he told me he had never handled a fatal accident before and that he was going to request that Major Accidents respond to the hospital. Even though as a passenger in the patrol car, it was my job to handle the paperwork for this, my partner thankfully took the reins and completed what was necessary.

Detectives from Major Accidents Investigation Unit, who investigate all fatal accidents, arrived shortly afterward and began their investigation. They asked the hard questions like the boy's name and birthday, how did this happen, and what did the car look like that hit him.

It turned out that this young family was visiting from Indiana. They had just finished a late dinner at a restaurant when dad went out to warm up the car. Mom waited in the restaurant for a few minutes and then carried their newborn in her arms as their 3-year-old son held onto her finger while walking alongside her. When the little boy saw his dad warming up the car across the street, he let go of his mother's finger and ran into the street toward him. That's when a silver sports utility vehicle struck him. The little boy was dragged underneath the SUV for about a block before his body came to rest on the cold pavement. Not wanting to wait for an ambulance, his father picked up his little body and raced him to the hospital in a cab. I found out months later that the driver of the SUV fled to Mexico after the accident. He later returned and was arrested.

I didn't speak of this incident the next morning while celebrating Christmas at my parents' house with my family. It would be the first of many events throughout my police career that I wouldn't speak of. Someday, God willing, years from now, my kids will be grown and read this story. And then they'll understand why daddy held their hands a little too tight at times and why they were carried across the street when they thought they were too big to be carried. Hopefully, they will understand how precious they are to me and how hard I've worked to protect them. And maybe years from now, if they see me staring off into space at a Christmas Eve party while everyone else is laughing and enjoying the celebration, they'll know that it's just that time of the year when their daddy must remember December 24, 1998, and the moments spent with that other little boy.

The following are the five situations that can have an adverse physiological effect on any law enforcement officer.

Being under Investigation for Allegations of Criminal Behavior, Indictment, or Incarceration

Police officers never imagine being on the other side of the law or being labeled a criminal. "I am one of the good guys, how can I be going through this, it's unbelievable." The fear of being arrested and convicted of a crime and feeling the despair of becoming an outcast within your own department and police family is extremely difficult to handle. Police are held to a higher standard as soon as they take the oath of office. The Constitution of the United States clearly states that everyone is innocent until proven guilty, but the general public often does not think that way when it comes to a police officer. The sentiment by the general public is that police officers often take advantage of their position of authority and that police should know better. In the mind of the public, the officer is most likely guilty.

An officer who is under investigation will most likely be stripped of his police powers and will have to turn in his badge and police identification card. The principle of innocent until proven guilty will take on a different connotation. The stigma associated with allegations of criminal misconduct will be difficult to handle, even if the officer is not guilty. The accused officer will always be looked upon as a "black sheep" and "bringing discredit to the badge."

Violations of department rules and regulations or impending criminal charges against an officer will often be highlighted in the news media. Allegations of police misconduct may also involve the initiation of a personal, civil, or federal lawsuit that may have implications for the officer and/or the police department financially. The officer has to contend with the likelihood of being fired from the job and the possibility of going to prison.

If an officer is fired from the department, he may have to personally incur the cost of an attorney along with the shame, embarrassment, and unpredictability of the trial. In many police stations, it is not uncommon for the officer's fellow workers to rally with a fundraiser to assist the officer financially through this difficult ordeal. A 10-1 (a code that signifies that an officer is in grave danger and needs help immediately) party will often assist the family of the officer by raising money for their legal defense or to assist with household expenses. It may not take long for an officer to fall into depression, especially when he is not working, bills mount up, and their future seems bleak. The following thought may go through the officer's mind:

- The reality of being alone, the officer's reputation of a once honest cop is tarnished.
- Suspension and termination from the police department.
- Financial obligations the officer will never be able to repay or recover from.
- In their mindset, the only solution would be to end the pain. It is an outcry of desperation.
  - "No one cares anyway if I end it all"
  - "I will be better off dead than living incarcerated"
  - "I can't stand the heartache any longer"

- "Where were my friends when I really needed them, where are they now"
- "Why me"
- "Just my luck"
- "I do not deserve this"

Sexual Accusations or Misconduct On- or Off-Duty

Police officers are always conscious of the situation they are involved in, especially with an individual of the opposite sex. In many police departments, officers must call in to their dispatcher their mileage and time if they ever put someone of the opposite sex in the back of their patrol car or cruiser, especially if they are transporting a child. When an officer is accused of sexual misconduct, he will have a difficult time explaining his innocence and expressing to fellow officers that nothing happened. The stigma of a police officer as a sex offender will always be his badge of shame.

An allegation of sexual misconduct carries the same stigma of a sex offender who is incarcerated, they are shunned and ostracized. Even if the officer is innocent, the dishonor of the allegation will always undermine his credibility. After a serious accusation, the police department will not allow the officer to work on the street until his case is finished. The police department will keep the officer on desk duty, in call back (just answering phones and doing reports), anywhere away from the public until the matter is resolved. An accusation of an officer as a sex offender can be extremely difficult for an officer's emotional well-being and stability. Police officers are always judged at a higher standard; the consensus of the public is "the officer should know better."

Lawsuits

Police officers take the oath of office to serve and protect. If police officers were to be sued for every questionable arrest or altercation with a citizen, there would be no one in law enforcement. Even though it is difficult to sue a police officer, it is not impossible. Police officers enforce the laws and there are limits to what an officer can do in the performance of his job.

If a police officer is performing his duty in a proper manner, he will be exonerated from any lawsuit, because he did not violate a person's rights. Every police department proclaims that their officers cannot be prohibited from doing their job and enforcing the law. There will always be times where police involvement will cause someone to get injured or damage property.

Officers have to make split-second decisions and mistakes will inevitably be made. Very often, an agency will be sued, and the officer(s) involved will have to testify to what occurred. Just being named in the lawsuit may still affect the officer emotionally even though no money will come out of the officer's pocket.

There are a few officers that have stepped back and are not as aggressive as they once were. Many officers have not been very assertive for the fact that their aggressiveness may wind the officer in unnecessary and unwanted litigation and the likely chance of being sued civilly. A police officer can be sued if there is a deliberate and unwarranted action taken by the officer that is outside of the law and his police powers. The officer may actually have to pay out of his pocket for an attorney, with a likelihood of losing any accumulated savings, losing his house and car or anything of value. A judge may determine if a police officer could be liable for his actions and if his actions were in the performance of his job. If a judge finds the officer liable, the case could go forward.

Lawsuits against police agencies often name the police officer in the lawsuit as well. Many of the lawsuits that are filed are for excessive force by police. This occurs when the victim that has been involved in some type of altercation with the police complains that excessive force was used unnecessarily. The victim claims to be unjustly beaten and his injuries were considered serious. There have been lawsuits filed on behalf of families that have sued because the victim died due to their altercation with police.

Lawsuits against the police may be filed because of malicious prosecution or false arrest. Victims may have been arrested because the officer did so for no other reason than malice, hatred, and dislike. The victim indicates that there was no probable cause and the malicious prosecution associated with their arrest violated the victim's Fourteenth Amendment rights in the process. The Fourteenth Amendment forbids anyone from denying a person's right to life, liberty, or property without due process of law.

Dr. Scrivner acknowledged that she has known many officers that have committed suicide because they have been threatened with lawsuits. Lawsuits are a growing phenomenon, and many police officers feel betrayed when they are part of a lawsuit because, in their mind, they did their job as they were taught and how they were supposed to. Then, when faced with a lawsuit, they may feel that others have turned their backs on them and that there is no one there to protect them, including the lawyers slated to represent them. They often lose confidence in the city or county legal system and fear not only a loss of financial resources, but also a loss of support from the police administration and the community they are sworn to serve. As those feelings of loss build up, either physical or psychological loss, an officer is more at risk for a behavioral crisis that could result in suicidal behavior.

Being Arrested for DUI, Substance, or Alcohol Abuse

Police officers are associated with being on the right side of the law. They invoke a higher standard of the law under which they serve but also by other members of the department and the general public. In the United States, our judicial system lives by the principle that everyone is "innocent until proven guilty." The very statement of "innocent until proven guilty" is often marginalized when police officers make immoral or unethical choices and wrong decisions. Any police officer accused of a crime or impropriety is most often assumed to be guilty. The reputation of a hardworking and honest cop will be tainted with mistrust and speculation caused by previous allegations. Almost no one will remember the respectable career he may have had, but they will never forget the stigma and disgrace they may have brought upon themselves and their department.

Not only will the possibility of a jail sentence for an officer lead to despair and confusion but the officer's future will most likely be unbearable and nerve-racking at even the thought of being incarcerated. If the officer is sent to prison, he will be the target of vengeance and torment every minute he is incarcerated. Just the thought of being physically and mentally harassed is enough for an officer in this type of predicament to take his life instead of enduring what is evident prognostication of his future.

Being Suspended or Terminated from the Police Department

For any police officer, being fired from the job comes with serious repercussions. The officer has either violated or broken particular rules or regulations or the officer committed a crime. A few examples of true stories that I have encountered working as a police officer are as follows:

An officer comes home after a rough day at work and has words with his wife that lead to another heated argument. The argument has been ongoing for the last few days but becomes more heated as the hours go by. The officer takes his gun out in frustration and points it at his wife as his two teenage daughters walk into the room. The daughters are crying, pleading with their father to put the gun down. Neighbors, hearing the loud screaming and commotion, call the police. The officers who arrive at the scene call for a supervisor when they realize that one of the parties involved in the domestic disturbance is a police officer. The patrolmen separate the husband and wife and begin to investigate the domestic situation when the sergeant arrives at the house.

After conferring with the wife and the two daughters about what happened, he spoke with the off-duty police officer. The off-duty officer admitted pointing his weapon at his wife but said that it was unloaded and that he only wanted to scare her. The sergeant ordered the police officers at the scene to confiscate the off-duty officer's gun, star, and police identification. The off-duty officer was soon led away in handcuffs to a district station where he was arrested and processed for domestic battery. The police review authority was notified and recommended to the police board that the officer be immediately relieved of all police powers and be suspended without pay.

The officer's wife filed for divorce soon after the incident and the officer's two children now live with their mother. The unpaid bills started accumulating, and the officer's house soon went into foreclosure for nonpayment of the mortgage. The officer will be afforded due process like any other citizen, but his case will eventually go in front of the police review board who will determine the officer's fate. What the officer did warranted being suspended for 30 days pending separation from the department. The police board recommended that the officer be fired for his actions related to the domestic battery. The superintendent upheld the police board's decision and fired the officer. Two days after being fired, the officer shot himself with his own weapon.

Father Dan Brandt* confirmed that another devastating blow to any officer is being stripped for something wrong he has done on or off the job. Officers being stripped and relieved of their duties are not prepared at all for the consequences that lie ahead. The department takes the officer's star, Firearm Owner ID card, and ID card. That is the officer's life, and it means everything to them. The only thing they do not take away is the officer's gun, which they eventually use to kill themselves.

Victoria Poklop† noted that if an officer is emotionally unstable, it could lead to further consequences and bad decision making that include police misconduct where an officer could be suspended or fired. The risk is high, and the consequences can be traumatic. Bad behavior includes being intoxicated at work, not showing up for work, and domestic and personal issues that involve the officer's career. Poklop specified that having therapists and counselors outside of the department has benefits. First, the officer can anonymously seek emotional help or counseling. And second, because the officer's department would not find out, the officer is more likely to follow through with therapy. The stigma of being fired weighs heavily with every officer, especially if they have to be admitted into a psychiatric facility. It is a traumatic, humiliating situation if they are mandated to go to a local hospital where they have transported others needing help. Their thoughts are, "I take people to this hospital, now you want me to go there?" Any psychiatric

---

* Brandt, Father Dan, Personal interview.
† Poklop, Victoria, Personal interview.

hospitalization should be discussed thoroughly with the officer and consideration to the location of the hospital should be contemplated by the department well ahead of a crisis to prevent traumatizing the officer.

Acute Stress Disorder

The continuous and gradual encounters with risk and anger will eventually take their toll on police officers. The culmination of constant stress, tension, and anxiety may cause law enforcement officers to experience acute stress disorder. For example, an officer encounters a terrible and horrific incident during his tour of duty. That incident stays with that officer for hours, days, and weeks on end. The incident, even subtly, has a ripple effect in the officer's time away from the job, affecting his mood and his ability to get a restful sleep. An example of a traumatic incident may be a situation where two people are burned beyond recognition in a traffic accident. Remembering and recalling the tragedy is common, especially if the officer is dispatched to a nearby location.

An officer may be impacted by 15–20 acute stress disorder episodes in the course of his career. Acute stress disorder transpires fairly quickly and dissipates over time. More often than not, the majority of police officers recover from the dangerous situations on their own time and in their own way, through internal assessment and acceptance. The thoughts of the traumatic incident may eventually fade through time, but the reality of the situation will never be forgotten. A small number of officers will recall the tragedy on a daily basis; not being able to forget the chaos and devastation will severely impact them the rest of their lives.

Everyone reacts differently to stressful situations. Every individual is unique in the way they handle nerve-racking circumstances. As officers, we build up our own unique defense mechanisms as we go through life. Pressure and stress can affect officers differently; what can be stressful to one officer may not faze another. After the tragic disaster of 9/11, many Americans are still affected by the memories, including on the anniversary marking the disaster. People remember where they were when they heard the news that the Twin Towers of the World Trade Center fell, similar to other fatal and destructive events that have occurred to our nation, or the day Pearl Harbor was bombed, or when President John F. Kennedy was assassinated or when Martin Luther King was killed. Extreme tragedy has a way of becoming a mainstay in a person's memory. Even the most stable officer can be affected by a steady stream of traumatic events that he encounters throughout a short period of time or by the time they retire. The sequence of many major episodes of trauma, devastation, and killing can lead to posttraumatic stress syndrome.

Posttraumatic Stress Disorder

Dr. Nancy Zarse said, "Let's face it, police work is very macho, and an action oriented culture that doesn't promote processing an officer's reactions and emotions. The negative emotional issues fester and eventually poison the officer. Police officers handle tragedies every day—tragic car accidents, horrific crime scenes, many victims of violent crimes—add that with bosses who complain, shift work, low pay, poor benefits, judges, attorneys, the list goes on. Police officers become powerless and rarely process or speak to anyone about their own emotions. Those are the ingredients that lead to depression, posttraumatic stress disorder (PTSD), and suicide." Dr. Carl Alaimo* said that the effect of stress is that it increases PTSD in law enforcement officers. Robert Douglas Jr.[†] noted that PTSD is directly associated with law enforcement and it is the greatest contributor (30%) to mental health issues that law enforcement officers encounter. As the toxic trash deepens for the officer, so does the desire to choose suicide.

Jeff Murphy[‡] said there are obvious signs of PTSD in many veteran officers. They take everything with a grain of salt. They are always looking for a person's motivation or where are they going with a statement. Lifelong police officers do not have the benefit of seeing the world with rose-colored glasses. Police officers see everything in black and white. According to the U.S. Department of Veteran Affairs (2014), PTSD can occur after someone goes through a traumatic event, like combat, assault, or disaster. Because PTSD is an anxiety disorder that can have long-lasting effects, it is often associated with military (shell shock) and law enforcement personnel. The human body can only process so many traumas. Everyone handles trauma differently. Instinctively, humans are similar to most animals when confronted by danger. The natural response to danger is to fight (stay and protect yourself) or flight (move away quickly from imminent danger). Trauma can affect this fight-or-flight behavior. A police officer who suffers from PTSD experiences the previous trauma of danger, even though that danger is no longer present or is not an issue. The officer is reminded in everyday occurrences of the tragedy that was experienced. An officer who experiences PTSD is continuously traumatized by recurring thoughts and nightmares.

- Intersection where a fatal accident occurred
- Reliving the same vivid memories over and over
- Nightmares, cold sweats, jumping up in bed
- Wanting to always be alone

---

* Alaimo, Carl Sr. PsyD, Personal interview.
[†] Douglas Jr., Robert, Personal interview.
[‡] Murphy, Jeff, Personal interview.

- Hard to focus on one thing, mind wandering
- Bothered by others or their problems
- Crying spells, lost interest in things they enjoy, lonely, left alone, pull away from family and friends
- Panic attacks, jittery, frazzled, and skittish, anxious
- Drinking to self-medicate, deal with problems by drinking
- Hard to stay focused. Not caring about personal hygiene

Bill Hogewood noted that PTSD is a condition where a random incident triggers a reaction that may last for a short to an extended period of time. Bill claimed that police officers who have 5–8 years on the job are still less likely to share their experiences, especially tragedies they experienced. We had PTSD before that acronym was even thought of. PTSD is a new title for an old thing. Many officers had frequent nightmares or trouble sleeping and a difficult time coping with family. Today, upper management may express concern for PTSD, but in my opinion, it is just lip service. They enjoy the spotlight in the media, but they do not step up to the plate when they need to sign off on needed services. If politicians really care about PTSD, they should allocate the necessary funds to tackle this problem. A fine example of this is in Chicago; they have 3 or 4 licensed clinicians for such a large department. In my opinion, there should be 8–10 clinicians for that size department.

In the military, PTSD can develop from the perils of war that include numerous fatalities, torture, and mass destruction. For law enforcement, it is working the streets, dealing with an undesirable population, drugs, gangs, and guns. Many environmental factors can be incorporated into how an officer handles extreme stress. These can often be seen in the formative years when a child is growing up and include emotional outbursts, depression, being withdrawn, head injuries from a fall, or showing any signs of mental illness. A common side effect of PTSD is having nightmares and recurring thoughts and flashbacks of the traumatic incident. These thoughts can trigger panic attacks, an increased heart rate (heart palpitations), uncontrollable sweating, and hyperventilating.

A police officer may experience feelings of guilt and remorse following what he did or didn't do at the scene of a traumatic incident. Many New York City law enforcement officers and their cohorts from the fire department continue to suffer from PTSD as they relive the trauma and the tragedy that occurred on 9/11. For example, the officer may feel guilt for not running into the Twin Towers of the World Trade Center to save lives like the rest of his team. Everyone on his team was killed, leaving them the only survivor. The trauma of the mass destruction, along with being the only survivor, may cause various symptoms of PTSD. The officer may always be reminded about the incident when he passes by the Twin Towers of the World Trade Center, or they hear a deceased officer's name, or the anniversary date. If the same officer saved a life during 9/11, the officer's emotional well-being may not be as taxed because in the face of tragedy, there was still a positive ending.

- Identify and deal with the guilt.
- Relaxation and the ability to accept what has occurred.
- Sadness, worry, and anger.
- Antidepressants are often prescribed to treat PTSD.
- Coping through any adversity.
- Enjoy different activities that are relaxing and fun.
- Confiding in others after the tragedy has occurred.

According to the National Institute of Mental Health, a person must be experiencing the following issues to be diagnosed with PTSD:

- At least one reexperiencing symptom
- At least three avoidance symptoms
- At least two hyperarousal symptoms (startled, tense, difficult time sleeping)

The National Center for PTSD (2013) stated that PTSD can occur after someone goes through, sees, or learns about a traumatic event such as

- Combat exposure
- Child sexual or physical abuse
- Terrorist attack
- Sexual/physical assault
- Serious accident
- Natural disaster

Officers that have exhibited signs of PTSD have a difficult time coping with even the simple stress of day-to-day life. It is not uncommon for police to have their sleep interrupted by nightmares and flashbacks of recurring and traumatic situations they were involved in or that they witnessed. It is not uncommon for an officer suffering from the effects of PTSD to have a difficult time trusting anyone.

Policemen will do anything to survive. The caveat of PTSD is that the person experiencing it often cannot handle the pain. I am not denying that the job of being a police officer has an impact on his life, but if you check the officer's background, most often it is not just the job. An individual's character may be the catalyst for the reactions to trauma. Many departments are aware of PTSD, but I believe it may affect a soldier to a greater degree. You hear PTSD associated mostly with soldiers, and I agree; there is more to the stress of combat and they have an unusually high rate of suicide. A positive step to recover from PTSD is that the affected person may need to relive his experience in order to recover emotionally from the trauma. PTSD is a symptom of mental illness, and persons who experience PTSD eventually have to address the adversity they experienced to restore any type of control in their lives. The same symptoms, to a lesser degree, and the time span for onset of symptoms and the length of suffering, occur in acute stress disorder, which probably should be the topic of conversation, research, and intervention.

Lt. Colonel Dave Grossman said that when an officer reexperiences a life–death situation, intense fear or horror that is not PTSD is a normal occurrence. PTSD only occurs when every symptom associated with PTSD lasts at least a month. PTSD is normal to an abnormal situation, and clinicians are very good at treating PTSD. Hundreds of thousands of combat officers and police officers have recovered from PTSD. The officer who was involved in a traumatic incident has to make peace with the memory. Part of the healing process is for that officer to separate memory from emotion. It is important and healthy for police officers to talk about tragedy and traumatic events that they have experienced and not lock down their emotions. Grossman suggests that the majority of police officers are strong and able to handle almost every situation and incident that they encounter. They have had extensive training in tactics and awareness; they have body armor and are prepared physically to do the job.

References

National Center for PTSD, www.PTSD.va.gov, National Institute of Mental Health, U.S. Department of Veteran Affairs website.

National Institute of Mental Health, www.nimh.gov/index.shtml.

Padar, Jim and Jay, Personal interview (2014), Chapter used with permission from the book *On Being a Cop*, Avia Publishing, Lake Placid New York.

Rufo, R. (2007), Dissertation, an investigation of online sexual predation of minors by convicted male offenders.

U.S. Department of Veteran Affairs (2014), www.USA.gov.

Violanti, John, PhD, Personal interview.

Nine Personal Issues That Can Be Detrimental to an Officer

6

RON RUFO

Contents

> Never tell your problems to anyone...20% don't care and the other 80% are glad you have him
>
> **Lou Holtz, Football coach**

Relationship Problems

Relationship issues and problems can be a major factor, especially if a police officer is contemplating suicide. In the police academy, I was told by my homeroom instructor that many officers who are married will be divorced by the time they finish their career. I wondered silently, why is this so, and is it due from the stress of the job? A vast majority of studies have indicated that my homeroom instructor was correct in his prediction. Statistics show that close to 80% of police officers who are married at the time they enter the Police Academy go through a divorce once they are on the job. Denis Adams noted that relationship conflict stressors include diminished and disrupted time with spouse and family, decrease in effective and relational communication, and unresolved or avoided problem about money, in-laws, child discipline, and intimacy needs.

Father Tony Pizzo* asked how many officers in reality do not take the opportunity to decompress after a negative experience. Officers need to process the pressure. It is a desperate situation; the officer indirectly takes his problem on the street home with him. It is the family and children that are ultimately affected. Many officers personify and project the attitude of being tough. This macho behavior and hardline assertiveness of "you can't get to me" can only last so long. In reality, that arrogance has to affect him; everyone has a breaking point. That constant pressure is not good. Officers must find a release, to reorient themselves in some way. It is difficult to live a normal life when a person has that much stress. It affects his or her professional and personal life, marriage, spouse, and everyone. They are carrying emotional baggage with him constantly. When officers become distressed, and cannot deal with the pressures of life anymore, that is when they feel the only option is suicide.

Dr. John Violanti† noted previous research has indicated that problems with interpersonal relationships may increase the potential for suicide. In New York City over the past 10 years, officers were involved in extramarital affairs, were recently separated or divorced, or had conflicts with supervisors at work. One reason for relational difficulties may be an emotional detachment from others. The role of a police officer calls for depersonalization—interpersonal relationships, on the other hand, call for personalization. The police culture socializes officers into not expressing emotion, to put up an emotional barrier to protect themselves from the human misery they witness. As a result, the personal relationships of police officers are not personal at all; they are more like transactions on the street. Significant others soon become less important to the police officer. Compassion is subdued in favor of the police culture, which takes precedent over most other emotional feelings. In some respects, the police role becomes a safe place to hide but at the same time does not allow for an outlet of emotions. The inability for police officers to use other roles to solve problems with a family person, friend, or lover may be behind many police relationship problems.

Sean Riley‡, founder of Safe Call Now, said that many first responders have the same problems as the general population, but many officers actually isolate themselves and rarely talk about their own frustrations, emotional pain, and lack of well-being. Besides working as first responders in scheduling

* Pizzo, Father Tony, Personal interview.
† Violanti, John, PhD, Personal interview.
‡ Riley, Sean, Personal interview.

and administration, police officers have to deal with family issues, relationship problems, separation and divorce, financial strain, and side jobs. Many officers often feel overwhelmed with nowhere to turn.

Domestic Battery Involving the Police

Police officers are called upon daily to respond to domestic situations that often involve a husband and wife, boyfriend and girlfriend, or other family relationship. It is not uncommon for police officers themselves to be involved in domestic relationship problems in their personal lives. Domestic battery takes on a different connotation and consequence when a police officer is personally involved in this dilemma; it can have a dramatic and damaging ripple effect.

It is not uncommon for any police officer involved in a domestic situation to have a supervisor of a higher rank notified and dispatched to the scene, often to the officer's home. The supervisor, when called to this situation, will have to make a judgment call as to the behavior of the police officer involved. The supervisor will determine if the police officer has committed assault and/or battery against his significant other or family member or if he is guilty of another crime. The supervisor must determine if the officer should be taken into custody, arrested, and have his gun and ID taken. A report will be written explaining the situation and documenting what the supervisor encountered at the scene. In Chicago, a complaint register number (CR#) will be issued against the officer if the supervisor determines that the officer has been the aggressor and is at fault in that situation. An investigation into the situation will begin immediately when a CR# is issued.

If the police officer is stripped of his weapon, they cannot work in the capacity of a police officer. In cases such as these, the police officer involved in a domestic situation can be assigned to administrative duties, can be ordered to undergo psychological evaluations, or may be suspended without pay (with the possibility of being fired from the department) until the investigation is completed. Unfortunately, these types of investigations can literally take months or longer to resolve. This is a very serious matter that can cause a financial drain on the officer. It is not uncommon for fellow officers to try to support an officer if this should occur by having fundraisers or 10-1 parties (10-1 is a code in Chicago for an officer down/or in trouble) that will try to help the officer with money, not only for legal expenses but other financial obligations. Brad Woods* claimed that domestic violence and divorce were common because the officer was rarely home, and when he was it was not pleasant for anyone in the family.

* Woods, Brad, Personal interview.

Separation, Divorce, and Custody of the Children

Not only do officers worry about the strain and stress of the job, but now facing the future alone is often more than they can bear. The beginning of the process can cause even the most even-minded and level-headed couples to fight and argue, coupled with the fact that lawyers initiate unnecessary arguments and accusations of deceit and exploitation, distorting the image of their one-time relationship. Sharing custody of the children or seeing his children on a limited basis may cause an officer additional stress, especially if his schedule dictates a time schedule he cannot manage. The court may dictate something that he cannot control—something an officer has a hard time relinquishing. The officer will often be obligated to pay attorney's fees and possibly lose half his pension, his home, and the custody of his children. The feelings of anguish and despair, coupled with stress at work, only add to his frustration.

According to recent statistics, a person who is divorced is three times more likely to commit suicide than a person who is married. A police officer going through a divorce will often go through one of the most difficult times in his life. Resentment; uncertainty of the future; strained relationships with past family, friends, and in-laws; animosity; resentment; and blame are filtered through the opposing attorney(s). New living arrangements and child support become issues in this stressful situation. Divorce proceedings begin to wear down what is left of a meaningful relationship. Once a loving couple, they are now feeling the despair of a strained relationship, constant fighting, bickering, and tormenting each other through arguments and threats that often get out of control. The strain of serious domestic violence issues can lead to the officer getting stripped of his police powers with the possibility of facing a suspension and/or being fired.

The financial burden of divorce may also become an issue. The police pension the officer has worked so hard for may now be part of the settlement, which may cause an economic wave of uncertainty about future plans. This financial uncertainty can also cause an aging officer, who was capable of possibly retiring, to now have to stay on the job and work longer. Side jobs may now be a necessity, instead of working occasionally just for added income. The very thought of losing their marital home, starting over from scratch, and what they had together to what he lost and the idea of seeing the spouse and children with someone else may cause additional emotional stress.

This new situation in the family can be difficult for the affected children as well. If there are children involved, there may be a custody battle. Each parent wants to spend as much time with their child/children as possible. There are some spouses who try to take the custody battle to the extreme, knowing that their actions can have a devastating effect on their past partner's emotional well-being. Out of fairness to both parents and the child (children), visitation and spending time with each parent may be difficult, especially with the uncertainty of the officer having to stay longer or work overtime because of a late arrest or a situation on the job. Each parent may become stressed trying to set aside sufficient time to be with their child. The police officer will always have to worry about manpower issues and staffing concerns that may prevent him from getting time off from work. The strain and constraints of picking up and dropping off a child or children at school, practice, music lessons, etc., at a certain time can be traumatic. The cycle of habitual arguments with kids caught in the middle of both parents they love, from seeing their child/children whenever they want to seeing him every other week, can cause havoc, especially when the court sets forth mandatory obligations.

Even the most grounded person may feel overwhelmed to the point of depression that includes suicidal thoughts. In the Police Academy, many recruits are told that 80% of married personnel who start the job eventually get divorced. When this researcher first heard that extremely high number, I questioned the validity of that statement. The emotional stress of his marriage coupled with the stress of the job may be too much for the officer to handle.

Jeff Murphy* said that the stress a police officer encounters continuously affects everything in his life. Divorce rates for police officers are higher than the norm. To avoid problems at home, many officers work more overtime, obtain side jobs, and volunteer for additional court dates, anything to stay out of the house. Police officers tend to isolate themselves from others by choosing to stay within their own immediate group of friends from work. Murphy stressed that many officers have the attitude that they cannot share their work-related problems with anyone at home or with anyone else, so they will take their problems to the bar with their other police officer buddies.

Loss of a Child

Losing a child is devastating for any parent but even more for a police officer, whose profession is to be the protector of everyone. The word *awareness* and *police* are synonymous with one another. A police officer who loses a child to suicide is often overwhelmed by the fact that "they did not see this coming, or how did I miss the signs, or why did I not act fast enough?" Police officers whose child committed suicide will most likely blame themselves, the long

* Murphy, Jeff, Personal interview.

hours on the job, the police department, supervisors and management, and the side job they were committed to and regret doing something different instead of spending more time with their child. The ultimate blame is often on their shoulders, not taking more time off when they could have. Officers experience guilt, blame, and helplessness, especially about working during memorable times in their child's life. The loss of a child means not enjoying special occasions, vacations, holidays, birthdays, or sporting events together anymore; each occasion brings back the constant pain of their child's death. Even a stable marriage or relationship may falter, with each parent blaming the other for not being aware of the problem or being able to prevent what happened. Life will never be the same as it was. Never. The pain is just too much to handle to continue without their child. Memories such as this may cause officers to go over the edge and ultimately take their own lives. Life is just not worth living.

Loss of a Spouse, Loved One, or Significant Other

Many officers look forward to spending quality time with their spouse or significant other (at least I hope so) when they are off duty. Coming home to an empty home after losing one's partner can be shattering. Again, the officer may blame his schedule, the department, or working extra side jobs to make ends meet when he could have been home. The blame of not being there or not being as thoughtful may often play on the officer's mind. The officer's life will change significantly; his future plans, vacations, and retirement are now changed or gone. "I was working when he needed me, I can't live without him, what is the use?"

Chronic Illness

A common issue with chronic health issues is that the illness lingers and often continues to get worse. Over time, anyone who experiences chronic illness often has a very good chance of controlling the illness with proper medical intervention, but there is little chance of being completely cured. Chronic illness can be extremely difficult for police officers to accept. Most police officers have led an active lifestyle during their careers. When a chronic illness develops, it may limit the physical activities the police officer was accustomed to.

Law enforcement officers may not understand:

"I do not know what happened, I used to be so active, I can hardly walk anymore."

"I can't work in law enforcement any longer, or any part-time jobs, this will hurt me financially."
"If this keeps up, I may have to get a caregiver, who is taking care of who now."
"I am truly a burden to everyone, especially my family, these are supposed to be my golden years."

According to the National Center for Chronic Disease Prevention (2104), chronic disease is the leading cause of death and disability. Some of the chronic and debilitating illnesses are arthritis, cancer, diabetes, asthma, blindness, and kidney and heart diseases.

Terminal Illness

The ultimate decision to take one's own life weighs heavily on the mind of a person who suffers from a terminal illness. Terminal illness often justifies why an individual commits suicide. In the process of writing this book, I discovered a popular and well-liked sergeant who was going in for tests for a tumor on one of his kidneys. His carefree and easy going demeanor was strained with the possibility that the growth could be cancerous. He was looking forward to retirement the following year, talking about traveling and visiting many cities that he wanted to see with his wife but never had the chance. The sergeant had 30 years on the job and was just 57 years old. The sad news came a few days later. The tumor was indeed cancerous. He immediately went on medical leave and began chemotherapy, but his future looked bleak and uncertain. The chemotherapy had a demoralizing effect on his overall well-being. The once jovial and outgoing supervisor was now sullen and forlorn. The cancer was quick to affect other organs in his body. The doctors took him off chemo and his oncologist gave him less than a year to live. He killed himself with his service revolver the next day.

Any illness, especially a terminal illness, is devastating. Police officers are taught to always be in control, but disease and terminal illness is something that controls us, an offender (terminal disease). Terminal illness definitely takes control away—something an officer has a difficult time relinquishing. The feeling of not knowing what the future holds, the thought of using their service revolver to end this dilemma once and for all, and the mindset of a warrior brought down by terminal illness can be illustrated in a simple statement that I am sure most officers that committed suicide felt before they killed themselves, "I do not want to be a burden, especially to my family and friends, I do not want pity and no one needs to take care of me, I do not deserve this, why is this happening to me…."

Financial Problems: Bankruptcy

"Money is the root of all evil" is a famous quote often uttered by those who are in a financial bind. Financial problems can cause a solid marriage and career to fall apart. It is not uncommon to hear in today's society that a person lost their home to foreclosure or that a person went bankrupt. It is a sign of the times, more now than ever, that many people have become victims of a financial crisis. Those in law enforcement are no different. Many officers have lost their ability to meet their financial obligations. An officer not being able to pay his rent or his mortgage will do more to hurt his pride in the community in which he serves. An officer losing their home or claiming bankruptcy can often lead to despair and depression. The officer takes on the added burden of working extra side jobs, with little or no time for leisure, recreation, or to just relax. Financial issues along with depression are contributing factors in police suicide.

Addiction to Prescription Medication

Sean Riley wanted to be the best cop that he could be. He was into body building and was often the first officer to work and the last officer to leave. The entire police culture soon caught up with Sean. He began drinking heavily and relying on narcotic prescription medication. Riley became addicted to prescription drugs, especially Vicodin. He began lying to doctors to get more prescription drugs and was eventually indicted for fraudulently obtaining a controlled substance and sentenced to 3 years of probation. Riley was trained in the Police Academy to never lose and never give up; he knew how to manipulate the system. Riley thought about suicide because of the situation that he found himself in; he thought about hanging himself or putting a loaded gun in his mouth, but he thought how he would look different in an open casket. This was a pathetic "low point" in his life. He knew he needed help; again, he was trained to be a survivor but felt that he was going through this situation alone. Riley knew through his experience that other officers were suffering in the same manner but most likely would not come forward to get help because of the stigma attached to seeking assistance. He realized that change was necessary and decided to do something about it. He went back to school for chemical dependency counseling and became a supervisor in a treatment center. Many officers have the perception that addiction is something they encounter on the streets, but as many as 20% of law enforcement officers have some form of addiction, be it gambling, drugs, alcohol, food, or others.

Alcoholism

It seems that more and more police officers are becoming overwhelmed and turning to alcohol to deal with their problems, but previous research indicates that alcohol only adds to an individual's problems. Alcohol has always been an issue in law enforcement. Officers who are experiencing problems or issues, both physical and emotional, may turn to alcohol for a false sense of comfort. The Chicago Police Department has four full-time alcohol and drug counselors who are on call every day to help officers who request their services. These drug and alcohol counselors often will see an officer when he has hit rock-bottom. The counselors work with police management and protect the officer's identity and begin a program for him to follow.

Jim Padar* began his career in the 18th District, fresh from the Police Academy. This district was diverse and incorporated the luxurious gold coast, Rush Street, and famous nightclubs as well as the impoverished Cabrini Green low-income housing. As the only member of his family to become a police officer, Jim was amazed by many things that he experienced firsthand. Padar mentioned that he was very surprised that drinking on the job was accepted. He said that a lockup keeper was pretty much inebriated most of the time when he was in lockup. The police culture was different then; the department enabled officers, especially officers who had issues with liquor. Instead of saying anything, supervisors paired up the officer who drank with someone that was sober. It was not unusual for officers to have a drink with their meal. Officers that needed help just sucked it up, never asking for assistance or showing their feelings or emotions. Today, it is completely different and drinking on the job would never be allowed and officers would be fired if that were to happen.

Dr. Ellen Scrivner[†] stated that traditionally, in terms of police culture, how officers would relieve stress would be to go to a bar after a shift with their buddies where they would drink, yell, and complain, then go home and not reveal anything that they had been through. They would not share anything with their families, because if they did, their family members would tell him to quit the job because the money is not that great. Yet, they go back every day and experience the same thing over and over because most in the general public, and sometimes even their families and friends, do not understand that public service, particularly public safety, is somewhat of a mission for most officers.

---

* Padar, Jim, Personal interview.
† Scrivner, Ellen, PhD, Personal interview.

Father Charles Rubey* confirmed that the high rate of alcohol abuse and suicide is adversely connected. Alcohol is often seen as a quick and easy fix to release tension that goes with police work. Dr. John Mayer† said that alcohol is another bullet to put into that loaded gun of despair and suicide. In the other chambers are hopelessness, stress, and life's problems. Many officers, who deal with stress at work, often do not want to deal with any problems, issues, or stress at home.

Jeff Murphy revealed that the supervisors and police officers working in the 1960s and 1970s were more tolerant of alcohol abuse on the job and in the department as a whole. Murphy said that if an officer showed up to work with liquor on his breath, no one stepped up and said anything or took responsibility. There was a heavy drinking culture that was silently accepted. The more aggressive the officer (tact, homicide, narcotics, specialized units, etc.), the more embedded he was in the drinking culture. Today, there is zero tolerance for alcohol, and supervisors will take necessary actions that could ultimately lead to the officer losing his job. The same equation holds true with police suicide. The more aggressive the officer, the more likely that he will commit suicide.

Brad Woods realized as a young officer and detective that if he wanted to be accepted, he ended in the bar with his entire team. At the end of the shift, the same officers that he worked with on afternoons were drowning their troubles at the local bar. It was not uncommon for bosses to drink with the officers they supervised. It was a vicious cycle that was a lot of peer pressure to be "one of the guys." Woods credits being promoted early in his career as a way of getting out of that drinking environment. There were many times where officers went into work hungover or not feeling well from the night before. Fellow officers would cover for the officer who was sick or hungover by not letting him drive or doing what they could to carry him through the shift. The "thin blue line of take care of your officers was apparent." Woods noted that drinking after work became a way of life for many officers; it was a way to handle their problems. Woods noted he could see how the police culture can be a detrimental factor in an officer's life. He noted that it takes a strong woman and wife to put up with that kind of life. Many officers were torn between their police friends, the job, and their family. Many officers chose their job and drinking. Domestic violence and divorce were common because the officer was rarely home, and when he was it was not pleasant for anyone in the family. Woods confirmed that alcohol creates the means to commit suicide, and the officer has that means in the gun on the side of their hip. Many officers use their own service weapon to take their life. They do not have to go far or be creative. Suicide is the

* Rubey, Father Charles, Personal interview.
† Mayer, John PhD, Personal interview.

final out. Woods stated that we may never know why or the real reason an individual officer took his own life; most times we can only speculate. Attempting suicide for different reasons is a way out. It is actually a "cry for help." Speaking with officers that attempted suicide, that is how we understand some of the issues officers are dealing with, but Woods insisted that the real reason why an officer takes his own life may never be revealed. An officer who commits suicide does not see the light at the end of the tunnel, and the only viable solution in his mind is "the world is better off without me." Suicide takes his problems away.

Dr. Frank Campbell* related that alcohol is the common denominator in many problems and crimes that we experience today. Research has proven that alcohol is a huge problem in our society; it leads to legal problems, crime, financial problems, sexual abuse, etc. When a person consumes alcohol, it lowers their impulse center, like they operate at the lizard brain level. They run with a monster, with lowered reasoning capabilities. The lizard brain adopts the "fight or flight" pattern of behavior. Many police officers begin to drink during their career in law enforcement because they are angry. Officers are set up to be angry because of the people they put up with every day. They start to think like criminals. The problem is angry people that are now dealing with angry people. Anger and suicide often live in a duplex in the mind. Campbell said: "the best way to have homicide in the community is to ignore suicide."

Dr. Robyn Kroll (2014) claimed that it is common to learn that officers admit they were alcoholics or have abused alcohol prior to their police work and, of course, minimized their drinking habits at preemployment screenings. It is also common to discover that there often exists a history of alcoholism in an officer's family. Alcoholism is a progressive, deteriorating disease, so officers with the addiction will likely decline with time, due to cumulative stress, dealing with extremes, and the negativity and violence they experience on the job, as well as the negative perception that some of the public and media have toward law enforcement. For new recruits who don't necessarily enter the force with an addiction issue, the acclimation to police culture can engender habit-forming behaviors. New officers want to fit in, so they may start hanging out at local police bars, and eventually the realities of law enforcement's social milieu become part of the recruits' lifestyles.

From an Anonymous Officer

He began his career on midnights and worked the paddy wagon for approximately the first 3 months. He had various partners for each month but one

* Campbell, Frank, PhD, Personal interview.

in particular stood out, and they did the same thing every day they worked together. "The first 4 hours we would gather 10–14 drunks off the street and put him in the back of the wagon. After that we would drive to a restaurant/bar and back the paddy wagon up to a wall so the drunks could not get out. The next two hours we would eat and drink, liquor included. After that, the last two hours we would arrest and process the drunks 'for drinking on the public way'." "When the tour was over we would go to a 'gin mill' and talk about our night, often going home somewhat drunk ourselves. This was our daily routine, right out of the academy."

He explained that being a policeman then was quite different than it is today. Back then it was not unusual for police officers to drink on duty. In fact, a good percentage of officers in his opinion drank on the job every day. Some guys would refer to their shift as the "4 to 4." They would start work at 4 p.m., work until midnight, then go to a bar and stay until the bar closed at 4 a.m. In some cases, the officers stayed even though the bar was closed. The bar stayed open after hours for the police. The door was locked and many guys were still at the bar until the next morning. Even supervisors would drink on the job. It was just accepted. Everyone met at the tavern. They would then go home, sleep it off, and be at work the next day. To get through the day, one officer would pour vodka in a coffee cup and have an extra bottle on the side.

There were watch parties while working, where officers would barbecue and party. If an officer could not drive, another officer would take him home. The camaraderie back then seemed much stronger than it is today. The officer remembers being taken home on the subway by a fellow officer. His wife was surprised to see the two officers at her door. This officer was involved in a few accidents and wound up in the hospital, injured, with his car totaled, after hitting a fire hydrant. He didn't remember anything that happened or how he got to the hospital or getting stitched up. He recalled never getting in trouble, or getting any citations. Drinking was being part of the crowd and part of the culture. Inspectors were working, but they seldom got stopped or written up.

The officer recalled that one day at the end of December, he came home in the morning drunk. He was supposed to attend a New Year's Eve party that evening. The officer slept most of the day and woke up late, missing the party. He was surprised to find his wife and a few family members waiting for him. His wife told him to "Get Out!" The officer joined Alcoholics Anonymous (AA) and attended several meetings a week. Over the course of several weeks, during much soul searching, he came to the realization that the efforts were worthwhile. From that point on, a serious effort was made to follow the teachings of AA, and his home life and job continued to thrive. Older members of his family also had problems with alcohol, and some became AA members, leading him to believe that the disease is hereditary. To this day he is thankful for all he has received!

Retirement

"The job of law enforcement will go on with or without me, time for the young cops to earn their pay" an officer bellowed at his retirement party.

Taking that oath of office for many police officers is a dream job come true. Today, many officers work between 20 and 40 years in law enforcement, or enough to secure a pension. Some officers just want to do their time and retire; other officers stay on the job until the last day they are eligible to stay, and they must retire (often from age restrictions). Officers who undergo retirement will begin a lifestyle change. Their fast-paced life will soon slow down; the officer will have to transition and adjust to a new way of life.

When officers start their police career, they are not thinking about retirement. Officers who have 15 years or more on the job will be contemplating retirement in the near future. Some officers begin planning for their retirement when they know they have a few years left of their career. In reality, many officers fail to plan for that inevitable day that they will no longer be in law enforcement but will start another phase of their life as a civilian.

Retiring from a career in law enforcement requires two significant conditions: financial stability and emotional acceptance. Many officers who plan for their retirement often do so with only the financial aspect in mind. They realize that they will be getting less money; some officers will receive 70%–80% of the pay they were making when they were on active duty. Some officers completely stop working, while others find full- or part-time work in security or a different field altogether. Many departments offer retirement seminars that focus on the financial necessities.

A few departments actually prepare their officers for the emotional letdown they are likely to experience when they retire. How officers prepare emotionally for a new chapter in their lives is important. They are able to spend the time with their spouse that they were unable to spend before. They left a position of authority, in the thick of things with their police friends, and now they are no longer needed, and they may feel like an outcast. A retired officer said, "As an officer, I had a job with authority, power and camaraderie. People listened to me, I meant something. Today I am working as a security guard, where I sit around all day, and no one cares."

The first 6 months of retirement are usually the most fulfilling for a police officer. This time can be compared to an extended furlough or vacation, having time to participate in sports, activities, hobbies, and travel, catch up on chores around the house, and attend grandchildren's sporting events or games. It is usually after the first 6 months that the officer begins to get bored. This does not happen to all officers that retire, but I have spoken to too many that have indicated that the 6-month mark is when they began to feel isolated and depressed. The garage is cleaned, and the painting is done. How much golf can I play? It does not take long before the retiree asks the question, "What do I do now?" The officer, who was rarely at home, is home all the time. This was the time that they were supposed to be with family again. Quite frankly, more than likely the family has had enough.

Dr. Dean C. Angelo*, Sr. said many retired police officers have difficult times accepting the fact that they are no longer the police. Being a cop is all that they know and all they have done for 25, 30, or even more years. Many officers may have been lucky enough to explore postcareer opportunities to keep them busy in retirement. For some, being retired from law enforcement is a major transformation, a total culture change. All of a sudden there are no bosses, no schedules, no court cases, and no crime scenes; they miss the rush, they miss their fellow officers, and they miss the routine. A few officers may wind up becoming depressed. They look for things to take up their time. I believe that there have been several studies that found that law enforcement members (both active and retired) are at the higher range of those who take their own lives. Angelo said that many officers get caught up with alcohol and addiction. Officers have a tendency to work hard, fight hard, and party and drink hard. In a bar they have to be the last one to go home; they feel that if they leave they might miss something. Sometimes they easily come to enjoy what was commonly known as "the 4 to 4 shift." They used to start their shifts at 4 p.m. and work until midnight. They would then head to the bars and look for a location with the extended hours and not leave until 4 a.m. They go home, sleep, and do it all over again the next day. Many cops go to the same bar, sit in the same chair, and tell the same war stories and stories after 30 years of being the police; many times the only thing that changes is that they are on their third wife, have three different families, and have gone from the beer days, to the beer and shot days and now are drinking cocktails with shot chasers.

Dr. Jack Digliani[†] also spoke about retired police officers. Some officers that have had honorable police careers become lost in retirement. They have lost themselves as well as their identity of being a police officer. They often feel cut off from other officers and the agency that provided them with a support system. They don't know what to do with their increased free time. Unfortunately, this time is sometimes filled with overeating, alcohol consumption, and other less than desirable behaviors. In the most serious of cases, the change from police officer to civilian can become such a challenge that it feels overwhelming. This can lead to thoughts of suicide. Digliani noted that it is inevitable that most officers will one day again become a civilian. If an officer does not die in the line of duty (something that all officers

---

[*] Angelo Sr., Dean C., EdD, Personal interview.
[†] Digliani, Jack, PhD. EdD, Personal interview.

attempt to avoid) or while the officer is still on the job, he will be a civilian again. Even though officers know this, Digliani said that many police officers remain emotionally unprepared for retirement. They are surprised by feeling what Digliani calls the "When you're out, you're out syndrome." This is the feeling on the part of retired officers that they are treated differently by working officers solely because they have retired. This leaves some retired officers isolated and without the social support they have known for many years. Retired officers may also experience family problems; they are home more than they ever were before, and their loved ones may have a difficult time adjusting to that. It takes a strong marriage to weather this storm and make the transition into something positive. Officers can better prepare for retirement and the challenges it creates by thinking and feeling through the anticipated changes, and this should involve spouses and other family members. Digliani suggested that officers should not retire *from* something; instead, they should retire *to* something. Having after-retirement plans and activities help officers through the retirement transition. Police officer retirement should be a time of celebration of a career that consisted of honorable service and positive contributions to the welfare of the community. If done thoughtfully, officers will enjoy their police retirement. As Digliani puts it, "there is life beyond police work."

Father Dan Brandt* acknowledged that officers deal with many different issues, but retirement from the job has made many former officers depressed and despondent. For many officers, being in law enforcement is all that they know, take that away from him and they're lost. Dr. Carl Alaimo† conveyed that officers who are nearing retirement have little preparation provided to them by their agencies for the inevitable transition from the job. Alaimo said that without some type of intervention, retirees may see an increase in substance abuse, marital problems, relationship and divorce issues, and a decline in their physical health. Officers will kill themselves because they are unable to process a lifetime experiencing the worst situations in life.

Jeff Murphy stated, "Today, police officers have a different mindset. Many are looking to do their 20 years and get out of law enforcement. Many veteran officers have a difficult time when they leave or are forced to leave the job. Forty years ago you would see claw marks on the wall when an officer was mandated to retire. Records of the number of suicides among retired officers are not very accurate but the number is significant. Murphy confirmed that another issue that many officers have when facing retirement is not being prepared for the next phase of their lives. Their career has kept him going at 100 mph every day, and then when they retire they go

---

* Brandt, Father Daniel, Personal interview.
† Alaimo Sr., Carl, PsyD, Personal interview.

down to zero. Hypervigilance is ingrained in officers from the first day in the Police Academy. That threat of something happening doesn't leave an officer, even after he retires. When an officer comes up to a stoplight, he is looking around, looking for any suspicious activity or unusual behavior. A retiree sees six guys in a car, and he wishes he could pull him over like he once did. Many departments, when they show their retirees the door, really do not know the difficulties the retirees will encounter.

Dr. John Violanti noted that there are a majority of police officers who do not prepare for that inevitable day of retirement. They become depressed; alcohol becomes involved. Violanti suggested that more officers who abuse alcohol also have relationship problems and may eventually contemplate suicide. Violanti stated that police administrations need to do a better job of preparing officers for a smoother transition into retirement. When an officer retires, there are a lot of changes in their lives; they lost their badge and police powers and authority, and they eventually miss the scheduling and the camaraderie. After 25 years on the job, retirement hits him hard. According to research conducted by Violanti and his colleagues at the University of Buffalo in New York, the life expectancy of a police officer is estimated to be 66 years of age. Violanti stated that the rate of suicide is higher for officers within 5 years of retirement. This is due to the stress of "what do I do now?" Just prior to retirement, an officer may feel indecisive. What does the future hold? Should I retire or stay on the job? Should I seek promotion? Many officers have their sights on a retirement date, but when that date draws near, they actually get cold feet.

Dr. Nancy Zarse* noted that there should be more attention drawn to officers that are near retirement or that are in postretirement. Many officers plan for the day when they will be retired. Most, if not all, plan for the financial spectrum of retirement, such as their future pay status and benefit package, but they do not plan for their emotional well-being. The first 6 months are awesome; retired officers become rested and rejuvenated. They do not have to deal with a jerk for a boss, they do not have a schedule, they do not have to worry about shift work, they can celebrate holidays with the family, and they can attend sporting events they have missed for years. Then, after 6 months, for many officers, the bottom falls out. The question is what do I do now? How much golf can I play? I have no mission; I miss the camaraderie. They are no longer in charge, no one takes them seriously, and they are spending more time with their families (this is unusual because they have never spent this much time with their families before, and honestly some family members wish they were back at work). What happens when they become lonely and isolated and they have a loss of

---

* Zarse, Nancy, PsyD, Personal interview.

focus? A large number of retired officers have no mission, no value, and no plan for their lives. This leads to depression, suicidal thoughts, and irrational behavior. Part of the mission of being an officer is having importance, self-worth, and honor. Retired officers may work a part-time security job at a concert, bowling alley, or retail store. This may get them out of the house, but they have lost that sense of importance. It all came down to this, still in security, but there is no value, no camaraderie like they once felt with their fellow officers, and no backup. I was a cop; I was valued at work. I had importance in my life, at work, controlling chaos, anarchy, and violence, and now I am keeping a few teens from being disruptive at a movie theater, or I am at a convention center checking IDs. As an example of false perception, the retired cop walks into a bar; all his friends express their envy about the officer's retirement, how he is playing golf and relaxing. The retired cop is bored with being retired; it is not fun or relaxing anymore. They have become frustrated with their life and they are screaming out for something to do. Many retired officers sign on with another law enforcement agency just to have something to do and to be in the company of "law enforcement and camaraderie" again. They have found that mission and importance of being needed and wanted again.

Robert Douglas Jr.* remarked that the job as a policeman defines who they are but not what they do. Police officers are often not accepted, and they feel their agency doesn't appreciate him. It is part of the police culture they are drawn into. They may "bitch and moan" but when they retire, they become quiet and withdrawn. The reality hits him pretty hard and they realize that they will no longer be a police officer. For many officers, being in law enforcement is all that they know. Douglas acknowledges that law enforcement officers must have a purpose in life after they retire. They must have their own identity and they need to make changes during their career, to prepare for the day that they will no longer be a police officer. Douglas gave an example of one officer that was drinking alcohol and was involved in a car accident that killed his wife. The officer said "that he felt physically alive and spiritually dead," the stress, hurt, and pain of being alone and someone not being there when you needed him. Douglas surmised that there are plenty of officers who love their job. Douglas said that he came in contact with one of his friends who he worked with when he was a police officer, who he has not seen in a while. He nonchalantly asked how he was doing. The retired officer said, "I do not miss the circus, but I do miss the clowns," the circus being the administration and the clowns being the police officers he previously worked with.

* Douglas Jr., Robert, Personal interview.

References

Kroll, Robyn, PsyD, Clinical Psychologist and Director of Interventions, Dr. Robin Kroll, Inc., Chicago, IL. *Managing the Dark Side: Treating Officers with Addiction* (2014).

National Center for Chronic Disease Prevention and Health Promotion, Centers for Disease Control and Prevention National Center for Chronic Disease Prevention and Health Promotion (NCCDPHP), Atlanta, GA, USA.gov. (2014).

Emotional Health and Concerns
A Cry for Help Is the First Indication That There Is a Problem

7

RON RUFO

Contents

And can it be that in a world so full and busy, the loss of one creature makes a void in any heart, so wide and deep that nothing but the width and depth of eternity can fill it up!

Charles Dickens

Emotional Health and Concerns

Father Tony Pizzo* noted that being a police officer is a difficult job, especially when officers are dealing with criminal activity, drugs, and gangs on a daily basis. Law enforcement officers are constantly bombarded with negative behaviors and it plays on their emotional health. People are always yelling, accusing officers of arriving late on call or for police misconduct. Many officers personify and project the attitude of being tough. This macho behavior and hard-line assertiveness of "you can't get to me" can only last so long. In reality, that arrogance has to affect them; everyone has a breaking point. That constant pressure is not good: officers must find a release, to reorient themselves in some way. It is difficult to live a normal life when a person has that much stress in his life. It affects his professional and personal life, marriage, spouse, everyone. They are carrying emotional baggage with them constantly. When officers become distressed and cannot deal with the pressure of life anymore, that is when they feel the only option is suicide.

Father Rubey† said that in today's police culture, I think there is not much support for the emotional well-being of officers. Many officers rarely seek any help or emotional support during their career. They prefer "to tough it out," keeping their emotions and the traumatic experiences they experienced to themselves. If an officer seeks any type of counseling or emotional support, he is deemed weak by his peers. That is not a healthy outlook or perception.

Captain Barry Thomas‡ noted that many law enforcement professionals are hesitant to share their inner emotions and have a tendency to hide their true feelings for fear of repercussions from their agency or peers. Historically, this has proven to be detrimental to the law enforcement profession as it leads to long-term mental health issues and opens the door for substance abuse.

Dr. John Violanti§ asked, "How many officers know the warning signs of impending suicide?" All of the training officers receive is to protect themselves on the street (which is also important). Officers are well aware of tactical training, protecting yourself and the public, shooting, driving. Violanti notes, "What about emotional training? There is not a lot of mental health training, stress management and well-being seminars. Training protocols should not be just a matter of street survival, but emotional survival as well. Many police departments and administrations have their priorities in

---

* Pizzo, Father Tony, Personal interview.
† Rubey, Father Charles, Personal interview.
‡ Thomas, Barry, Captain, Personal interview.
§ Violanti, John PhD, Personal interview.

the wrong order. How difficult is it to have separate training on emotional awareness? This subject needs to be addressed. It is a great idea to come in and talk, just for a mental health check, but especially after a police shooting. The most important aspect of any debriefing or meeting is that it must be confidential. An officer should be able to air out any concerns he is having without being punished. The element of trust and an element of fear among officers are difficult to achieve and accept. If a department does not have enough psychologists, they should use members of Peer Support as an alternative."

Lisa Wimberger* noted that many departments continue to reinforce the tactical side of policing, but often are not entrenched in the emotional well-being of their officers as they should be. Soft skills or emotional survival are often prioritized at the bottom of importance by many police administrators. An officer's emotional well-being has a dramatic effect on sick time and an officer's time away from the job. Psychological issues and emotional trauma can become a costly proposition to any department and this problem needs to become a priority. In the long run, it will most likely cost the police agency far more money paying out disability benefits than if they addressed the problem sooner. The only way to cut back on police suicide is for police administrators to invest in prevention.

Showing Weakness

If an officer admits that he or she is in need of any counseling services, it may be viewed by his or her fellow officers as a sign of weakness. Showing weakness is something that officers will never openly admit to—remember police officers are warriors and problem solvers. In a police officer's mind, wimps are weak, and officers cannot show anyone that they are weak or are in need of help. Many officers will disguise any personal problems or issues they are experiencing. Police officers are clever in their efforts not to be branded a *loser*. If word gets around that an officer is in need of counseling for whatever reason, many of the other officers will most likely refrain from working with him. The officer may also be worried that if he seeks help about emotional instability, he will risk a chance to be promoted. The stigma of going for counseling will most likely remain with that officer for a long time, even if he transfers to a different district or location. The fact that no one wants to work with a person seeking counseling or being associated with that individual may cause the officer to be even more depressed, as he suffers his emotional pain in silence.

---

* Wimberger, Lisa, Personal interview.

Dr. Jack Digliani* indicated that police culture has developed from a long history of tradition. Included in this tradition is the idea that officers must be tough and show no weakness. This is especially true in the area of occupational and personal stress. Thinking that "asking for help" is a "sign of weakness" is the reason that many police officers will not seek or otherwise ask for help, even when it is clear that they need it.

Asking for Help

Many officers, even if they do go for counseling, will not reveal that they are seeking help for fear the department will eventually find out. The fear is that if the department finds out they may be experiencing psychological or behavioral problems, the administrative powers will order that their stars and weapons be taken away. Any officer who is placed on medical leave cannot work in any capacity outside of the police department. Not being able to work side jobs could add to financial problems for the emotionally strapped officer. In his mind, going for counseling or seeking help will only complicate the problem. An officer's response to handling a crisis in his life may be "I can handle my own issues and affairs the best that I can…. I am not taking a chance the department will ever find out."

Dr. Digliani confirmed that "asking for help does not mean that the officer is "unfit for duty." Some officers will not ask for psychological help even when they think they should because they have concerns about being "found out" and perceived as unfit for duty. Although it is possible for police officers to develop psychological symptoms serious enough to become incapable of performing their jobs safely, there is no comparison between asking for help and being unfit for duty. Seeking appropriate support and intervention for any reason, be it physical, psychological, emotional, or substance-use related, does not automatically make an officer unfit for duty. The fear of being perceived as unfit for duty by reaching out for assistance during stressful times or asking for help with a stress-related issue is an unwanted manifestation of police secondary danger. This idea must change to effectively reduce the secondary danger of law enforcement."

Superintendent Terry Hillard† noted that law enforcement officers need to seek help for any difficulties that they experience throughout their careers. It is not a sign of weakness to ask for help. "I saw a need to address this problem of depression and police suicide when I was Superintendent of Police for Chicago. Many major cities such as New York and Los Angeles already had programs in place for officers who were experiencing emotional trauma.

---

* Digliani, Jack, PhD. EdD, Personal interview.
† Hillard, Terry, Personal interview.

I had two exceptional officers in my command staff, Jim Powers and Brad Woods*, who implemented programs to address emotional issues that many police officers were experiencing in their careers, especially alcoholism and depression. Police officers need to get away from that macho image of keeping their inner emotions to themselves and get away from the stigma of seeking help." Police officers experience the bad elements of society; they deal with the stressors of shift work and eventually everything takes a toll on the officer. Then when the officer goes home, he has to deal with family issues. The stress level is constant. Seeking help due to stress and job-related issues is recommended. Asking for emotional help at a time of crisis is not weakness. It should not be held against an officer if he wishes to discuss issues that are bothering him. Emotional issues should not be bottled up and kept a secret. Officers need to let someone know they are in a crisis.

Brad Woods stated that officers are taught early on in their career to not talk about anything and to not trust anyone. It does not take long for police officers to realize that showing their emotions and feelings may cause them to be branded as a sissy, or being weak. Captain Barry Thomas indicated there is a cultural shift in law enforcement, especially regarding the stigma of officers asking for help.

An Officer Not Getting the Help He Needs

Most police officers fear that double-edged sword of asking for assistance. The first and foremost crisis is the possibility of having the officer's weapon taken. This may have a detrimental and cascading effect in that the officer without a weapon may be stripped of his police powers and the possibility of not continuing in law enforcement. Another concern is where officers may fear losing an assignment, a detail, an assigned post, squad car, or unit. An officer who is cited for psychological or behavioral concerns may not work on the street for quite a while and may spend a substantial amount of time assigned to desk duty, the call back unit (report taking only), or nonconfrontational positions within their department. The rumors of being psychologically unfit may cause the alienation of other officers willing to partner up or work with the individual officer and/or the consideration for future promotions that include pay raises. With the consequence of seeking help comes the added emotional trauma of the situation.

According to Dr. Violanti, police culture is one of the primary factors that prevents officers from getting the necessary help they need. Violanti understands the cultural pull that police officers experience and sees this as a

---

* Woods, Brad, Personal interview.

genuine problem. "We need police officers to change the attitude and culture of seeking help. Asking for help is an indication of strength, not of weakness." Violanti stated that if an officer asks for help, other problems may arise for that officer, such as the following:

- Other officers may question the confidence they have in that officer as a backup.
- The officer asking for help may keep them from being promoted.
- Leadership and the administration may look at that officer in a strange way.

Mike Holub* said that police officers are expected to hide their feelings and emotions under a shell and they are expected to have a Turtle Wax exterior. Many officers work their entire careers keeping their sentiments hidden, especially on the job. Officers are expected to be tough, but in reality, many officers are not as tough on the inside as they portray. The police culture practically dictates this behavior. Many people look at police differently, but as Holub said, "We are human, we have problems, we cry, we bleed, we have family issues, we are not super human, and we are like everyone else. People see us in a fishbowl, but in actuality when we are put into a pond, we are like everyone else."

Dr. Ellen Scrivner† revealed that the emotional part of the police culture is "suck it in, don't show emotion, or others will think you are weak." There are a range of issues related to police suicide including personal issues, breaking up a relationship, Post-Traumatic Stress Disorder (PTSD), or financial issues. More recently, however, I have seen more officers who have committed suicide because they have been threatened with lawsuits. Lawsuits are a growing phenomenon and many police officers feels betrayed when they are part of a lawsuit because, in their mind, they did their job as they were taught and how they were supposed to. Then, when faced with a lawsuit, they may feel that others have turned their backs on them and that there is no one there to protect them, including the lawyers slated to represent them. They often lose confidence in the city or county legal system and fear not only a loss of financial resources but also a loss of support from the police administration and the community they are sworn to serve. As those feelings of loss build up, either physical or psychological loss, an officer is more at risk for a behavioral crisis, which could result in suicidal behavior.

Pam Church‡ noted that there are resources available to all officers; however, most will not take advantage of them because of the stigma attached to

---

* Holub, Michael, Personal interview.
† Scrivner, Ellen, PhD, Personal interview.
‡ Church, Pam, Personal interview.

those officers who want to seek assistance with emotional wellness. Church indicated that she introduced a program called *Career Coaching*, which is designed to keep an officer on his career track and to address issues such as career burnout; however, many of her officers are suspicious of the program and do not want to participate in it. Victoria Poklop* affirmed that when an officer does seek counseling, he often finds immediate relief from the tension of holding everything in for so many years. There are many officers who become amenable to help only when they cannot handle the inner troubles. They are more likely to open up to someone they already know and can trust. Poklop said, "I am the confidential liaison for my department, I direct our officers to confidential counseling through our many outside resources." Poklop's philosophy is that nipping any problems an officer may have in the bud before it becomes enormous or too much for the officer to handle protects the officer from further harm. She wants officers to develop healthy coping skills that will keep them emotionally safe and secure. Officers can improve their coping skills by being able to ask for help in a safe environment, but only if the environment is safe.

Dr. Nancy Zarse[†] acknowledged that part of the culture is the misinformation about getting and receiving help through counseling and therapy. The police culture discourages anyone from receiving help, and most officers are afraid that their department will punish them for seeking help. Documented contemplation of suicide can lead to an officer being stripped of his Firearm Owners' Identification (FOID) card, which means he cannot carry a firearm, and thus, his time as an officer may soon come to an end. The department realizes that the officer may become a liability. There needs to be a safe haven. As officers, they should be able to say they are in bad shape emotionally and not be punished for seeking assistance. There needs to be a shift in the department's way of thinking, keeping the officer from losing his FOID card and keeping the star and job. I wish we could put therapy on par with medical services. I never expect someone to tough out a broken arm and still go to work. How would I expect them to tough out a broken heart? The attitude of police culture is to "tough it out." They are constantly reminded that this is what they have signed up for. Handling a bus accident with 20 dead children, or a DUI driver that was decapitated, a mother putting a hot iron on a baby's cheek because she was crying, or a spouse that abandoned his or her family is often not out of the ordinary over an officer's career. Officers experience and live the evil that often surrounds their world, and it does not take very long for them to eventually become depressed and despondent, especially with their families. Most people drink when they are depressed and alcohol is a depressant,

* Poklop, Victoria MS, Personal interview.
† Zarse, Nancy, PsyD, Personal interview.

which just adds fuel to the fire. An officer may be thinking that he does not have the guts to pull the trigger, until he starts drinking alcohol (liquid courage). Then he has all of the bravado he needs.

Sean Riley* acknowledged that he knew through his experience that other officers were suffering in the same manner but most likely would not come forward to get help because of the stigma attached to seeking assistance. Sean started Safe Call Now in April of 2009 in the hope that no other first responder would have to face a crisis alone. Riley realized through his own experience that law enforcement takes an emotional and physical toll on many of its officers. He noted that asking for help is often seen as a sign of weakness by many in law enforcement but has learned now that it is an act of courage. The job is stressful, and many officers will not risk their career by admitting they need help.

An Officer Seeking Psychiatric Assistance

Most major police departments have counselors, alcohol counselors, and psychologists on staff and available 24 h a day, every day; if not, they may be on call if certain situations warrant their services. Because of liability, employee assistance program (EAP) services are confidential and the department is not informed of the officer's attendance. The officer does not have to worry about notes or anything written down or what he has said. The counseling services offered by EAP are free for any officers and their immediate family.

There is a way to ask for help and a way not to ask for help. If an officer wants to hurt himself and admits he is experiencing some emotional trauma, he can seek out the police department's EAP section. The EAP counselors and psychologists have a patient–client confidentiality privilege. Anything that an officer reveals about his personal and private life will not be revealed to anyone. No records or notes are taken nor are they kept. A police officer seeking help to resolve issues should not be punished. The clinicians at EAP know what to do to protect the officer who comes into their facility seeking help.

Anyone involved in the EAP will definitely recommend seeking treatment, but they recommend that an officer who finds himself or herself in this dilemma see them first. The staff at the EAP office wants to help the officer before he becomes a suicide statistic. Many officers have a misconception regarding reporting their thoughts or seeking help because of behavioral or emotional issues. Many officers are disgruntled and bring the negativity

---

* Riley, Sean, Personal interview.

of police culture home with them, affecting their home life. The children struggle as well as the officer's significant other. EAP can help the officer in many ways. Not only can EAP assist the officer in overcoming the impulse of suicide, but they will help the officer keep his job and get the additional counseling needed to stay focused and productive as a policeman. The difference from an intake hospital and EAP is that EAP does not notify or release information to the police department.

The following story is an example of how the EAP intervened in a serious incident involving an officer with suicidal thoughts. A young officer with a few years on the job made strong indications that he was going to kill himself. The officer called members of his police team and left messages saying good-bye; he also left notes for his wife and kids telling them "he loves them and good-bye." One of his officers on his team notified his sergeant. The sergeant found out where the young officer was, took his gun, and called the staff at the EAP office. The EAP office made a makeshift room for the officer to stay in and worked with him until he was well enough to be on his own. The officer is mentally healthy again and is working. EAP does not write anything down and they do not take notes or make any type of diagnosis.

If an Officer Enters a Mental Health Facility or Psychiatric Ward

There are many misconceptions regarding thoughts of suicide. It basically comes down to who is notified. According to the staff at the EAP, if 911 is notified, the police officer's district will be notified, and the officer will be psychologically evaluated. An average stay for inpatient treatment can be up to 3–5 days. Any time an officer is admitted to this type of facility, they take on the risk of being fired or released from the police department because of his actions.

Once an officer, spouse, or family member alerts 911 or the police department directly that he has some emotional or psychological troubles and needs hospitalization, his career as a law enforcement officer may be in jeopardy. According to Illinois State law, if an officer is remanded or requested to attend a hospital and psychiatric treatment facility or program, the hospital is required to formally notify the officer's department and authorities about the treatment received. A normal stay in a treatment facility may last only 3–4 days, but this hospital evaluation will most likely have a devastating effect on that officer's career.

The wheels will be set in motion to relieve the officer of his police powers. In Illinois, a peace officer seeking psychiatric help at a hospital must relinquish his FOID card. This will cause a downward spiral for the officer, because now without his FOID card, he is not allowed to carry a weapon and continue his duties and continue to work as a law enforcement officer. Most police departments will not allow an officer hospitalized for emotional or psychological issues to work in the capacity of a peace officer because of liability concerns.

State law mandates that the hospital or psychiatric facility notify the police department where he is employed. In Illinois, to be a police officer, an officer needs a valid FOID card. Entering an inpatient psych ward in a hospital or a psychiatric facility for treatment invalidates the terms and conditions of the FOID card. Simply stated, you are not allowed to legally carry a weapon; therefore, you cannot carry on your job as a police officer. The Chicago Police Department follows this standard as it is clearly a case of liability for the city if something should happen because this officer has a weapon.

Because that officer no longer can work in the capacity of an officer, he has added to the problems, causing more of a crisis and traumatic situation. Now the officer has no means to support himself, or his family. It is not impossible, but it would be an extremely difficult and time-consuming experience trying to get the officer's FOID card back and trying to get him reinstated again as an officer. The entire ordeal can take 3–4 years and the officer still may not be successful returning to the previous career as a law enforcement officer.

An officer who seeks a private psychiatrist may have to report any work-related issues and document his sessions by notes, information, and making a diagnosis. A private psychiatrist can possibly have his information, reports, and diagnosis subpoenaed by the courts by the officer's department. Any information received by a private psychiatrist can be detrimental to the officer's career because it is in writing. Identification and communication can be documented and acknowledged. Perception is everything.

Symptoms of Mental Illness

Father Charles Rubey declared that research has proven that 95% of people who complete suicide do so as a direct result of some form of mental illness, be it chronic depression, bipolar disorder, or whatever the diagnosis. Many families who are survivors of a suicide do not want to accept the stigma of mental illness that is associated with their loved one's death. Their loved ones who committed suicide often kept the signs of mental illness to themselves. Survivors did not see the signs of their loved one's impending suicide, but the vast majority never envisioned that their loved one would take his or her own life. They may have hidden their intentions from everyone. Men tend to hold their emotions in, and women are more likely to express their feelings.

Dr. Carl Alaimo* revealed that the attitude and understanding toward police suicide has dramatically changed in the past 20 years. While we are more educated about mental illness and suicide, law enforcement suicide still remains three times higher than that of the general population. For example, on average, 11 people out of 100,000 citizens in the general population commit suicide. Our law enforcement and correctional professionals exceed these numbers. Jeff Murphy found that many successful law enforcement agencies were using varieties of the critical incident training (CIT) that is in place today. Murphy† said, "We have swept mental illness and police suicide under the rug for years." Crisis Intervention Training deals with an officer who is in crisis. Crisis Intervention Training offers a different approach, which is conflict resolution, de-escalation, and bringing the officer to as calm as possible, even if it means negotiating an action.

Dr. Bruce Handler‡ noted that police officers are very good at portraying the persona of being tough, independent, and in control. There is a stigma that still exists with mental illnesses, and in spite of an officer's stress from his chosen career, he fears he will be seen as weak if he admits to needing help for his emotional problems. Asking for help, to many officers, is admitting to the pain of depression, and officers who suffer emotionally in silence risk suicide in the end. Barney Flanagan§ said that depression is the common cold of mental illness. We take medicine for allergies and back pain. Why are we afraid to get help when we are troubled emotionally, especially with chronic depression? Many officers are afraid to say anything about taking antidepressant medication or going to EAP for help. We are afraid to be painted with the term mental illness. Mental illness is more common than anyone would believe. If everyone would admit he or she is suffering from some type of emotional distress, we would need to build hundreds of high-rise institutions. We have been experiencing a nationwide epidemic of suicide, not only police suicides, but in the general population as well. Every year we lose 35,000 people to suicide across our nation.

Terry Hillard affirmed that mental illness can be treated. Cops need to be taken care of; in our society, there are programs that help everyone else, why not police officers who need the help. We can utilize resources such as Peer Support, EAP, and wellness seminars. The help the police department provides needs to be confidential where it is not to jeopardize the officer's livelihood. We do not attempt suicide—we commit suicide!!!

---

* Alaimo, Sr., Carl, PsyD, Personal interview.
† Murphy, Jeff, Personal interview.
‡ Handler, Bruce MD, Personal interview.
§ Flanagan, John Barney, Personal interview.

Risk Assessment

Dr. Ellen Scrivner noted that it is also important for supervisors to be trained in that type of risk assessment, in how to recognize early signs of problems their officers are experiencing, and how to support early intervention initiatives. Their ability to be able to recognize signs of trouble in an officer's life is meaningful and wellness checks, EAP, and Peer Support are critically important. However, there are always a few officers who will not take advantage of these opportunities because they may feel that it would jeopardize their career. It is then that the supervisor needs to enlist early intervention. Beyond training officers and supervisors in utilizing wellness checks and/or individualized risk assessment, we also need to promote change in the culture. When an officer is killed in the line of duty, in the police culture, he is viewed as a hero and rightly so. However, when an officer takes his or her life, the culture does not respond positively and often attaches a stigma. Many officers rarely want to talk about it, much less why it happened. They may feel guilty because they missed the signs that a fellow officer was in emotional trouble; or they may fear that what happened to that officer could also happen to them.

Personal Concerns and Behavioral Intervention

Many departments do not want the liability of an officer being depressed or emotionally unstable protecting their citizens. Most police departments will offer the officer the opportunity to seek psychological help without any implications or repercussions. There is a stigma regarding police suicide. It is something the police department, or any of its supervisors or command staff, remotely wants to talk about or address. Regarding police suicide, it is something rarely brought up or discussed by anyone in the upper levels of the police department, and there are often no statistics on how many officers have attempted or committed suicide.

Police administrators, command staff, and supervisors have an obligation to their department to ensure the emotional well-being of all of their officers and make certain that they can function safely at work. An officer who seems emotionally and mentally distressed can be ordered by a supervisor to report to EAP and seek professional help. The officer may be a danger to himself, fellow officers, or the community. Not taking appropriate action on an officer's unusual behavior can put liability on the police department, especially if the officer is exhibiting symptoms of psychological instability. A few issues that may cause concern for supervisors who are monitoring officers on or off duty are as follows:

- The officer's actions that have been reported or observed, counter-productive behavior. Is the officer able to function safely at work?
- An officer's being ineffective in the ability to perform his or her job; continuously being late, unexcused absences, coming to work drunk or with liquor on his breath, lack of alertness, missed calls, sleeping on the job, continuous violations of the department's general orders.
- Excessive force and verbal abuse complaints.
- Obvious signs that there are emotional issues, moody, unstable, uncooperative, always depressed, not themselves, continuous anger, hostility or violence, volatile, unbalanced.
- Domestic violence, relationship or personal issues that require police action or service continuously.
- Hospitalization for psychological problems or a danger to themselves or others, anxiety. Suicidal ideation, suicide attempts.

Brad Woods developed an early warning system that would get help to an officer before the officer's situation became worse. The Personnel Division would handle this intervention, not Internal Affairs because that would only increase the stigma attached. This unit dealt with officers who continually were accused of using excessive force, abused the medical system, had many unusual or explained absences from work, or had performance issues. In his role as a commander, Woods would have to strip the officer of police powers. Woods said that he had to do *right* by the officers. Woods said, "There were officers who did not like me, I became the enemy. I had one officer who thanked me for saving his life, and he received help and returned to full duty status. An officer may lose his family, his house, but his last stronghold is his job, and he would do anything to keep it. He would be threatened with suspension or dismissal if he did not get help." But in this case, he should be placed on involuntary hold if he needs to be hospitalized. In most states, the bar is set fairly high for taking an officer off the street. At this point, the officer should be taken off active duty and guns taken away, but that officer should still have an opportunity at a later date to be reassessed for a fitness for duty evaluation and have a chance to possibly have his job back. If an officer breaks his leg, naturally he will be off on medical leave until he is healed. The same concept applies to an officer who has experienced extreme emotional problems. He too should undergo a fitness for duty evaluation to be allowed to return to active duty. A team of mental health professionals should make this determination. It should not be made by a single therapist. Every police department should have a fitness for duty evaluation procedure in place. Some officers have extreme issues or they have deteriorated to the point that their problems cannot be resolved or fixed long term. The officer in this type of situation often winds up no longer being able to work in law enforcement. He should be put on medical disability or work in another field. Some people cannot be rehabilitated and coming back as a policeman should be decided on a case-by-case basis. If an officer seeks counseling for marital problems, drinking, depression, or any other issue he is experiencing, this information should always be confidential. If an officer seeks counseling, it does not mean he is not fit for duty; he should never be punished simply for seeking help. Many people can be rehabilitated for drinking, depression, and family issues that will not necessarily affect their jobs in law enforcement.

Dr. Carl Alaimo said that police regulation is archaic, especially what we know about recovery in mental health and what behaviors need to be treated. Taking an officer's gun away for seeking help is the same as taking the tools away from a tradesman; he can no longer work or do the job. An officer's mindset is "You tell me you want to help me, but you punish me if I ask for help." Cops get caught up in addiction because they get caught up in the job. They begin to use chemicals to manage their stress. The stress of being pulled from the job is a real obstacle. Research shows that an individual in law enforcement will have an increase in dependency (addiction), financial problems, loss of social relationships, and health issues. If he ignores the problem that will not subside, but only get worse. To ease this pain, the majority of retired officers choose suicide. No one will take responsibility for making a cultural change, yet a change must take place in the law enforcement culture in asking for help.

Resilience

Resilience is defined as the capacity to adapt in the presence of risk and adversity. It is the ability to recover quickly from difficulty. Dennis Adams[*] said that resilience is defined as the capacity to adapt successfully in the presence of risk and adversity. Resilience is a broad, multidimensional concept that reflects the ability to

- Adapt and overcome
- Successfully adjust to difficult or challenging life experiences
- Confront and handle stressful life challenges and adversities
- Endure traumatic events

Dr. Alexis Artwohl[†] implied that police officers must become hypervigilant to work on the street and learn how to control their stress level. This is often

[*] Adams, Dennis, LSCW, Personal interview.
[†] Artwohl, Alexis, PhD, Personal interview.

through experience, as an officer is the master of his environment. He is resilient and in control. An officer will always act in a way to keep himself safe. If an officer stays on the job for 20 years or longer, he will naturally get tired of the day-to-day grind. Officers who have worked this long have seen a lot of negative things and are feeling the stress of the job. Things become routine; they are fed up with the administration and their supervisors. This is normal in every profession; they are not as enthusiastic about this job and are often looking for excitement or something new in their life. The best thing we can do for officers, and others, is to destigmatize mental health problems, officers trained Peer Support groups like alcohol recovery teams, and try to ensure access to top-quality, confidential mental health care. Once an officer trusts a mental health professional, he will be happy to open up about issues that are bothering him. Officers want to know how to fix their problems and get on with their lives.

Lt. Colonel David Grossman* declared, "We are human and must deal with the psychological problems that we encounter. Psychological problems can hurt every one of us, there has to be a balancing act. If there is a problem, we must deal with it." Police administrators need to create an environment for their officers who need emotional support to receive it without being punished. Psychological concerns can cripple anyone, especially a police officer, but there are many ways to get help without saying an officer is suicidal.

Sean Riley, founder of Safe Call Now, believes that many of the officers' problems are treatable and that officers have a resource to get help, especially if they are worried about confidentiality issues. Safe Call Now provides a confidential means and has trained personnel who understand what police officers and first responders and their families are going through and they understand the demands of law enforcement. Safe Call Now is a not-for-profit organization and they are funded through private donations and fund-raisers, conducting nationwide training and grants. This organization works with public safety groups, mental health, and substance abuse facilities. They provide a safe place for police officers and their families to call when they are experiencing an emotional crisis or just need to speak to someone that is willing to listen. They can provide the necessary resources that can be most beneficial to the first responders and their families.

Lisa Wimberger (2010) emphasized that the battle to win law enforcement agencies' ears and budgets continues. It is understood that there is a need to invest dollars into street safety training and special skills training. It makes sense to be prudent with budgets. But there must be a way to get officers and first responders the emotional training they need in order to remain

* Grossman, Dave Lt. Colonel, Personal interview.

healthy and productive individuals. This dilemma is now 20 years into its own debate if we begin counting at the government's recognition of this crisis. Over these last 20 years, the status quo methods have done nothing to lower the depression rate, burnout rate, or suicide rate of sworn personnel. Clearly it is time for a change.

Police versus Fireman

Dr. Frank Campbell* made a comparison to the difference between police and fireman.

Firefighters: Although firemen have an extremely difficult job when they are called out to fight a fire, when the fire bell rings and they are called out for assistance, they all go together as a team. In the mindset of firefighters, if it is predictable, it is preventable often with a limited range of risk. Their conditions are conducive to normal behavior. Eighty-one percent of firefighters would do it all over again. They train as a team, fight fires as a team, and trust one another. Often there are about 10 firemen assigned to a shift in the firehouse, working the same schedule. They stay in the same firehouse or quarters together, start their shift at the same time, and leave for home at the same time. A typical fireman works an average of 84 days a year. The firehouse is where they live for 24 h on duty, with 48 h off duty. They are sent into danger together; they come back as a team together. When firefighters come back from a fire, they come back to the firehouse and discuss what happened by sitting around and talking as a group (group debriefing). It also allows them time to digest what they have been through. They most often receive adequate sleep; eat breakfast, lunch, and dinner as a unit; and exercise together, hang out, talk, laugh, and watch TV together. Firemen have more of a group behavior and mentality. Often when a tragedy does occur or there is a structural fire, the entire firehouse is affected.

Police officers: Often work by themselves in a squad car answering dangerous calls, not knowing if their next call could be their last. Police are more likely to eat by themselves during a quick ½ h lunch break, consuming fast food because of the time limit allowed. Police officers continuously deal with the worst elements in society, often handling numerous critical incidents in their career. Debriefing in law enforcement does not touch on the emotional trauma the officer had to deal with, but what the officer could have done better or what he could have done to achieve a better outcome. The officer rarely shares the traumatic incident with anyone,

---

* Campbell, Frank, PhD, Personal interview.

often keeping his emotions bottled up. Debriefing in law enforcement is not the same or achieve the same benefit that fireman encounters. When the officer goes home, he is emotionally drained and detached, often keeping to himself. Being on guard all the time, the body has to rest. Police train in the academy together. Trained to stand alone, they call for help only when necessary. Police officers often start their shift with roll call, where they gather with their fellow officers as supervisors, hand out their assignments and disseminate current information, mostly about crime in the area and offenders to be aware of. Roll call has changed throughout the years. Previously, roll call meant talking with fellow officers sharing "war stories on the job", today roll call has become a quite solemn place where many officers have cell-phones in hand, mesmerized by the small screen in front of them.

Importance of Peer Support

Most major police departments have counselors, alcohol counselors, and psychologists on staff and available 24 h a day, every day. Because of liability, Employee Assistance Program (EAP) services are confidential and the department is not informed of the officer's attendance. The officer does not have to worry about notes or anything written down or what he has said. The counseling services offered by EAP are free for any officer and his immediate family.

The Chicago Police Peer Support program was created in April 2000. This program is part of the professional counseling employee assistance (EAP). This program is modeled after the one instituted at the Bureau of Alcohol, Tobacco and Firearms, who also provided the initial training. All Peer Support team members work on a strictly voluntary basis as a way of giving back to the Chicago Police Department family. Peer Support members come from varied backgrounds. This ensures that when a police officer or family member is in need of assistance, someone is available to him with the appropriate expertise, qualifications, knowledge, and awareness to offer the necessary resources.

The primary objective of the Peer Support program is stress reduction in the form of immediate emotional assistance and support. The Peer Support team members use active listening skills as they help fellow officers who are involved in critical incidents that range from normal reactions to abnormal behavior. Peer Support team members offer immediate on-scene intervention to fellow officers and their families after any traumatic incident or any other problem they are facing personally or professionally. The cornerstone of success to any program like this is confidentiality. Peer Support team members are trained and required to maintain strict confidentiality in all Peer Support communications. It is important for all department members to feel safe in their efforts to seek help in their time of crisis.

Father Dan Brandt said Peer Support is a great asset and they have done wonders addressing police suicide awareness and prevention. Dr. Campbell said that many officers are confused about seeking help for emotional problems they are experiencing. Officers have no idea where to go for help and who they can turn to and it can eventually lead to deteriorating behavioral issues. An officer who takes his own life does so because it appears to be a solution. They feel they are not worthy. Most officers do not have a deep understanding of suicide until they have personally been touched by a suicide. Campbell mentioned that he was with an officer waiting for funeral home personnel to take a person away that committed suicide. Campbell noted that he was wearing a coroner's jacket, and it must have appeared to the officer that he was not just a civilian, but someone that he could relate to and trust. Campbell asked, "How are you doing?" The officer said, "Do you know that this person used the same revolver that my dad did to take his life?" The officer broke down crying because he kept the suicide of his father pent up inside since he was a child. The officer felt that if he talked about his father's suicide, it would be a sign of weakness. The officer, whenever asked about his dad, would always say that his dad was killed in a traffic accident to avoid any questions about his father, who died at a young age. The officer could not say the word *dad*.

An officer will always remember his first suicide call, the same as he would remember his first homicide scene. It is something haunting and intrusive, and like most officers, they accept it as part of the territory, part of the job, "just suck it up." Anyone wearing a uniform, police, fire, EMT, or military soldiers, is exposed to traumatic loss and is vulnerable. Distress from the traumatic event can be a formula for disaster. People who enter the police force are not trained to handle the trauma that goes with critical incidents. There is no "open support," especially if police culture to "suck it up" continues. If that attitude worked all the time, we all would be saying it.

Police officers do not share with anyone, especially anyone that is not a police officer or their immediate inner circle. Officers need to talk out scenarios that they encounter on the street in a safe setting. That is why Peer Support is so important; it is a gatekeeper that opens the door to the EAP and crisis intervention training (CIT). Police need to speak with someone "who has been there" and who has experienced what he is going through. Campbell said it is similar to an alcoholic seeking help. Would he rather speak with a recovering alcoholic who has been there, or a counselor who does not drink? It is the same with police officers; they want to speak to someone who "has been in their shoes" and "who understands what they are going through."

Bill Hogewood* noted, "In 1983 I was asked to be in a project where many of us were trained to support our sisters and brothers in the aftermath of a trauma and also in the ongoing problems of life. After all, a police officer is still a person with ongoing relationship, financial, child rearing and the daily pressures of life. Add to that, death, horrific scenes, career criminals, and those that need help in a variety of ways. Compounding this are the media outlets that seem to thrive on the mistakes that officers make. Certainly more so than the attention paid to doctors, lawyers, professionals and blue collar careers." "Peer Support teams are made up of personnel working in a specific agency. Members volunteer and are selected through an application and interview process. They can be sworn and non-sworn members of the agency. They must display maturity, compassion, a willingness to be available and they have to be emotional risk takers. They also should be honest, credible, patient, trustworthy and not presently under investigation. Finally, and most importantly, they should be able to understand and utilize the concept of empathy. Empathy is sometimes defined as: One's ability to recognize, perceive and directly feel the emotion of another. It is the ability to relate to the common denominator of mankind, which are feelings.

The use of empathy and other skills can be taught and utilized by those willing to learn. These skills are essential to assisting the affected person in the process of ventilating or sharing, thoughts and feelings. This ventilation process is found to be emotionally cathartic."

"Peer Support for Public Safety" by William Hogewood

Peer Support is essential to the overall stress management program. It does not work in a vacuum, but alongside the professional mental health staff, the chaplains and other support groups such as substance abuse clinicians. It is not a competition for services; police officers and their families should be able to choose to find help where they feel comfortable. Peer Support is not just for intervention in the aftermath of critical incidents, but for assisting the police family through any bumpy roads. In my opinion, formed through many years of experience in local and federal law enforcement and from experiences assisting those in need, departments of any substantial size should provide these services and these choices to their personnel and

---

* Hogewood, Bill, Personal interview.

the families. Why? My experiences with interventions in suicides, deaths, Columbine, Katrina, and World Trade Center tell me it's just the right thing to do for them.

Train the Trainer

Hiram Grau* suggests that there are many programs that would ensure police officers receive training but one in particular that he spoke about is "train the trainer," where more information can be provided and distributed regarding a police officer's emotional well-being. He indicated that this type of training emphasizes increased communication and understanding of a persistent problem of dealing with his emotions when they are off duty. A nice part about this type of instruction is that it can be incorporated during roll call training sessions. Grau also suggested reinforcing emotional training by formulating a question on promotional exams. He noted that this would confirm that the police department is truly serious and concerned about the well-being and welfare of all of their officers. Officers need to be reminded that there is help available to them. It is often a double-edged sword; the officer is worried about seeking help because the administration can take away his FOID card (this card lawfully allows the officer to carry a weapon). Many officers are concerned about seeking professional help or counseling for this very reason. The law enforcement officer would be in a predicament, because he may be perceived to be psychologically unfit to work in the capacity of a police officer. Grau stated that officers who see unusual changes in their fellow officers should say something to someone, especially if they see an officer who is conveying obvious signals or warning signs that they need help. All officers must take these warning signals seriously. Grau stated it is better to err on the side of caution, especially if it means saving another individual's life. The reporting officer knows in his mind that he did the right thing. A good officer should be always looking out for his partner on the street as well as their emotional well-being.

Personal Early Warning System

Pam Church and her staff use a "personal early warning" system. This system identifies officers who may be in need of agency intervention in the form of either an informal or formal referral to the EAP. This program

---

* Grau, Hiram, Personal interview.

takes into account a number of factors, such as an officer's pattern of inappropriate behavior or discipline, performance evaluations, use of force incidents, accidents (including workers compensation and traffic), and citizens' complaints. This personal early warning system is a total overall picture of checks and balances that alerts the first-line supervisor and the administration of possible struggles that an officer is experiencing before they escalate and become detrimental to the officer and the department.

Make it Safe Program

In 2013, Dr. Digliani developed the "Make it Safe" Police Officer Initiative. The Make it Safe initiative is designed to reduce the secondary danger of policing. It is a reflection of the Below 100 initiative, an initiative that was created in 2010 with the goal of reducing police line of duty deaths to less than 100 a year. The Below 100 initiative addresses the primary danger of policing.

The "Make it Safe" program would change police culture by encouraging law enforcement agencies to initiate and maintain programs that would be aimed at reducing the number of suicides within their ranks. The Make it Safe program would literally make it safe for police officers to ask for psychological support and counseling. Digliani suggested that the police culture should (1) make it personally and professionally acceptable for officers to engage peer and professional psychological support services without fear of agency or peer reprisal or ridicule, (2) reduce officer fears about asking for psychological support when confronting potentially overwhelming job or other life difficulties, (3) change organizational climates that may discourage officers from seeking psychological help by reducing explicit and implicit organizational messages that imply asking for help is indicative of personal and professional weakness, (4) alter the profession-wide law enforcement culture that generally views asking for psychological help as a personal or professional weakness, and (5) improve the career-long psychological wellness of officers by encouraging police agencies to adopt long-term comprehensive officer-support strategies.

The Make it Safe initiative is dedicated to making it safe for officers to request and engage appropriate psychological support when dealing with difficult circumstances. Digliani stated that an officer does not need to be suicidal, have an alcohol or other substance-use problem, or be experiencing the emotional aftermath of a critical incident to benefit from this change in the police culture. The men and women of law enforcement need to rethink what it means to be a police officer. Officers should be able to ask for help without fear of negative career consequences and without feeling that asking for help is a personal or professional weakness. He proposed 12 elements to positively change the police culture. These elements collectively comprise the Make it Safe initiative.

The Make it Safe initiative encourages

1. That every officer *self-monitor* and take personal responsibility for his mental awareness
2. That every officer seek psychological support when confronting potentially overwhelming difficulties (officers do not have to "go through it alone")
3. That every officer diminishes the sometimes deadly effects of secondary danger by reaching out to other officers known to be facing difficult circumstances
4. That veteran and ranking officers use their status to help reduce secondary danger (veteran and ranking officers can reduce secondary danger by openly discussing it, appropriately sharing selected personal experiences, avoiding the use of judgmental terms to describe officers seeking or engaging psychological support, and talking about acceptability of seeking psychological support when confronting stressful circumstances)
5. That law enforcement administrators better educate themselves about the nature of secondary danger and take the lead in secondary danger reduction
6. That law enforcement administrators issue a departmental memo encouraging officers to engage psychological support services when confronting potentially overwhelming stress (the memo should include information about confidentiality and available support resources)
7. Basic training in stress management, stress inoculation, critical incidents, posttraumatic stress, police family dynamics, substance use and addiction, and the warning signs of depression and suicide
8. The development of programs that engage preemptive, early warning, and periodic department-wide officer-support interventions (e.g., proactive annual check-in, "early-warning" policies designed to support officers displaying signs of stress, and regularly scheduled stress inoculation and critical incident stressor management training)
9. That agencies initiate incident-specific protocols to support officers and their families when officers are involved in critical incidents
10. That agencies create appropriately structured, properly trained, and clinically supervised Peer Support teams
11. That agencies provide easy and confidential access to counseling and specialized and psychological support services

12. That officers at all levels of the organization enhance agency climate so that others are encouraged to ask for help when experiencing psychological or emotional difficulties instead of keeping and acting out a deadly secret

Chiefs Lead the Way

Dr. Marla Friedman*, a licensed clinical psychologist, has written an article about the complex subject of police suicide for *Command* Magazine, a publication of the Illinois Association of Chiefs of Police. Dr. Friedman explained that more law enforcement officers are killed by their own hands than in the line of duty. She said, "Many prevention programs have tried to assist departments in understanding the causes of police suicide and developing plans to combat these high numbers, but we are not even close to where we need to be." Dr. Friedman explained that one police chief said, "Realistically we need more than the checklist; a catalog of symptoms for depression and trauma is not enough. Attempting to identify behavioral signs that precede the act is just too late."

The sources of suicidal intentions are varied. The exposure to trauma and pain on a daily basis, grief, financial strain, family and marital conflict, availability of guns, job stress, and uneasiness about retirement can all contribute to the belief that life is unmanageable. Alcohol abuse, gambling, and sexual addictions are common coping mechanisms that lead to greater depression and anxiety. Ultimately, we are still left with the question of what we can do to stop suicide attempts and completions.

Currently, Dr. Friedman uses an approach called the *Proactive Health Check-In*. This is a methodology developed by Copsalive.com and Badgeoflife. com. She has added some modifications to the program and uses it when training chiefs of police.

This protocol includes the following features:

1. A visit to a psychologist to *develop* a relationship that can be relied on if needed in the future.
2. A *confidential* meeting that does *not* initiate a record or report.
3. It is *not* a fitness for duty evaluation. It is a *check-in* not a check-up.
4. There does not need to be a problem to go for the *check-in*.
5. It's just a *discussion* about what's happening in your life.
6. Participation is fully voluntary and *encouraged*.

* Friedman, Marla, Personal interview.

It is the first step toward *building* and *maintaining* good mental health. Many law enforcement officers are leery of mental health care professionals or counselors who work at EAPs. They feel that their information will be shared with their superiors. The ethical and legal statutes of confidentiality bind all mental health professionals, but if officers still have their doubts, then the program won't work. Concerns about appearing weak, crazy, or labeled unfit for duty are obstacles that have to be confronted and dispelled.

As a result of these issues, Dr. Friedman developed a program called "Chiefs Lead the Way." It is based on the idea that chiefs, as mentors and leaders, are uniquely qualified to role model healthy behavior. They represent parental figures, authoritative and strict, or one who provides support reassurance and comfort. Chiefs do not have to be perfect to encourage positive actions. Like the concept of the "good-enough mother," she just asks them to be "good-enough chiefs."

The program works by having each chief go for his or her own Proactive Health Check-In and then return to his or her departments and during roll call, or individually, review the features of the check-in. Then he promotes and urges all personnel to follow through with a visit to a psychologist. Chiefs' participation helps reduce the stigma of asking for help and allows officers to take responsibility for their own emotional well-being. It reduces bullying between peers in the department and normalizes the quest for a balanced work and family life.

A case example of how this might work would be as follows: a chief encourages his officers to go for a proactive health check-in. An officer then goes for a visit with a psychologist. The officer has not identified an issue, but follows through with the appointment to prepare for a time when a crisis might erupt in the future. The session goes well. The officer talks about what is happening in his life with no particular focus on a specific problem. Some of the uncertainty about seeing a psychologist dissolves as he talks and realizes that it really *is* just a check-in. The psychologist answers any questions that are asked and clarifies that no record is being kept and no information goes back to his chief or anyone else. No evaluation is done and the appointment finishes. That is the end of the experience. Hopefully, the officer will leave feeling like he has someone in his corner if needed at a later date.

To continue our case example, the following year the officer is involved in a shooting that results in the death of an offender. All of a sudden there is stress, confusion, and inquiries to deal with. Most law enforcement officers perceive themselves as effective defenders of the community. The reality is that death is not easily integrated into their views of themselves. While intensive training prepares them to act decisively and effectively in the moment, it's the subsequent consequences of the act that may disrupt their functioning down the line. Dr. Friedman explained that this is true whether the incident is judged to be a "good or bad" shooting. In any police involved in shooting, the news media will likely highlight the actions of the officer. Following proper procedure is not a safeguard against a campaign of ongoing investigation, scrutiny, or blame. Possible lawsuits to the department, personal liabilities, or concerns about being terminated will also plague the officer. The department they work for will be under fire from the community and the chief of police will be battered from all sides. Dr. Friedman says the stress is cumulative. Add this experience to years of handling deaths due to car accidents, sexual assaults, and domestic violence cases. Most officers will tell you that one of the top stressors is dealing with the deaths of children. These are images that can haunt an officer forever.

Then, along with the shooting incident comes a host of conflicting thoughts and emotions that undermine the confidence of the officer. It is not uncommon for the officer to have difficulty sleeping, insomnia, nightmares, exhaustion, and oversleeping in an attempt to escape the effects of the whole situation. Panic attacks, obsessive thoughts, depression, guilt, and shame are common reactions. Flashbacks of the incident and a sense of unreality may also be experienced. There can be a total numbing of feelings and withdrawal from friends, family, and other law enforcement officers. Anger at the offender for initiating these current problems is not unusual, though it may be confusing to the officer who has just done his job. Agitation, reckless behavior, and problems concentrating can occur as the officer tries to understand and integrate what has happened. A fear that normal life will never return destabilizes the officer and the risk of relying on ineffective coping mechanisms may begin. Dr. Friedman reminds us that these are normal responses to trauma. Few first responders have none of these reactions.

This is the critical juncture. Choices about how to cope with this accumulated trauma are made in this moment. Early education and intervention is the key to how the officer will cope overall. That is when the knowledge that a prior relationship exists with a psychologist can make a difference between seeking support or spiraling into feelings of hopelessness and despair. Without assistance the officer may increase alcohol consumption, overuse prescription drugs, engage in extramarital affairs, and begin or increase gambling as well as other high-risk behaviors.

Dr. Friedman says, "Imagine that the officer who was involved in the shooting begins to doubt his ability to be a good spouse or parent. His children require his time and attention and they don't understand why he missed their dance recital or soccer game. No amount of explanation to a child ever satisfies the child, or relieves the guilt of a parent. A threatened divorce may be added to this mix and it is just a matter of time before things start breaking apart. The officer's work life is overwhelming and his emotional defenses are already weakened. Add fears about finances, the future and eventual retirement, can you see how the thought of suicide could become a viable option?" Without a well-devised health plan that is already in place, the choices of what to do become limited by exhaustion, depression, and fear. She stressed that most officers are not involved in shootings, which initiated our case discussion here. Still, the effects of prolonged untreated stress that are associated with a career in law enforcement are undeniably devastating. Dr. Friedman is currently introducing the "Chiefs Lead the Way" campaign to national leaders in police suicide prevention and is hoping that a joint effort between the psychology and law enforcement communities can stimulate research and comprehensive programming, which will lead to a major change in how law enforcement personnel are trained and supported by their local departments. Hiram Grau stated "As police chiefs, championing our officers should be among our top priorities. We simply have to do a better job of that. It's important to remember that our people are the most important asset. The real work is done by the men and women who drive our police vehicles, the men and women who answer the phones, who talk to the public. Our job is to make their job possible. We are responsible for not only their physical well-being but their mental and emotional well-being as well. It's important to remember that it is not about you, it's about the officers who deal the real work."

Reference

Wimberger, L., *The Future of Stress Management for Law Enforcement*, 2010. Founder of The Neurosculpting®Institute, Denver, CO, and TPCG a subsidiary of Ripple Effect, Author of *New Beliefs New Brain*.

Suicide Is Never a Dry Run

8

BOBBY SMITH*

Contents

I have never seen my son's face. Nor have I ever laid eyes on my wife's beautiful smile. If I wanted to be really dramatic, that alone would be enough to make me stick my Glock 9 millimeter in my mouth and blow my brains out. I have found that never seeing my son laugh or even our dog's furry mug is reason to feel deeply sorry for myself, if I let it. Never experiencing the look of love in my wife's eyes as she looks at me so sad.

---

* Bobby Smith, PhD, a Louisiana State Trooper, has written three books after being permanently blinded by a shotgun blast from a cop killer in 1986. This chapter is reprinted with permission from Dr. Bobby Smith's book, *The Will to Survive.*

For those of you who have loved a child, whether it was your own or someone else's, can you imagine having a baby and *never* being able to see its face? Think about how beautiful a sleeping infant is, when he is learning to walk. How would you feel being so close to that little being, yet so far removed at the same time? I remember the joy of seeing my daughter, Kim, go off to kindergarten with her big smile and her front tooth missing. It was one of the most precious sights I have ever seen and will forever be branded on my memory. Unfortunately, I have had never had the pleasure concerning my son Brad. People have told me that he looks just like I spit him out of my mouth, but God, if only I could experience that for myself. What I wouldn't give to see our family portrait!

Now, obviously I'd never consider killing myself over not being able to see my family, despite the fact that it irks me and always will. But, I'll tell you, when emotional stresses stack up on top of each other, one after the other (with no end in sight), there's no telling what you'll do.

But It Will Never Happen to Me

Well, I've got some good news, I am just surprised as you may be when I tell you that in my research, I've found a little bit of good news—cool news, even. Not about the numbers, because they are definitely too high. But about the *why*'s behind this phenomenon of suicide. I think when you read about what's been driving this epidemic, you will breathe a sigh of relief and more hope if the statistics have been bothering you. This chapter will take away some of the mystery and drama associated with suicide, which is a scary topic for us cops, based on the sheer number of us who fall victim to this form of self-destruction. How can we be so smart and do such a dumb thing? How can we be so tough, yet so weak to destroy ourselves? This chapter will help you wrap your mind around the problem, ensuring that you'll be better armed so that regardless of what cards you're dealt, you will never be seriously tempted. You're reading about a guy (me) who has every reason and then some to kill himself. Odds are that if I were seriously tempted (which I was) and didn't succumb (obviously), you won't either, especially if you read on.

I know that some of you are thinking, "Even so Bobby, I think I'll skip this chapter because suicide will never be an option for me." I used to think the same thing. I'd be at an officer's funeral and wonder why the deceased had taken the cowardly way out by leaving everyone in such despair. I absolutely couldn't relate. But I was soon to learn the hard way about the allure and temptation of the perceived *freedom* that comes with ending it all.

So, please read this chapter in its entirety, even if you're hesitant. Think of it like eating your vegetables. You don't want to do that either, but you do because it's good for you. Along with the good news, I'm going to be telling you the bad stuff, too, and straight up, because frankly, some of you don't have much time to waste. While I promise to keep it as short as possible, there are some things you *need* to know, especially if you are having a hard time or know someone who is. Even if you aren't anywhere near the danger point of becoming a statistic yourself, you could encounter suicide on the job at any time. In other words...suck it up. It can't hurt to read a measly little chapter. I promise what you'll learn will be both fascinating and valuable.

We Are Our Own Worst Enemy

It is true that the majority of you reading this book will never attempt to take your own life, but that being said, nearly *one thousand cops will kill themselves this year* and every year after that, unless knowledge like this becomes commonplace. Knowing this information could be the difference between life and death for you at some point in the future. In case you think that I am being melodramatic about the psychological dangers we face, think on this (and the following points): Today, while reading this book, two or three cops will kill themselves! To put it in less dramatic language, my first little self-published autobiographical book, *Visions of Courage*, has sold somewhere around 22,000 copies. If you go by the stats that means that 22 cops who read my book will kill themselves. That's 22 sets of parents who will be devastated and many more spouses, children, siblings, and friends who will forever miss their loved ones, some never getting over it.

Few Alarming Points I Hear Frequently throughout My Travels

1. Suicide has become one of the great *secrets* of law enforcement.
2. As many as 600–800 cops kill themselves each year, and that is a conservative estimate.
3. Out of the 25,000 potentially lethal attacks on police officers in 2001, only 150 were deadly.
4. Suicide is the leading cause of death for police officers.
5. We have the highest suicide rate of all professionals. (Did you really believe dentists could outdo us? Come on!)
6. We are the boogeyman waiting in the dark. Suicide kills more cops than all of the dangers we face combined.

In 2000, according to executive director, Robert Douglas, of the National Suicide Foundation, in Pasadena Md., 418 police suicides occurred that year. But the actual numbers may be double that, as many suicide-related deaths are misrepresented as accidental death. (How many times have you questioned an "accidental death" when you heard the details: a skilled cop is cleaning his gun but somehow shoots himself in the temple, an officer's car hit a tree dead on, resulting in immediate death, but there aren't any skid marks to show that he tried to stop or swerve. You look a little deeper at the officer's personal life and hear about how he is losing his kids in a nasty divorce or being reprimanded publicly for a wrongful act on the job. Suddenly the *facts* of the case seem a little less factual and a lot fishier.)

Why the hush-hush? The stereotype that police are too tough to have emotional problems is a hard one to break, made more problematic by the fact that we don't typically acknowledge our stressors to anyone but each other. Talk about the blind leading the blind!

Very few of us want to talk about the fact that more cops die each year at our own hands than killed in the line of duty. The stats are hidden, altered, and eased, for the sake of the victims and those who love and employ us. The question becomes, why? Why do we do it? Suicide happens in great part because we don't know how to deal with the anger that comes from holding all of the stresses we deal with. According to recent FBI findings, *87 percent of American law enforcement officers suffer from posttraumatic stress disorder* (PTSD). In my counseling work with cops, I get to see the results of locked closets and horrors of cops who never cry or get help and who eventually try to kill themselves, often succeeding.

In short, the most powerful perpetrator lives in the psyche of the officer, as the hazards of the job are often unbearable and our rage has few outlets. But it doesn't have to be this way.

Why Are We So Susceptible? A Bizarre but Potentially Positive Twist

I'm about to tell you "cool" news. It's rather tragic, actually, especially for the people affected by suicide, the part of the world I'm going to tell you about. But for the rest of us, there is a powerful lesson here that can bring great relief and, I believe, hope.

On the South Pacific Islands of Micronesia, suicide has truly become a phenomenon. Young men, specifically, seem enamored by the possibility of killing themselves, as if some mythological power has them spellbound. Those who find themselves feeling suddenly powerless in a situation sometimes find the allure of taking control over their own death too tantalizing to ignore.

In a gripping account told by author Malcom Gladwell (*The Tipping Point: How Little Things Cam Make a Big Difference*, Little Brown, 2002), the Micronesian epidemic of suicide and what it means to the topic in general is thoroughly investigated. It turns out that as recent as the early 1960s, suicide on the islands was nearly unheard of. Once it was introduced by one *heroic* 17-year-old boy named Sima; however, "it began to rise, steeply and dramatically, by leaps and bounds every year, until the end of the 1980s there were more suicides per capita in Micronesia than anywhere else in the world." In comparing suicide rates between the islands and the United States, for example, a September 2003 report from *BMJ Publishing Group* (*British Medical Journal*) in Australia stated that for every 100,000 males between 15 and 25, there are 200 suicides in Micronesia, a number that exceeds U.S. rates by 20 times. How could this be? We're talking about beautiful islands here, not some horrible place ruled by an evil dictator.

What makes these numbers even more staggering is that suicides are often the result of *small* incidents: an argument with a parent, a breakup with a girlfriend, or a failed grade. It has become a kind of a ritual of adolescence. One 11-old boy who lived through such an attempt explained that he did not want to die but was merely "trying out" hanging, as if it were an experiment. With each new suicide, the myth takes on greater allure and rates continue to climb.

Although this almost casual way of viewing suicide in Micronesia is markedly different to the way suicide is seen in the United States, several similarities exist. As police suicide rates in America continue on their yearly ascent, there appears to be a kind of cancer at work. *Suicide leads to more suicide.* It's as if the mere fact that it exists, like a cancerous tumor, feeds continued growth. According to anthropologist Donald Rubinstein, as quoted in *The Tipping Point*, "As the number of suicides (in Micronesia) have grown, the idea has fed upon itself, infecting younger and younger boys, and transforming the act itself so that the unthinkable has somehow been rendered thinkable." In a series of papers, he writes, "Thus as suicide grows more frequent in these communities the idea itself acquires a certain familiarity if not fascination to young men, and the lethality of the act seems to be trivialized."

What does all this have to do with us? Plenty! Have you ever stopped to think about how often the reality of suicide has come into your life? How many times have you answered a suicide call on duty? How many times have you heard your fellow officers talking about one of their suicide calls? How many funerals have you heard of or attended where the officer shot himself in the head? Chances are suicide has become all too familiar to you. Now in comparison, how do you think your numbers rate against the general population? How often do you think your grandmother or your first grade teacher's life, for example, was touched by suicide? How many dead bodies do you think they have seen in their lives? Now you're getting the picture. The average person doesn't have this subject on their internal "computer screen" very often, if at all. For you, on the other hand, dead bodies and suicide are a real part of your everyday life and one that has become far too real and *way* too much of the option, especially when you're walking around with survivor guilt, repressed anger, and PTSD. *The unthinkable has somehow been rendered thinkable.*

The act of taking one's own life is obviously contagious under some circumstances, whether you believe that or not, whether you like it or not. Because suicides invariably lead to more suicides, we need to be mindful of this epidemic and mentality and emotionally protect ourselves from being easily influenced by the mindless actions of others. All sorts of statistics exist that prove the contagiousness of suicides on our shores. Right after Marilyn Monroe's death, for example, researcher David Phillips discovered that our nation's suicide rate temporarily increased by 12%—predominately from white women taking their lives in greater numbers that month (from *The Influence of Suggestion Suicide*, in the *American Sociological Review,* 1974). And think of how often you hear on the news that a man has shot his wife and children before killing himself. These stories are becoming more and more common. This isn't just a problem concerning a small group of islands. This is a global issue.

But this is good news for us. This is something that once we are aware of, we can have power over! Now that we know that we're dealing with a virus, or sorts, we can choose the emotional vaccine. I can't tell you how exciting this is to me. Suicide has merely become an option for us because that's what we've seen. It's become an option for us because we've become numb to how truly outrageous this is! Are you listening to me? Do you see how crazy and unconscious this has become. Do you understand that we have had the act of taking our own lives as an option because we thought it was rational. What would you say to your young daughter if she said that she wanted to kill herself? You'd say, "What are you kidding? Have you lost your mind? Nothing could be that bad, Don't take yourself so seriously!" But that's just what we do. We take it all too seriously, and that's crazy! Believe me, when you're suicidal, you're not thinking rationally. I know. I have been there.

Losing My Mind

When I was a kid, nighttime was always scarier to me than daytime. The closet that seemed totally safe and normal during the day was the place where monsters hid in the dark. From time to time, I would have myself totally convinced that evil, scary creatures were living and breathing somewhere in the space above my shoes and under my clothes.

In going back in time for a minute, one of the worst things about going blind was that it was always pitch black dark, no matter where I was or the time of the day. Thus, I was thrown often right back into these childhood fears of hidden evil entities who were coming out to prey on my poor, helpless little self. After all, evil lurks in the darkness and is afraid of light. I no longer had the ability to turn on the light switch and remove my darkness. Paranoia is common after trauma, and mine, encouraged by the onslaught of constant darkness and pain killers, started right away in the hospital (and creeps in from time to time). I had to be watched 24 h a day because I have been known to go into a rage and pull the IVs from my face and hands. I had no consciousness of what I was doing, and when I awake, I'd be confused, disorientated, and sweating. One evening, I sat up and was told that my brother Terry was sitting at the foot of my bed; only I didn't know who he was.

"Who are you?" I asked.

"Bobby, it's me, Terry," he replied. "What's wrong?"

"Why are you holding me here?" I asked.

"Holding you where?" he said.

"Holding me here, in the concentration camp," I said.

I was serious. I was certain that everything Terry was telling me about a shooting and losing my eyesight was crazy and that I was really being held against my will in a concentration camp. I wanted out something fierce! I stood up, pulled the IVs from my arms, tore the bandages off my face and hands, and yelled at Terry that he could no longer hold me against my will. I could feel pain, and suddenly, everything got really confusing because I could "see" that the room was painted in yellow and black checkers. Talk about being paranoid! As the nurse rushed in, I growled at her to get away from me and disregarded her assessment that I was hallucinating. It was only after they called in an officer that I knew I could trust that my memories started returning and I began to believe their story and accept the fact that I had been indeed shot.

Returning Home Brought Its Own Kind of Paranoia

In the deep quiet and stillness of the nighttime, without my wife's presence, I discovered that a mind can play horrible tricks on a person. Even though I couldn't see the difference between night and day, there was something sinister about nighttime now. Bad things always seemed to happen at night, and I couldn't figure out why. My paranoia was so intense that nearly every time I lay down, I would hear the most awful noises. (I could make a monster sound.) I remember like it was yesterday, hearing footsteps of a heavy-set man walking down the hall. As the steps grew closer, I could hear the man enter my bedroom, walk over to me, and stand right over my bed. I could actually hear him breathing right over me! Terrified, I lay motionless, wrestling with what to do wondering if I should stay put or chance it by reaching for the phone. Sometimes I did nothing only because the fear was paralyzing.

I don't know what it was about nighttime; if it was because the phone would stop ringing and the noise of the neighborhood would cease, but whatever the reason, this is when the dragon was unleashed, along with his buddies fear, anxiety, paranoia, and insomnia. I couldn't shake the fact that I was in this mess because I had been able to see from the glare of the high beams that night on the highway, and now I *really* couldn't see. Did this mean I'd be harmed again? Could it be worse the next time? I was so worried, knowing that I wouldn't be able to arm myself against an attack if it were coming. Certainly my guns would be of no use to me now.

I felt so vulnerable and at the mercy of any psychotic madman who could decide to hurt me. It had happened once before, and now I was imagining 101 ways in which it could happen again. As you can imagine, my biggest fear was that I was going crazy and would end up getting beaten up somewhere in a nut house that I couldn't escape from.

Just Walking to My Mailbox Brought on Panic Attacks

Coming home was a brutal reality. I hated every minute of it! I was getting bruised shins by attempting to navigate my way past the coffee table to the television set. I was feeling like an idiot groping for the toilet seat and peeing on the floor. (Have you ever tried to stand in front of a toilet with your eyes closed? Do I have to explain that one?) Hearing my wife sob hysterically in our bedroom down the hall before she gave up on me entirely, I knew that life would never again be lived on my terms. The smallest actions—getting the mail or going to the garage—became terrifying. Soon I developed agoraphobia and panic attacks, making it impossible to be self-sufficient. I was emotionally chained to the couch—my security blanket—and had to have my lifelines to the outside world, my remote control and phone, within reach at all time.

Couldn't Make It through the Night without Calling My Buddies

I don't think I'd be here today if it weren't for my buddies. These guys held my hands and held me up when I couldn't take care of myself another minute. When you've spent your entire career identifying with yourself as "the man," it is not easy to suddenly live life as a dependent person. My panic attacks were so relentless during the middle of the night that I often couldn't make it without calling my friends for help. Too many nights they had to race over and hold me, cry with me, and make sure that I felt safe. Trooper Mike Epps, for one, came over so many times between 2:00 and 3:00 o'clock in the morning that I lost count. This guy worked deep under cover in narcotics for years; he is *not* a guy who is going to show you his emotions. He has these real dark, deep-set looking eyes and a linebacker mentality. Think Tommy Lee Jones. He's always lean, mean, a fighting machine, and a real athlete. Believe or not, his favorite snack was yogurt raisins, so that's the bait I used to keep him coming back. I would call him sobbing on the phone and although I couldn't even talk, he knew it was me. Who else would be on the line snotting and wailing in the middle of the night? Mike would be asleep and answer in his sleepy tone saying: "Bobby, Bob," I'll be there in about twenty minutes. I'm en route, but don't call Jackie I don't want to have to deal with both of you wimps bubbling on the couch."

Of course, I had usually already called my partner, Jackie. What a mess we were! Mike would walk in the house and I'd be distraught with snot running down my face (sometimes Jackie would already be there, sniveling alongside), and he'd say, "Would you just stop all that damn crying." Without a beat, he'd walk straight to the pantry to the big container of yogurt raisins. He loved those things. As I'd hear him walk across the kitchen, I'd say to myself, "Oh God, I hope I'm not out of yogurt raisins because if I am, he is going to throw a fit!"

"Bobby!" he'd yell. "This really pisses me off! You call me over here at 3:00 a.m. in the morning and you don't even have any damn yogurt raisins!"

What angels my friends were to me! I never personally heard Mike cry, but I know that he did. Jackie couldn't help but cry. He was always such a softie; I often wondered how such a nice, sensitive guy could be happy being a cop, but he still loves it to this day.

Wrestling with the Five Stages of Grief

As we've already discussed, losses add up. I was starting to feel that mine had stacked so high that I was unable to deal with the enormity of my pain. Let's indulge in a brief recap, shall we? Let's see. I had never grieved the death of my mama, who had died on my 10th birthday. The only job I ever had loved had just been taken away from me because I could no longer perform the duties necessary to be a cop. I lived in a world of total physical darkness and dependency and would never again see *anything*. My second wife had just left me, and I was now living alone with terrifying panic attacks and agoraphobia. Oh, and monsters came to visit nearly every night. Dang, "my life was nasty!"

I'm sure you've heard about the five stages of grief. In a nutshell, none of us gets passed these suckers when dealing with trauma and devastating events. I had gone through several by this time, but I was far from being through with the grieving process! Let's look at the stages (four of which I had already encountered), and while you're reading, see if any of these are familiar to your life:

1. *Denial*: My best buddy! I loved hanging onto this one, but like all things, denial evolves, sticking around only until you're ready to deal with your loss. Eventually I had enough courage to stare reality in the face and look at my options, but that took a long time. Denial serves a purpose, however, and for a while it kept me from going totally mad by making me believe that I would get both my sight and my job back. In the end, it just wasn't worth trying to live in a fantasy world when the facts told a different story. That doesn't mean that I don't pray every day for the restoration of my sight, but I no longer depend on the outcome for my happiness. I no longer expect to be able to see again. If that happens, it will be the icing on a cake of a good life.

2. *Anger*: Okay, this is a given. As soon as the shooter's red car nearly hit us at the checkpoint, my blood was boiling. My memory is such that from the minute I woke up in the hospital, I was still furious. I was always a fighter, my shooting put me over the edge. I began taking my anger out on the people I loved the most (especially my sister Betty), which made me feel terrible. She would cry and then I would cry, which fed into bargaining and depression, the next two stages.

3. *Bargaining*: This is one stage I embraced right from the start! When I was face down on the highway, I bargained as if my life depended on it. Lying on the cold pavement, I told God I'd do *anything* if He'd just make it all okay and keep me alive. Later, my plea became more about how I can get back what I've lost. I can't count high enough to tell you the number of times I begged and pleaded with God to heal my situation. Even though I was willing to do whatever it took to get my job back, we all knew how that one turned out.

4. *Depression*: This is anger's twin and where you end up when you realize that bargaining ain't getting you anywhere. You can't have depression without anger. Depression is anger turned inward as a result of fear. It was pretty obvious that I had some attachment to this stage because any guy who curls up in the fetal position in the corner of his room to cry for hours at a time (which I did) has a little challenge with depression. Oh my Lord!

The stages don't necessarily follow chronological order, but all have to be fully worked through before the loss can become fully accepted. It would take some serious time before I explored the fifth and final stage: *acceptance*. That, and the issue of finding hope once again, was a little more elusive.

I Had So Much Shame about Who I Had Become

It is safe to say that I hated myself, not understanding that the nightmares, flashbacks, cold sweats, and hallucinations I was experiencing were normal.

I thought that I was the weakest cop ever to walk the earth. Another thing that was gnawing away at my self-respect was that I had lied about my shooting. It was a stupid lie, but an honest one (if that makes any sense) because it was all born out of denial. You see, when I was shot, the first bullet missed me, but I fell to the ground anyway. I had convinced myself that the first shot had ripped into my hand, spinning me around, and leaving me more vulnerable to the second shot.

The reality was that the second shot hit me in the hand *and* in the head. Even though getting hit by the first shot seemed like a stretch to me, that was my byline, my 10 s sound bite. Mostly everyone bought it, and that was fine with me because that's I wanted to believe. I just couldn't accept that I fell from fear. "Bang, bang you're dead" was too simplistic for my mind. It may have been the script we followed as kids playing cops and robbers (when falling to the ground upon hearing those fake bang, bang shots were part of the rules), but I hated to think that I didn't know better as an adult. It took me several years of therapy before I could admit that the first bullet (the one that brought me to the ground) missed me altogether.

Some of you may be thinking that we're trained to hit the ground when shots are fired, and you're right to think that. But I was still mad at myself for being so robotic in my response and ashamed to admit, even to myself, that I had fallen out of fear. I couldn't get it out of my mind that the fact that my knees had buckled out from under me may have contributed to my getting shot.

So, Mr. Superman state trooper thought he was a coward. As I lay in my bed or on my couch and cried (something I didn't seem to have any control over), I knew that people were standing around me crying. I felt so badly for them. They hurt for me because I was hurting, and I hurt for them because they were hurting. It was a vicious cycle of spiraling emotions and helplessness. When I talked, they tried to console me. When they talked, I tried to console them. It was never ending and totally depressing!

The Straw That Broke the Camel's Back

After Debbie left me, I didn't know what to do. It was obvious to everyone who knew me that I just couldn't stay home alone and do nothing. I needed a job; I was desperate to keep busy and find value in my life again. Too much time on my hands had left me paralyzed with fear and self-loathing. I needed to find a way to be of service, to contribute to society, and experience camaraderie with others.

Sgt. Aubrey Futrell, who trained me at the academy, and Sgt. Vic Summers came by one afternoon and asked me if I would be interested in going to Baton Rouge and doing a training video with the state police concerning my incident. Despite my fear of facing my memories in that kind of detail, I knew that I was getting stronger and that my story could help save lives in the future, so I agreed.

The ride was very enjoyable, and I thanked Aubrey for all of the training he had given me at the academy, telling him that if it hadn't been for the intensity of his leadership, I may not have survived that night on the highway.

The taping was a success and I was glad that I had made the trip. On the way back home, Aubrey asked me if I'd be interested in going to work for the state-police academy in Baton Rouge. I was so excited that I could hardly believe it! Maybe I could still be a Louisiana State Trooper after all! Even if I weren't in the field, at least I'd still be with the state police. I was elated, and we planned for me to move in with his family. It was fairly clear that I'd be a blind school dropout anyhow because in the short time I had attended the building where they were supposed to teach me how to walk around with a stick and read little raised dots with my fingers (yeah, right), I had rebelled against all of the rules and kept arguing with the teachers. I was sure that I was about to become the first person on earth ever to be kicked out of blind school, so I had no qualms about leaving. Besides, I had a job to go back to now! This was a dream come true.

I Moved to Baton Rouge and Moved In with Aubrey and His Wife

The director of the academy, Captain Rutt Whittington, knew about my background interest in psychology and my experience with PTSD and thought that it would be beneficial for the training academy if I did some work with Aubrey, so he put a desk for me in Aubrey's office. It was so great to finally feel that I was a part of something again, especially being a part of the Louisiana State Police! With time, I began to regain some of my old self-confidence. Captain Whittington came to me 1 day and asked me if I'd like to be a permanent part of the academy. Almost nothing could have made me happier, and I accepted right away. I was told that I would need to produce a proposal for the colonel, to show him how I could be of service to the department. I was determined to write the best proposal the department had ever seen.

Sgt. Vic Summers, who was an English major at LSU, helped me to complete my detailed proposal; we worked so hard on it and made sure that it covered every possible point that could help my case. On the day of my meeting, I was scheduled to speak to the new cadet class at the academy. My job was to inspire them to be the best cops they could be and to learn from my example. It was a blast. In full uniform once again, my dream was already coming true. The cadets loved the talk. As I stood in front of the room, I was overcome by feelings of joy and tears began to well up in my eyes. These were happy tears. For once!

When I finished my presentation, Aubrey and I went straight to my meeting with the colonel. I walked into his office feeling confident, excited, and nervous because this guy had my future in his hands. It soon became clear that something was wrong and that my future wasn't so important to this authority figure after all. I handed him my beautifully typed proposal, and he threw it across his desk without so much as looking at it.

"Bobby, I know why you're here. I received a call from the Governor. It's just not going to work out. Let me be very honest with you. We have the tape [referring to a training tape I made about the incident]; we just don't need you anymore."

Holding back the tears, I turned my back and walked to the door, thinking, "You don't deserve to see me cry." I was devastated, knowing that all of my dreams were now crashing around me. The daggers of his words had pierced my heart and I was furious that I had lost my eyesight in the line of duty and this was my thanks. He then informed me that he was in the process of finishing my retirement papers and that he wished me well. I wondered how someone could be so heartless, without empathy or compassion. *Sticks and stones may break your bones, but words will never hurt you. What a lie!*

I left headquarters and was suddenly thrust back onto the roller coaster of emotional turmoil. I had finally been accepting myself as a blind person and this one person had just taken a world of hope away from me. In a matter of second, what had taken 6 months to build was wiped away. To add insult to injury, I was told that I wasn't eligible for the retirement watch, even though I was now officially retiring, and I had to travel 230 miles to Monroe to sign my papers.

I could not believe what happened next. My colonel flew to the event in his helicopter with his personal photographer and had the audacity to take pictures of me shaking his hand as he handed me my retirement papers! In a big facade, the public was supposed to see how "gracious" the state police was being to a poor blind man.

I Sat on the Edge of My Bed with My Revolver in My Hand

I had never contemplated suicide before my shooting. As I said earlier, I never understood how anyone could be so irrational. But now, after being rejected, nothing seemed to be going my way. I felt like I was doomed to a life of failure and dependency. Thoughts that would have seemed totally irrational to me earlier now seemed completely rational. Death seemed like the only way out of my traumatized life. What was the point? My life only brought misery to me and all those I was dependent upon.

I knew it would be simple; countless cops before me had proven that. All I had to do was put my trusty loaded revolver in my mouth or hold it to my temple and fire, quick and easy. I reached for my familiar Smith and Wesson .357 Magnum. I didn't want to die; I just wanted the emotional pain to go away. Since there was no light at the end of my tunnel, I figured I'd go looking for the supposed light on the other side. I saw death as my only real option.

Just as I was planning to put the gun toward my head, I heard a voice. There wasn't anyone in the room, so it appeared the voice was in my head. But it didn't sound like my voice. It was strong, forceful, and certain. It said, "Go get the poem." I remembered that my daughter had given me a poem after my shooting called *Footprints in the Sand*. I knew it by heart and had been so moved at the end of the poem where God reveals that the reason there is only one set of footprints in the sand during times of trouble is because God is carrying us. I hurriedly found the poem, held it to my chest, and cried and cried. Kim was still alive at that time, and yet she had no idea how many times her small gift to me proved to save my life.

What Have You Done Lately to Reach Out to an Officer in Trouble?

I'd like you to think about your attitude toward officers who are experiencing trauma. Have you been willing to listen to a buddy in pain? Or did you exit the east entrance of the station when you saw one of your troubled brothers or sisters coming through the west entrance? If it weren't for my buddies, I never would have made it out alive.

I get letters all the time from cops who've heard me speak and want to share stories with me, often baring their souls concerning issues they've bottled up inside. One particular letter still stands out as one of the more heart wrenching.

A female officer wrote to tell me that she had gone to high school with a popular guy she didn't really know. A self-proclaimed geek back then, she wasn't included in his social circle. One afternoon she saw this man, now a fellow police officer, at a police-sporting event. They had a great time talking about their children and about the many comical things they each experienced in their respective departments. He mentioned that he had been divorced, and before leaving that night, he gave her his home phone number, saying that he hoped they'd get together. She thought that was a great idea, and when she got home, she put his number on her dresser so she'd remember to call him. She never got around to making that call, however, and it soon became too late because she heard that he had committed suicide. This woman was devastated and wrote to me about her regrets about not following up. She, like most people affected by suicide, wondered if maybe she could have made a difference.

We all get so busy; it can be hard to know when a situation is indeed dire. I'm quite certain, too, that in this man's misery, he never would have believed that in taking his own life, he'd be hurting people as remote as this female officer he barely knew.

If You Think You Are a Burden Now, Wait until after You Pull the Trigger

Okay, you're doing dang well if you are still reading this thing! My hat goes off to you. It isn't so bad, is it? Now I have to talk with you a little bit about the stark reality of what suicide really looks like to the people left behind. Please indulge me. This is my feeble attempt to write my own version of *Scared Straight.*

Cops aren't afraid to die, but we don't handle death well either. We're mostly afraid of being weak, of feeling shame, of letting people down. Ironically, we're terrified of being a burden to others, but the reality of suicide is that you become the ultimate burden, as you'll see.

Think back to a time when you've felt badly about yourself. Maybe you felt fat or sick or depressed and didn't think you were able to contribute enough joy or skill or money or emotional support to those around you. Maybe you felt that your life put undue stress on others—a spouse or coworkers, children or parents—and that life would be easier without you. I can see how that mentality forms. I've been there! When I had lost it all—my eyesight, my job, and my wife—I thought that killing myself would be a win-win situation of sorts: bringing peace and ease to those I was dependent upon, and the freedom from the pain that I so desperately craved. Freedom is a big one for us cops because it ties in with being independent. I was used to being "da Man," not "da burden."

I had never depended on so many people, from doctors, strangers, and coworkers to my friends, my brothers, and my sister. It seemed that no matter what someone offered, I always needed further assistance. Friends would bring me groceries but then I needed help putting everything away. Someone would help me find what I needed in a store, but then I couldn't count my money. If I asked for help getting to a bus stop, then I needed someone to make sure I was going to the right destination. I was constantly at the mercy of others and felt like a leach, which was ongoing and unbearable. Thankfully, however, I never totally lost sight of the bigger question.

How Do You Want to Be Remembered?

It all boils down to this one question, doesn't it? What do you want your legacy be? The sad truth is that most people who kill themselves are found by their children or spouses. I can't imagine a more selfish, horrible legacy to leave to your loved ones. Now, it's important to keep in mind that when you're depressed and suicidal, you are not thinking clearly. There's a chemical imbalance that takes place in the brain when a person is severely depressed and thinking irrationally, we deny that we have a problem. Suicide begins to look rational, and a cop will say to himself: "I'm the decision maker. I'm used to taking control. There is nothing wrong with thinking about taking my own life." It's like trying to convince a drunk that he's too drunk. He doesn't believe you because the alcohol has dulled his rational thinking.

So, in your irrational moment, maybe you don't think your family will be adversely affected if you die. Maybe you don't care what happens to them in that moment. Maybe you're mad at them; maybe they've hurt your feelings or let you down. You're so irrational that you can't even see that 2 days from now, everything will look brighter. You're talking yourself *way* too seriously!

You Take Your Gun Out and Shoot Yourself in the Head

Once you actually pull the trigger, you are now a hideous mess—waiting to be discovered. Your youngest child finds you lying on the floor of your bedroom. She's terrified. But, you're not dead yet. You're bleeding to death and incoherent, but you're still alive, thrashing around and convulsing. The top of your head is blown off, splattered on the wall, and your daughter runs screaming from the room and calls the rest of the family, who all scream and cry upon finding you. What happens next?

The paramedics come, as do the neighbors and the media who heard it over their police scanner. People are hysterical. Your family wants to ride with you to the hospital, knowing that this might be the last time they see you alive. But they aren't allowed to come. Why? Because your spouse and older children have to go into the station for questioning. The police on the scene can't be sure that you're responsible for your shooting. For all they know, someone in your family has tried to kill you. The investigators, who are your extended family, would sometimes rather believe that your wife killed you rather than imagine that you took your own life. Imagine the panic you've instilled in everyone involved. So, while you get wheeled away in the screeching ambulance, your family is hauled off in a somber squad car and taken in, where they will have to sit for hours in their bloody clothes, answering questions and trying to prove their innocence.

Do you really want to avoid being a burden? The only opinion is to get your act together and get some help! Suicide is an option, but not a very good one. There are better ways to leave an unhappy life, like divorce or a job change, for starters. The guy I just wrote about couldn't have left a more tragic and hideous legacy if he had paid Stephen King to write a horror movie of his life. His family will never forget that nightmare day and its aftermath. No matter how happy they may become down the line, these images will never, ever, fully disappear. This one very selfish act set this guy's wife and kids up for a lifetime of haunting flashbacks and regret. *Now that's irrational!* Is that really what you want to leave behind at the end of your life?

Unfortunately, this ripple effect is largely unimaginable to a suicidal person because desperate people don't see past their own misery. But all you have to do is look around at your next suicide call and imagine those aftershocks taking place in your house.

If Kim's Death Didn't Push Me over the Edge, Nothing Will

Thankfully, I had done a lot of work on myself and healed a lot of my old pain when I found out that my daughter was dying in the hospital. Although I spent many dark moments grieving over the loss of her life, never once did I consider killing myself when she died. Probably because I had worked so hard on myself and learned how to handle the largest stressors that life could dish out. *Thankfully once again, the option of suicide had become unthinkable.* (Later, I realized that she had previously been the one to stop me from killing myself with the poem and that strength still held strong years later.) I have been able to stay rational and see the beauty of my life, even against the backdrop of the worst tragedy I had ever faced. Kim's death was emotionally devastating, but I had been to this place before; I had walked this familiar trail already. I could tell myself, "This is going to be hard, but it can't take me out."

In hindsight, Kim must have known on some level that she was going to die. On her last birthday, she said to me very seriously, "You know Daddy, you're a much better dad blind than you were sighted." A month before her accident, we had dinner together, and she told me that she was sorry for the bad choices she made in her life and that she had forgiven me for not always being there for her as a child. I had no idea it would be our last meal together.

I'm so grateful that my daughter and I were given emotional closure. Although I'd like nothing more than to have her alive, I found the strength to move forward, just as Kim would want me to. I think about my mama's words, oh so many years ago, and I know what she meant when she said to me, "God never gives you more than you can handle." No matter how bad it looks, we have the fortitude to get through it.

Suicide Is Never a Dry Run

No matter how bad it looks, suicide is never worth the aftermath. I pray that no matter how terrible your life might seem to you, no matter what you've done, who you've hurt, or what kind of mess you may find yourself in, you will keep your wits about you and remember my situation. Remember that the one pair of footprints in the sand are not yours but God's, as he cradles you.

If I didn't take my life after becoming a groveling, snot-nosed dependent wimp, you can get through whatever is going on with you. I never could have known at my lowest points the joy I currently live with. I have so much fun on a daily basis, so much laughter, such love and success around me that sometimes I feel like one of the most blessed men in the world. I challenge you to stay open to the good your situation can bring to the world and trust that there's a plan. There is always a plan, and being six feet under before your time ain't part of that plan.

I'm certain of it. Hang in there, no matter what, my brotha (I say that with affection for the ladies as well). This too shall pass. It's going to be okay.

Bobby E. Smith PhD

Footprints in the Sand

One night I had a dream.
I dreamed I was walking along the beach
with the Lord.

Across the sky flashed scenes from my life.
For each scene, I noticed two sets of
footprints in the sand,
one belonging to me, and the other to the Lord.

When the last scene of my life flashed before me,
I looked back at the footprints in the sand.
I noticed that many times along the path of my life
there was only one set of footprints.
I also noticed that it happened at the very lowest
and saddest times in my life.

This really bothered me
and I questioned the Lord about it:
"Lord, you said that once I decided to follow you,
you'd walk with me all the way.
But I have noticed that during the most

troublesome times in my life
there is only one set of footprints.
I don't understand why
when I need you most you would leave me."

The Lord replied:
"My precious child, I love you and would
never leave you.
During your times of trial and suffering,
when you see only one set of footprints, it was then
that I carried you."

Mary Stevenson

Footprints in the Sand was added to this section by Dr. Ron Rufo. There are numerous authors who have claimed to have written this poem. I have submitted this poem from Mary Stevenson.

Dr. Ron Rufo

Police Suicide

RON RUFO

Contents

The clock of life is wound but once, and no man has the power to tell just when the hands will stop, at late or early hour. Now is the only time you own. Live, love, toil with a will. Place no faith in time. For the clock may soon be still.

The Clock of Life, Robert H. Smith 1932, 1982

The Lakefront: by Jay Padar

To my left, the waters of Lake Michigan encroached upon the sands of North Avenue Beach and then slowly receded. On my right was an endless line of headlights, which traveled north up Lake Shore Drive. My right arm was planted firmly upon the blue metal railing as my left arm wrapped around my brother's shoulders. We swayed back and forth as we listened and sang along with the band in front of us. I needed this. I needed to return to this beautiful lakefront under better circumstances. I don't believe my brother was aware that just 24 h ago, I had stood on the lakefront just a mile north. I wasn't smiling or singing then, just staring.

Eight minutes out of roll call the night before, I had heard the dispatcher send a job to a beat car. She assigned me to that same job without even asking me if I was available. I tapped the screen on my computer to retrieve the call just as she began reading it over the air. The caller had just found a suicide note left by a family member. He was nowhere to be found. He was a Chicago police officer.

All available units responded. Some went to the caller's house. Others went to the park where the note said the family member was headed. We scoured the park on foot and in cars, looking under every bush and up into every tree. We were searching for something we didn't want to find. When our initial search was completed without success, we called in the K-9 units just to double check. The marine unit was summoned to check the river and its banks, which bordered the east side of the park. Patrolmen from other districts in the city responded to assist in the search. A unit was stationed in front of the police officer's home, just in case his family heard any good news.

When our initial search yielded nothing, the family informed us that this officer also spent a lot of time at the beach. We notified all of the districts along the lakefront. The officer had left his house on foot and shouldn't be too far. It was still like looking for a needle in a haystack. We searched every late night bar and stopped every person on the street. We woke up every homeless person, asking whether he had seen anything. We sent a formal flash to all units citywide, asking for their eyes and ears. We had nothing.

It was 6:03 a.m. A beat car searching the lakefront pulled up on a man sitting against a tree with a gun in his hand. He wasn't moving. A towel was over his head. The officers called out but got no response. They approached slowly and pulled the towel from his head. They immediately called for an ambulance. I was notified and responded with my lights and sirens wailing. I didn't want it to be him.

To my left the waters of Lake Michigan slowly rolled up onto the beach. To my right was an endless stream of morning commuters traveling north up Lake Shore Drive. In front of me was the lifeless body of a Chicago police officer, a bullet in his head. My right arm was planted firmly on my squad as my left hand covered my mouth. I stood motionless and watched as officers strung crime scene tape from tree to tree. A steady flow of squad cars with flashing lights pulled up onto the lakefront.

I gave my brother a little hug, smiles, and fought back a tear. We swayed back and forth, still singing with the band. He was unaware of where my thoughts were, but he hugged back and smiled at me. I was trying to reclaim the lakefront. I was trying to erase the tragic scene I had just witnessed. I was trying to see the lakefront as it should be seen. This was not just another image of a dead body to be filed away in my mind. This was a Chicago police officer. He was a protector of the weak, a crime fighter, and a friend to many. He could have been my backup had I ever needed help. He was a fellow officer whom I couldn't reach in time when he needed help the most.

My Friend George: by Matt Walsh-Lieutenant Cook County Sheriffs Police Recalled This Story of a Friend and Colleague

Matt said that he and George were friends, and they would often work side jobs together and have a few cocktails occasionally after work. He was extremely happy in the police academy and when he finally realized his dream as a police officer. George, 41 years old, came from a police family; both his father and grandfather were police officers. George was a marine and always wanted to be a policeman. George was an aggressive officer and did well in his district. He was married and had six children. George was injured on duty, eventually was assigned to desk duty where he accepted that role. He apparently forged a document relating to that incident. After the forgery was discovered, he was suspended from duty upon investigation, and it was recommended that he be fired. George never asked anyone for help or guidance after the forgery allegations. George began drinking heavily and became reclusive and was not his jovial self. After a few months of being suspended, he was terminated from the department. George used his service weapon and took his life in 2006. One of his children found him.

My Son: by John Barney Flanagan

John Barney Flanagan* lost his police officer son Kevin to suicide. Officer Kevin Flanagan started his career in the 11th District and soon signed up

* Flanagan, John Barney, Personal interview.

for a special unit that often was dispatched to high crime areas in Chicago. Kevin wanted to be a policeman all of his life, especially wanting to help the citizens he served. Kevin, a young 25-year old, good looking man, had many good friends, and had everything going for him. Flanagan had a special relationship with his son, they were great friends, and they did a lot together. Kevin was a comedian and the life of the party. He was well liked by everyone. When Kevin got there, the party began; it was like New Year's Eve every day!!! If this could happen to my son, it could happen to anyone. Kevin took his own life in his apartment, on the night of February 23, 2004. Flanagan said that when you lose a child, there is a sudden emptiness in your life. Flanagan remarked that the Chicago police department has averaged two–six suicides per year consistently since the 1970s. Kevin's close police friends as well as personal friends were deeply affected by his death. Flanagan commented that all of Kevin's friends are hurting emotionally, and he sees a definite change in their behavior and outlook on life. Flanagan was dismayed that he did not see any tell-tale signs that Kevin wanted to take his own life.

Twelve Possible Warnings Signs of Pending Suicide

1. Relationship issues (domestic violence, order of protection, separation or divorce). Relationship issues often play a major role in many police suicides.
2. Lack of sleep—Being sleep deprived also can affect the judgment of the officer. His reasoning skills and thought processes are ultimately affected. The conflict in his life becomes even greater than it appears; he is always tired, angry, and living on the edge. Indeed, this is a true combination for disaster.
3. Overwhelmed by financial problems, bankruptcy, etc.
4. Anxiety, anger, hostility and violence, "short fuse," hostile, argumentative, confrontational, belligerent, extreme stress.
5. Withdrawal from family and friends, indifference, coldness, lack of interest, isolated.
6. Changes at work, not caring, reckless conduct, don't care attitude, unnecessary risks, verbal complaints, aggressive behavior, calling off sick, loss of assignment or position, fired or separated from the job, fear of retirement, lawsuits.
7. Giving away prized possessions, life having no meaning or worth, hopelessness, their lives are out of control, defeated, formulating a plan, saying "when they are gone" or talking about suicide.

8. Obvious symptoms of distress, depression, symptoms of mental illness, feeling sorry for themselves, impulsive, and irrational behavior.
9. Consuming large amounts of alcohol, and addictive behavior.
10. Noticeable change in mood, strange behavior, habits or personality, neglecting their appearance, activity uncharacteristic of the individual.
11. Family history, prior attempts, etc.
12. Comments, "I will not be around to see that," "Don't have to worry about that," indicators, cry for help.

Physical Ailments That May Lead to Police Suicide

Poor eyesight
Hearing loss
Cancer
Crippling arthritis
Stroke
Heart attack
Diabetes
Kidney failure
Ulcers, stomach issues
Weight gain

Dr. Ron Rufo's *Ten D's* of Suicidal Ideation

Suicidal ideation is a medical term for the condition of having suicidal thoughts. Emotions are the only part of a crisis that an officer can control. Smaller issues are only symptoms of a bigger problem.

1. Desperation
2. Despair
3. Dejected
4. Demoralized
5. Devastated
6. Depressed
7. Discouraged
8. Distressed
9. Decline
10. Downward spiral

Three Ms of Police Suicide

Denis Adams* mentioned the 3 Ms associated with officers who contemplate suicide:

Motivation: The motivation or the incentive that triggers the officer may be to silence the personal emotional struggles that he has been experiencing at the time. The stimulus could be the mounting personal conflicts they could not control. An example could have been a recent divorce that an officer did not want, but had to accept.

Method: This is the method in which an officer decides to take his own life. How an officer may plan his death, how he will be found, and who he plans to discover their body: a loved one, a colleague, or friend. At times this choice may be based on an impulse to end the emotional pain.

Means: How the officer intends to die. Often officers will use their own service weapons to end their lives. A majority of police officers who commit suicide use their own service resolvers that are easily accessible, convenient, and are clearly close at hand. Dr. Frank Campbell[†] noted an amazing statistic: that police officers are five times more likely to use their service weapon on themselves than on an offender in the line of duty. Dr. John Mayer[‡] believes that when things get out of hand at home and blow up, that's when police officers want to kill themselves. Sad to say, a police officer knows the means, and has the accessibility of his service weapon to complete the act. The fact is that police officers have seen or heard about suicides on the job. They have read reports and seen how it has been done. Police suicide has become a reality and the possibility for the police officer. Just like the copycat phenomena in suicide, because it is in the profession, it becomes the mindset. At a scene of suicide, how many officers say underneath their breath? "Look at that lucky bastard, that guy's or girl's problems are over." An important point witnessing the aftermath of suicide, what effect it has on the human mind, "That doesn't look so bad; they died peacefully because of the overdose."

Police Suicide

In Chicago in 2013, the Chicago Police Department thankfully did not lose any officers in the line of duty, but regretfully, the Chicago Police Department lost six of its police officers to suicide. Most police suicides involve an officer using his own weapon (often to the head), hanging,

---

* Adams, Dennis, LSCW, Personal interview.
† Campbell, Frank, PhD, Personal interview.
‡ Mayer, John, PhD, Personal interview.

stabbing, drug overdose, carbon monoxide poisoning, or his death is made to look like an accident.

According to Suicide, Finding Hope (2013), they noted that there has been a silent statistic within the law enforcement profession that has been unspoken for decades. A line is drawn deeply and permanently between two deaths, namely one, whom we call a hero when dying in the line of duty, the other a mere whisper of an officer who has died. When an officer dies by suicide, the family not only grieves the loss of their loved one, but must also deal with isolation and abandonment of their police family. Law enforcement is the only profession that has a written funeral protocol based on how the police officer dies. Shouldn't these men and women be honored for how they lived?

Bill Hogewood* noted that the general population and police officers share the top three reasons why suicide occurs: relationship issues, financial problems, and terminal illness. He remarked that suicide is one of the most researched, yet least understood phenomena affecting society today. Each day there are horror stories of suicide attempts or success that shock those who are close to the victim, yet when retrospectively evaluated come as no surprise. Each day, one who supposedly has it all, takes his own life. Father Tony Pizzo believes that when officers become distressed, and cannot deal with the pressure of life anymore, that is when they feel the only option is suicide.

Nichols (2014) said that the decision to end one's life represents an unendurable amount of emotional pain in the form of an overpowering sense of helplessness, hopelessness, futility, desperation, and despair. It is not unusual for these emotional feelings to possibly not have existed at the same level of intensity just a few days earlier or even the day before. The individual proceeds with disconnecting from almost everything, and in doing so becomes vulnerable. Consequently, the option to formulate alternative approaches becomes so constricted that a second thought is not sufficient to put out a cry for help. Indeed, it can be said that once the final decision is made, the individual can almost feel a sense of relief as well as surge of energy, the latter necessary in order to carry out the act. Often this can be seen in those persons with depression by way of their mood appearing on the upswing.

Father Dan Brandt† said he had been called out and involved in some capacity in the last 5 out of 6 suicides that occurred last year. When Operations Command calls me at 3:00 p.m., I know that most likely, it is a mundane call, but if the phone rings 12 h later at 3:00 a.m., I know that this is going to be an "oh shit" moment. I know whatever call that I have to

* Hogewood, Bill, Personal interview.
† Brandt, Father Daniel, Personal interview.

respond to will not be good. Everyone has stress in his or her life, no matter what line of work a person is in, so I am not 100% sure that we could blame the job for every suicide. Other occupations have to work harder to find the means to kill themselves. Police officers have the means to kill themselves, because their tool is on the side of their hip. Other stressors take over, and that quickly they are gone, suicide was the solution to their problem. All six officers that killed themselves in 2013 used their own weapons to end their lives. Alcohol plays a major role in police suicide, because it impairs their decision-making process. Alcohol makes depression worse as it breaks down the wall of resistance. Last year, four of the six officers that committed suicide were drunk when they pulled the trigger. Brandt said every suicide is difficult, but one that was devastating to him and the young officer's family was when the officer tried committing suicide but he failed to die after he shot himself the first time. Wounded and dazed, he walked around the house, smearing blood across the wall of almost every room in his house. A short time later, he walked back into the kitchen and shot himself again, this time it was fatal. This young man had everything going for him, and actually had plans to redo his landscaping at the table where he killed himself. It was a shock to not only his family, but everyone he worked with and his many friends. After seeing what I have seen, especially with police suicides, I have to go through a debriefing (spiritual direction) as well. Nationwide, twice as many officers kill themselves as are killed by offenders. And again, "they" say that statistic might be more than *three* times since some are classified as accidents; driving a car 100 mph into a pole with no seat belt on and if no suicide note is there, then, though unlikely, it might have been an accident.

Dr. John Violanti acknowledged that as a result, the personal relationships of police officers are not personal at all; they are more like transactions on the street. Significant others soon become less important to the police officer. Compassion is subdued in favor of the police culture, which takes precedent over most other emotional feelings. In some respects, the police role becomes a safe place to hide but at the same time does not allow for an outlet of emotions. The inability of police officers to use other roles to solve problems with a family person, friend, or lover may be behind many police relationship problems. Below is an example of a relationship problem which ended in suicide:

> Two weeks before his death in mid-April, this officer, 26 years old, told friends he wanted to kill himself. He felt caught, he said, between two women. He was deeply involved with one but planning to become engaged to the second. He had been on the force four years. A colleague of the dead officer spoke of stress on the job. "Unfortunately," he said, "the department does not teach how to deal with it well. It's a big organization and some people get lost."

Some police suicides may be therefore based on shame or inability to fulfill role expectations of the organization, police peers, the public, or oneself. Below is a case of police suicide that involved perceptions of bringing dishonor to the role of police officer:

> This suicide involved an officer who was thirty years old and a recent graduate of the Police Academy. Two days after graduating from the Police Academy and a day after being assigned to a Precinct, the officer became intoxicated, and struck another car, slightly injuring two people. Instead of stopping, he sped off and later reported his car stolen. New officers are on probation for their first two years and the charges would have been enough to end the officer's career. He apparently shot himself in the chest with a handgun in his basement apartment amid empty beer cans. Nearby was a display of his uniform and his equipment set up in such a way that one official described it as "a shrine to the police department." He left a note apologizing to his parents and the department for any disgrace he might have brought them.

Dr. John Violanti said it is considerably difficult to disentangle the complex causal web of police work and suicide; however, one point remains clear: far more research into every aspect of police suicide is necessary. Such an effort is crucial if police work is to become an occupation where individuals can work with satisfaction and psychological health.

> Caught by surprise, you hear a rumor at roll call that Officer Ben Shields is dead; you hear that he killed himself last night. He was recently divorced. You remember working with Ben years back. He didn't seem the type to take his own life. The phone rings, a mutual friend calls and confirms that indeed Officer Shields killed himself last night with his own weapon to the head. His ex-wife and two kids are taking it hard. Peer Support and the Chaplains unit are called to visit his immediate family at their home. Everyone that knew him is in disbelief. An anonymous female police officer declared "No one tells you or talks about police suicide…..no one here expects you to deal with feelings or show feelings…they wall up"

Lt. Colonel Grossman* said that police peers likely contribute to feelings of shame and guilt. Statements found in police suicide notes like "I let the guys down" confirm the need of officers to fulfill their police identity. The potential for suicide may be the result of a perceived unforgivable offense against the police role and the job. Police culture restricts flexibility in thinking about the world from other than the police view, and the use of other life roles in dealing with stress. In summary, these factors impair the police officer's ability to deal with psychological stress. As a result, the potential for

---

* Grossman, Lt. Colonel Dave, Personal interview.

suicide may increase. Regarding police suicide, let's learn from what happened to that officer. Not every officer is going to commit suicide, there must be a balance. There are resources out there that officers can take advantage of: Employee Assistance Program (EAP) and Peer Support. Peer Support needs to be implemented and used more often if police departments have them. Grossman insists that we need to protect ourselves, like body armor for the mind. "We can get officers to calm down just by talking over a drink or a meal. Just by separating memory from emotions is part of the healing process. It should not be a pity party, no macho man belief; officers just need to regain control."

Dr. Alexis Artwohl* said that the threat of police suicide should be taken seriously. There are a relatively small number of police officers who are bothered by suicidal ideation, delusional thoughts, who are psychotic or seriously intend on harming themselves or others. Artwohl noted that suicide is associated with other mental issues, such as chronic depression or manic depressive disorder that may be too difficult to treat and will lead that person to commit suicide. Rarely does someone have a serious suicidal crisis "out of the blue." An officer in a drunken stupor who calls 911 for help is obviously in a suicidal crisis. A police officer who has a chronic alcohol abuse problem is more than likely on a downward spiral. This type of officer will eventually destroy his health, his family, and often hold it together until the last thing that he loses is his job. Alcohol or drug problems can be genetically driven. Artwohl said that the tragic death of Robin Williams, who was very talented and successful, had a great sense of humor, a gentleman by most accounts, yet it was sad that he took his own life. There was no outwardly obvious reason for his suicide, but the sad truths now have come out: a lifelong history of (1) substance abuse, and (2) depression, both of which have significant genetic contributors and are known serious risk factors for suicide. He was not able to overcome these illnesses in spite of being able to afford the very best of mental health care. Undoubtedly, he had some situational problems and stressors like the rest of humanity, but many people are in far more desperate circumstances, yet carry on. There are many other examples of people who have much going for them, yet take their own lives. Artwohl stated that some occupations and/or demographic groups have higher suicide rates than others for mostly unknown reasons. For instance, men commit suicide at four times the rate of women, yet no one really knows why. There is plenty of speculation, but no scientific proof. This is why I think it is not accurate to say that job stress is the primary cause of police suicides. Any stressor can be a suicide precipitant for vulnerable individuals. Job stress in and of itself is not likely to cause otherwise healthy individuals to kill themselves. Mental

---

* Artwohl, Alexis, PhD, Personal interview.

health problems are complex, and we are far from having a clear understanding of them. In spite of this lack of understanding, there are things we can do to treat and support people who are struggling with these issues.

Jeff Murphy* said that throughout his 40-year career, he has attended 4 funerals for officers that he knew personally who were killed in the line of duty and 12 officers who have committed suicide. The biggest killer is not the threat of dealing with deadly force, but the stress of intense police work that leads to suicide, and other health issues such as heart attack, stroke, high blood pressure, diabetes, migraines, and other physical ailments. Stress is a major concern that shortens the lives of police officers.

Father Rubey† articulated that we are experiencing a high rate of suicide among police officers. Unfortunately, suicide is still considered a sin under extenuating circumstances. Fifty years ago, the church did not allow for Christian burials if someone took his or her own life. The church reinforced this stigma by limiting the support and the services for the survivors of suicide. Many families that experience the death of a loved one by suicide also share in the guilt of not seeing the signs beforehand. Questions that are often asked after the death of a loved one are, "What did I miss?" "What should I have done?" "I should have seen it coming." Guilt often overwhelms survivors of suicide as the grieving process often never ends. The goal of the grieving process is to develop a comfort level regarding the person that died. Survivors need to talk about it and remember their loved one in a positive way. The survivors of suicide cannot stop living their lives. Rubey recommends a ritual honoring the family member that died, because it is important to remember them: recognizing the anniversary of their family member's death, wedding anniversaries, birthdays, holidays etc., some way to remember their life. Rubey gave an example of one family that celebrated their son's 16th birthday at the cemetery, with a birthday cake and fond memories of their life together.

Father Rubey cited the writing "The Elephant in the Room." (Author unknown)
"The Elephant in the Room"
There's an elephant in the room.
It is large and squatting, so it is hard to get around it.
Yet we squeeze by with,
"How are you?" and "I'm fine," and a thousand other
forms of trivial chatter. We talk about the weather. We talk about work.
We talk about everything else, except the elephant in the room.
There's an elephant in the room.
We all know it's there. We are thinking about the elephant as we talk together.

---

* Murphy, Jeff, Personal interview.
† Rubey, Father Charles, Personal interview.

It is constantly on our minds. For, you see, it is a very large elephant
It has hurt us all.
But we do not talk about the elephant.
Oh, please let's talk about the elephant in the room.
For if I cannot, then you are leaving me....
alone...
in a room....
with an elephant

Thirty years ago, not mentioning the person who committed suicide was part of the culture. Our society has gradually become more open about suicide. Rubey said it is important not to make the person's death an elephant in the room. Rituals address the elephant in the room for many family members who need other people not to be worried or feel uncomfortable about discussing the topic.

Rubey gave an example of a lady who lost her husband by suicide. The first wedding anniversary since his death fell on Labor Day. Her five children, aged between 8 and 19 went about their business, not once mentioning the anniversary to their mother. The next day, the widow asked if they forgot it was their parent's wedding anniversary. Each child expressed that he did not want to bring it up for fear of causing more pain, anguish, and guilt. Clearly a worse tragedy than suicide is not remembering the person after they have died. Rituals help to remember in a positive way the person who died.

Father Rubey noted that we need to address the impact of police suicide and bring it out of the darkness. Rubey said that we need to address this topic openly, honestly, and candidly. Police suicide needs to be transparent, where we take the shame away. As a society, we need to do what we can to lessen the stigma of police suicide. Suicide is a result of mental illness, and the person who ends his or her life only wants to end the pain he is experiencing. It is a human issue that should not be covered up. It has gotten better, but we still have a long way to go.

Statistics

Recent studies indicate that police suicide is seven times the national norm and it is the ninth leading cause of death in the United States. In 2012, the average age for suicides among police officers was 42 years old, with 16 years on the job and was often in the patrol division. Many of the officers that took their own life were married, or were in a committed relationship. Many suicides were done while the officer was drunk or alcohol related. Statistics from the study done by Badgeoflife indicated that in 2012 study, there were

126 police suicides throughout the nation. The study revealed a few different stats than previous years in that

- 91% of suicides were by males.
- The age group that was most at risk was from 40 to 44 years of age.
- The most at risk time on the job was from 15 to 19 years of service.
- 63% of the suicide victims were single.
- 11% of officers who took their own lives were also veterans.

Dr. Frank Campbell found that women attempt suicide more often than men, but men actually die by suicide about three times more often than women in the United States. Research shows that smaller police departments have higher rates of suicide than larger departments. Violanti (1996) examined data from five police departments in the United States and found most police officers who committed suicide were Caucasian males, of lower rank, used a firearm, and had alcohol involvement.

New York City Police data indicated that 77% of police officers who committed suicide were less than 35 years of age and 73% had less than 10 years of police service. In 2012, the New York City Police Department had four officers kill themselves in a 1-month period.

- One officer killed himself after his shift was over.
- A father of 5-year-old twins, with over 20 years on the job, shot himself at home.
- An officer killed himself on duty after an anonymous caller reported that he was depressed.
- A young officer took his life in his parents' home after he was involved in a traffic accident.

Misclassification

When pressed for a response, the Chicago Police Department, like other police departments, will retreat into a corner for good reason. There are a few reasons why suicide is rarely acknowledged by police departments across the nation. Police departments will neither confirm nor deny any suicide or suicide attempts. The vast majority of police departments do not want to admit they have a problem involving suicide within their department. If a police department highlights the issue that many suicides have occurred throughout the year—they are admitting that there is a problem that needs to be addressed. Administration within the police department will need to reinforce that there are many confidential counseling services, programs, and seminars available to their personnel. The police department will need to show what is being done to combat the problem of suicide and steps to ensure that any officers experiencing a personal crisis in their life are given the opportunity to seek support or help for the crisis they are experiencing.

It may be difficult to fathom how many police suicides are actually mis-labeled. If an officer's death is deemed a suicide, many police agencies do not want to air out their "dirty laundry." This may be true for a variety of reasons.

1. *Officer's family*: Suicides that are misclassified as "accidental" or "uncertain" to protect the officer's family. This may be for emotional reasons and/or possibly for monetary and insurance reasons.
2. *Police family*: Suicides that are misclassified as "accidental" or "uncertain" may be initiated to protect the morale and reputation of the police family, especially if low morale is a major concern of most officers. They do not want other officers thinking about killing themselves.
3. *Public perception*: Every police department or police agency is wor-ried about the number of suicides within their departments. Police departments do not want the parade of rumors that may validate the thought that *maybe* there may be a problem in our department.

Dr. John Violanti did a study on the misclassification of undetermined deaths and found that 17% of these undetermined deaths were actually sui-cides. Misclassification of what really happened protects the officer and the officer's family. Suicide is the most preventable death, it is the top leading cause of death in the United States. Police administrators continue to bury their heads in the sand, because the sad fact is that we lost 141 officers to suicide last year. Suicide is higher among active duty officers than retired officers. Violanti stated that the rate of suicide is higher for officers within 5 years of retirement. This is due to the stress of: "what do I do now." Just prior to retirement, an officer may feel indecision: what does the future hold? Should I retire or stay on the job? Should I seek promotion? Many officers have their sights on a retirement date, but when that date draws near, they actually get cold feet.

Dr. Ellen Scrivner* said that we need to take the curtain down and shine the light on this issue, since it is not going away. We do not know the full extent of the number of suicides, since some are covered up to look like an accident for the protection of officers' families or to preserve their benefits. But, what we do know is that police officers see many victims of suicide and may be internalizing it as one way to solve a problem, since when you kill yourself, the problem is over and you are out of a very painful situation. We need to ensure that officers do not adopt this mode of thinking about

---

* Scrivner, Ellen, PhD, Personal interview.

problem solving and the best way to do that is, again, take the curtain down, shine the light, and start talking about it. Those actions will represent a very positive change in direction for the police culture.

Bill Hogewood acknowledged that his department at one time had fewer officers and naturally, they had fewer suicides. He acknowledged that on the job, we did not know about suicides, it was not openly discussed. The administration did not want the public or the officers to know about officers wanting to kill themselves. As far as the police department was concerned, they do not want to scare the public into thinking that there are a few homicidal maniacs walking around. Hogewood expressed "that the police suicide statistics are skewed; Suicide stats show that police officers kill themselves four times more than the line of duty related deaths, this does not include traffic accidents. If you include traffic accidents, the line of duty deaths is only 1½ to 1 of the general population. In my opinion, if you take accidents into consideration, the rates of suicide by police officers are comparable to the general population, especially with the officers that fall into the age group of those who are 23–45 years of age." Bill Hogewood expressed that the emotional conflicts and problems an officer may experience are often swept "underneath the administrative rug." He surmised that police departments may not be totally honest when reporting what really happened to one of their own. Instead of a "self-inflicted gunshot wound, a report may read accidental discharge." There is not a police department in the nation that wants to be known for suicide among its officers. "We do not have this problem in our department." Suicide gives any department a proverbial "black eye," especially if officers are killing themselves at a relatively steady pace. Police administrators may be uncertain how to even address this issue. Keeping police suicide within the department is often hard to do. Police officers begin to talk, rumors spread, and become rampant. The concern of all police department personnel is to keep suicide in their department at an all-time low. This may be an attempt to spare the officer's family, friends, and fellow officers the gruesome details of what happened. A vague report may ensure the officer's family will not be in danger of being denied any compensation or monetary settlement from the officer's death.

Captain Barry Thomas* believes the number of underreported suicides may be as high as three to five times those that are actually reported. Even with that in mind, considering the actual number of reported suicides, law enforcement officers are two to four times more likely to die by suicide than from an adversarial encounter. Thomas believes this is unacceptable. Lisa Wimberger stated that police suicide is definitely an epidemic. Statistics can be argued, and are often not accurate. Either way one suicide is too many.

---

* Thomas, Captain Barry, Personal interview.

Retired police officers who commit suicide are not statistically included in police data, because they are no longer in the job. Their death by suicide could conceivably have resulted from an officer's inability to cope with retirement, or to the trauma they experienced in their career. Police suicides are definitely out of proportion with in-line-of-duty deaths.

Mike Holub* suggested that many police departments falsify the real report, stating that the officer died as a result of a gun cleaning accident, an accidental shooting, a hunting accident, or the officer accidentally mixed up his medication. There may never be a true account of how many police suicides there are because of these incorrect classifications. Holub noted that we should not stigmatize the tragedy any more than we need to. If we hope to fix this, we have to acknowledge that, as tragic as it is, the officer took his life by a self-inflicted gunshot. Holub insisted that, "Like any kind of issue, the first step is to acknowledge, recognize and identify that a problem exists, the second step is to find the root cause of the problem, and the third step is to do something about it. We cannot be in denial about police suicide, which I call the 'ostrich syndrome,' where we bury our heads in the sand and pretend that it does not exist. We need to find a solution, not have a Band-Aid approach."

Jeff Murphy explained that police departments across the country have virtually covered up suicides by misclassifying how the officer died. Police reports may indicate that the officer died cleaning his weapon, or in a one-car accident or by drowning in a swimming accident. The department may have saved pension or insurance issues and extended grief by misclassifying their report, but unintentional or not, it creates a situation that cannot be ignored. Besides the support of the Gold Star Families (families that have experienced a loss of a police officer on duty), no one is there to light the darkness for the families, but we do more than in previous years."

Police Culture

A police officer's job is demanding and stressful. An officer may commit suicide from issues or discipline related to problems at work, stress from past or current relationships problems at home, mounting financial burdens that may take many years to resolve or recover from. What seems to be a clear and sensible solution can become clouded with doubt and uncertainty. The emotional state of a suicidal officer is that this pain will only be gone if he takes his own life—there is no light at the end of the tunnel.

In Illinois COPS Police Magazine (February 2013), there was a letter titled *Closing Arguments Regarding Suicide of a Fellow Officer's Close Friend,*

---

* Holub, Michael, Personal interview.

"We are not without emotion, but we put up a pretty good front. When I got on the job, I was given advice like that which many of us received: You need to have thick skin. This message was received well. I have tried never to take jokes too seriously, criticism too harshly or punishment too resentfully. After working on the street for a time, the rose colored glasses are removed and you see the things that most people will never see; some sights that could make tourist people cry, the angry expressions of disdain and hatred cast upon you by those you have never met before. Are you there yet? All of these jeering words of abrasion you have drowned in cannot be unheard. All of these sights of turmoil you fell victim to, cannot be unseen.

Despite all that tough skin you have developed over the course of your tours, you are not without flaws. Sometimes the surface cracks. We are only human. When we go home, we take off our badges, vests and guns and we are left only with the aftermath of our fallout. I cannot stress enough that how we feel from that point forward is absolutely critical to the healthy relationships that we have with ourselves and with others. There are times when life will give you lemons and you will know what to do with them. Though there will be times when life gives you rusty nails and you will need to decide: what is the purpose and what will you do with them? Being human may be our biggest weakness, but it also may be our greatest strength. It is vital that we remind each other that when the chips fall where they may and the proverbial excrement 'hits the fan,' we will be there to pick up the pieces and help clean up the mess. Regardless of whether there are numbers against us, blocked on all sides and shrouded with darkness, our will and strength will see us through the light." (p. 38)

Taking Deliberate Chances

A depressed and disgruntled officer, who does not want to be labeled a coward by taking his own life, may make a deliberate attempt at being killed in the line of duty by taking risky and unnecessary chances. The officer will make a concentrated effort to appear as if his death was caused by an accident on duty. An example would be the first person busting down the door attempting to enter a gang/drug house or driving dangerously with lights and siren blaring, hitting a retaining wall at full speed. If they get killed, their family will be financially taken care of by the city, county, state, and federal government. They will be revered and recognized as a hero with their star being displayed with other fallen officers that have lost their life serving the people of the community. An officer's premeditated attempt to end his life takes away the label of a coward, and takes on the marque of a hero.

The Pain Is Gone; It's All Over

A suicidal officer simply does not want to continue with the emotional or physical pain that he is experiencing. The feeling of hopelessness overwhelms an officer in this mental state. It is often the burden of his despair and depression in an attempt to find a resolution to his dilemma that put him over the edge. Depending on the individual, an officer may contemplate suicide after a cycle of extremely bad luck, emotional and/or financial setbacks, and problems that in his mind cannot be resolved. Suicide is the ultimate end that finally stops the pain the individual officer is feeling and suffering. There are many complex issues and deteriorating circumstances that can cause an officer to commit suicide. Justifying his actions to relieve the pain, problems, and suffering he is enduring can come at a weak moment in his life, thinking irrationally that there is a better place if he were gone. An officer who takes his own life may feel he has become a burden to his family or friends; it becomes a strained situation. A police officer may want to end the apparent conflict in his life that may be caused by mental and/or physical pain and anguish he is enduring.

Crisis coupled with anger frequently turns into depression, which is often the major component in suicide. Untreated depression is the leading cause of police suicide. Depression is considered a mental health disorder that is associated with constant and persistent feelings of sadness and despair. It can be linked with a chemical imbalance in the brain along with a myriad of stressors and or trauma that a person encounters: grief, divorce, and relationship problems can be factors. Other factors that can lead up to depression and erratic behavior is when the officer is overextended financially, causing him to work additional hours doing security, spending less time with his family. Alcohol complicates the issue as it elevates depression, enhancing suicidal thoughts and actions.

Not all police suicides end in the officer placing a gun to his head and shooting, or using a rope or a duty belt to hang himself. There are many officers who are alcoholics and will drink themselves to death to take away the pain. The officer who drinks to die will not necessarily have the stigma of committing suicide to fellow officers that do not know of his addiction. If an officer dies from a gunshot wound, his fellow officers will know immediately about the suicide attempt, if the officer never wakes up from alcohol poisoning, their fellow officers would not necessarily associate their demise to suicide, they may just look at it as an untimely and unfortunate death of a friend and fellow officer.

Lt. Colonel Grossman said that depression plus suicide is a volatile mixture-add stress, now you have a toxic cocktail called the treacherous trio that lead to suicide. Police officers will often mask any signs of depression, rebellious relationships, or alcoholism as an escape mechanism. Police have a higher suicide rate than the general population that is often associated with a number of stress factors. Police encounter the stress associated with imminent danger associated with criminal element on the street, the lack of control they experience from their department, and the uncertainty and isolation from family as their police career moves into high gear. Eighty percent of policemen who were married before they get on the job will most likely end up divorced. The emotional well-being must also be included in police training. Father Dan Brandt declared that officers kill themselves, because they can no longer take the pain. So many of our officers choose suicide: it is the opposite of what we are proficient at, it does not make any sense. We are the only species who choose to take our own lives.

Selfish Act

Committing suicide is considered by many to be a genuinely selfish act, because the officer may have taken the easy way out (kill the pain that has been haunting him once and for all), but the shock, aftermath, and stigma of their suicide will continue to plague those that they loved for years to come. Dr. Dean C. Angelo, Sr.*, noted that police suicide is a sad, final act. He doesn't think that people realize the wake they leave as a result of taking their own life. Officers have easy access to their firearm. It is a shame, but they feel that it is the only way to end their problems. It is rough, especially if the officer who took his own life has family on the job. Sometimes there might be extra stress in the officer's life if his family member was on the job and they were high ranking, but the officer under stress is not. The officer wants to emulate a hero and does not want to disappoint them for their job performance. Many believe that it is a selfish act that conveys a feeling of guilt for everyone who had known that officer. Coworkers think that they should have done something: that they should have seen or that they missed the signs. Everyone carries around that guilt forever.

Notable Occasions

Suicide is prevalent around any holiday season, most notably being Christmas, Hanukah, and News Year's Eve, considered happy, joyous, and exciting times for many. Statistically, this time of the year can also spur depression, loneliness, and despair for a variety of reasons. The holiday spirit takes on a different

* Angelo Sr., Dean C., EdD, Personal interview.

meaning for police officers who find themselves alone. Remembering previous holidays that were happy, joyful, and fun are now filled with resentment and loneliness. Depending on the officer's seniority and shift, he may have to work, while everyone is getting together to celebrate.

- Being forced to work additional hours because of the lack of time on the job.
- Not being home to partake in holiday festivities, celebrations, or parties because of their schedule.
- Not spending time with the children or spouse during the holiday season.
- Not having enough money to make ends meet or to buy gifts, trying to take on extra jobs.
- All of the pressure of the job, lack of sleep, and grueling schedule may be more than the officer can bear.

Aftermath and Aftershock

A normal reaction by family and friends of suicide is shock and disbelief, leaving them with grief and guilt. The family of the officer who committed suicide may ask:

- "Why did this happen?"
- "Why did I not see any signs or indication of trouble, how did I not see this coming?"
- "I should have been more aware."
- "What could I have done to prevent this tragedy?"
- "Was I to blame?"
- "What was the trigger that caused them to do this?"

Location of Suicide

Suicide is often seen as a solution, not a problem. A police officer in crisis may plan his demise, formulating a specific place and time that has meaning or significance where he can end it all. Most suicides by law enforcement officers take place in a memorable or common site, often a familiar site of comfort or pain. It could be a place where the officer confronts his fear, grief, or demons. Suicide often occurs in a bedroom, bath, or basement of the home.

There is often a method to the madness, especially if the officer committing suicide wants to be found by a certain individual. That individual could be the officer's wife/husband, significant other, a family member, relative, friend, or another member in the law enforcement community. A few officers have taken their lives in a wooded area, often indicating that they did not want anyone experiencing the mess and the lasting trauma of the clean-up surrounding their death. Lisa Wimberger noted that the probability of knowing someone who has attempted suicide or committed suicide is significant. The officer often lacks the coping skills necessary to relax and wind down from the graphic details and traumatic events he has experienced. Suicide is often not as impulsive as someone may believe. Many officers use alcohol as a way to cope, but alcohol is a depressant. Many officers have a plan, and the alcohol just makes it easier to carry out that plan.

Why?

Suicide does have an effect and impact on immediate family, relatives, friends, and the police department and on the community. I personally feel that a family that has been touched by suicide never gets past the emotional trauma. The aftermath and aftershock impacts the officer's immediate family. They are devastated and often angry as they question why their loved one went to such extremes to end his or her life. Why he chose death as a logical conclusion to end his life. Now the immediate family is left trying to tie up loose ends that the officer left behind, at the same time trying to grieve for the person that died. The immediate family of an officer that has committed suicide may need some form of crisis resolution or psychological assistance.

Committing suicide may be the ending of the officer's issues and problems, but his family will encounter many unanswered questions. An officer who commits suicide will leave behind a void within his immediate family. The survivors of a suicide not only feel remorse due to the loss of a loved one, but feel guilt that they could not help or see the signs of the suicide before it happened.

A person may acknowledge the death of a loved one, but will always question the officer's motives and the reason he took his own life. Many of the deceased officer's friends and family will question themselves as to why they did not do more to inquire what was wrong. It is often after the death of the officer that the little signs begin to surface, like putting the pieces of the puzzle together. Life could not have been that bad, as speculation runs rampant. If the officer has a child or children, it is not uncommon for them to shoulder part of the blame.

Victims of Suicide

When an officer decides to take his own life, he leaves a multiple number of victims. Suicide is a tragedy that validates the mortality of an individual that was often seen as the strength and pillar for others. Their loss creates a rippling effect. The victims of police suicide include: husband/wife, significant other, parents, children, immediate family, relatives, close personal friends, and the police family and coworkers that are so much a part of the deceased officer's life. Regardless of the statistics, the death of a police officer has a significant impact, not only on the family and close friends of the victim, but also upon the entire department.

Other victims: Dispatcher taking the call, officer making out the report, supervisors, and detectives called to the scene, the fire department, Emergency Medical Tech (EMT), any other police officers responding to the scene, medical personnel taking out the body, the family being notified, the person notifying the family. Incidents that involve murder/suicide or multiple suicides affect the entire community.

Steve Stelter, Chief of Police for Brookfield, Illinois, stated that there were two very good officers who committed suicide. Both officers had everything going for them. With all that they had going, the main question is "Why?" One officer had a wife, two kids, one graduating grammar school, and the other graduating high school. Stelter stated that nothing is so bad in someone's life that something cannot be worked out. This officer was demoted and was worried about not being able to make enough money. The officer was despondent. In his mind, this problem is something that could not be resolved. The other officer was having personal problems, she had two wonderful daughters. Her oldest daughter said, "I never thought the first funeral that I would have to go to would be my Mom's." Both officers had everything to live for, both were very good cops. Everyone is still hurt and upset by their deaths. The topic of suicide is relevant and it is something that can't be just brushed off, it is a serious problem.

Bill Hogewood noted that suicide affects many, not just the victim and each time an attempt or a successful suicide occurs, there are multiple victims. The person taking the original complaint or notification is victimized. The family who has to be notified is victimized. The person who has to make the notification and the person who has to treat the injuries or remove the body is victimized. The police officer, fire fighter, or emergency medical technician who comes face to face with the attempter is victimized. In fact, the system itself becomes a victim by tying up resources, for the attempted or completed suicide, that could otherwise be devoted to providing support for those intent on living.

Dr. Bruce Handler implied that police suicide not only impacts the officer's family and loved ones, but it affects the entire law enforcement community. We need to focus and concentrate on education and training that dispels the misconceptions regarding mental illness, depression, and suicidal thoughts. Dr. John Violanti remarked that suicide causes a lot of grief within a family, grief for the department, and it causes low morale. It affects everyone involved in that officer's life. If a department does not care about the life of an officer, it should care about replacing that officer. Not only is the department losing the experience that officer had, but the cost of replacing that experience with a new officer on the street is compromised.

Father Dan Brandt articulated that many parents that have encountered suicide have said that parents are not supposed to bury their children. Many families rely on their faith when the despair of suicide takes hold. Father Brandt said that one Atheist patrolman he spoke with said, "With all of the shit that I have seen on this job, I am starting to doubt my disbelief." Father Brandt does not necessarily believe that God does not give us more than we can handle. He said that some folks are dealt losing hands time after time.

Dr. Frank Campbell revealed that suicide leaves survivors with more questions than answers. His research ranked the top 10 relationships to the deceased who are most likely to seek help following suicide. He noted that after reviewing over 400 cases, the following list describes those relationships that came to the Crisis Center seeking help following the death by suicide of a loved one:

1. Mother of the deceased
2. Sister of the deceased
3. Wife of the deceased
4. Daughter of the deceased
5. (Tied) Friend-Son of the deceased
6. Father of the deceased
7. Brother of the deceased
8. Girlfriend of the deceased
9. Stepfather of the deceased
10. (Tied) Cousin-Fiancée of the deceased

Active Postvention Model

Those individuals who experience the loss of a loved one by suicide are often reported to be eight times more likely to commit suicide themselves, which includes friends as well as family. Dr Frank Campbell initiated the Active Postvention Model concept, which involves a team of first responders who go to the scene of a suicide and provide support and referral for those bereaved by the suicide. The goal has been to shorten the elapsed time between the death and survivors finding the help they feel will help them cope with this devastating loss. The Active Postvention Model has been shown to have a positive impact on both the team members (most often bereaved individuals who have gotten help and now provide hope to the newly bereaved) and the newly bereaved. The model has now been replicated in countries as diverse as Australia, Singapore, Northern Ireland, and Canada.

Reactions after a Suicide

Anderson (2014) acknowledged that suicide is a serious problem that is not often talked about in police circles. It is very hard, if not impossible, for us to understand why someone chooses to end his life. Shock and disbelief are usually the first responses to an officer's suicide. Reactions to suicide can sometimes be irrational and destructive. Remember, no one can "second-guess" or take responsibility for another person's reactions to the events that are happening in his or her life. And suicide is not the only response to life's problems. Suicide is the ultimate act of violence that hurts many people around the victim. Anger and guilt are two very natural and normal responses to suicide. Yet, these emotions are very difficult for police officers to talk about. However, many friends and family members of the suicide victim talk about having feelings of guilt for not preventing the suicide. They believe that they should have seen it coming. Sometimes suicide is an impulsive act, one that has not really been planned out by the victim. A major difference between the general public and police officers is the immediate availability of a weapon. When a police officer decides to commit suicide, he doesn't have to go out and get a gun—the means are available at all times. In fact, the number *one* method of suicide by police officers is their gun. Anger is normal after suicide and should be expressed—it's part of the grieving process. Sometimes the anger is directed toward the victim. It doesn't mean that you didn't love the person because you're angry. I don't believe that people who commit suicide understand the pain it causes for family, friends, and children; a parent's suicide leaves a lifetime legacy of torment. Many child survivors have told me that their parents didn't love them enough to stay and persevere through life's problems. Sometimes anger is misdirected at family members, friends, colleagues, or organizations. Anger can be very isolating, since it can distance people from each other. It's not pleasant being around someone who is always angry. Talk about your anger to someone who can help you understand it. Otherwise you may say or do things that you will regret later on. You have every reason to be angry—that's okay. (Anger is often a common emotion for police officers anyway.) What's not okay is taking out your anger unfairly on yourself or others. Your anger is not going to go away on its own. Unless you find a way to express it, you may suffer emotionally or physically from its effects. You could become verbally abusive to citizens or family members. When you find yourself short on patience, quick to lash out and criticize or lethargic and emotionally down, it's time for professional help. Another response is emotional numbing where you just don't feel anything. Reactions after a violent suicide, especially for those who find the person, are more complicated and intense. While most police officers have seen the aftermath of violent suicides, it's much different when the victim is a fellow officer. The shock and horror upon discovering the victim and the image that is engrafted in the mind can be overwhelming. Grief becomes more complex when this occurs. The mental picture will remain with the person, sometimes accompanied by flashbacks, nightmares, and thoughts. Police officers all too often stuff their feelings so as to not appear weak. But emotions are normal and in order to heal, you must unburden what you have had to endure—you must tell the story. Discovering the body of a friend or loved one is shocking and painful—an experience that you will never forget. It is important to share the powerful emotions that this experience brings.

Grief

When it seems that our sorrow is too great to be borne, let us think of the great family of the heavy hearted into which our grief has given us entrance, and inevitability, we will feel about us their arms, their sympathy, their understanding.

Helen Keller

Grief plays a major role in stress. Grief is what we feel when we experience any kind of loss, especially when a police officer takes his life without any explanation.

Mourning the Loss of a Loved One

And can it be that a world so full and busy the loss of one creature makes a void so wide and deep, that nothing but the width and depth of eternity can fill it up

Charles Dickens

Death stings the victim only once, but those left behind feel the pain of loss with every passing memory every day.

Author Anonymous

Everyone mourns in their own way. I have found that mourning often encompasses a three step process that will begin the healing process.

1. *The first step is the acceptance*: The reality of any loss for immediate family members is often devastating. The initial first step in the healing process is acceptance and the reality of the loss that will not change. The pain and grief of police suicide will be long lasting for the family and friends of that individual.

2. *The second step is adjustment*: Even though the initial shock of the police suicide was devastating and overwhelming, the daily routine of life continues on. Adjusting to life without that special person, paying the bills, raising the family, and continuing on with a void

3. *The third step is adapting and acclimating and eventually moving forward*: The memory of the person never goes away, but the start of acclimating to a new life, as difficult as it may be, life goes on. The healing process is like a deep cut, the memory is the apparent scar that is a constant reminder of the loss that has occurred in their life.

Healing and Recovery

Anderson (2014) said to be gentle with yourself and your fellow officers. Grieving is a long process—one that is very personal and sometimes difficult to understand. Talk to friends, coworkers, and family about the suicide. While traditionally this is very hard for police officers to do, it's a vital part of healing and recovery. Unlike a "line of duty" death, police suicides are often enshrouded in shame and silence. While social attitudes have become more informed about suicide, there remains a stigma that people must deal with. All too often people are quick to form judgments. Survivors are left to somehow make sense of this terrible tragedy, maybe even feeling responsible in some way for contributing to it. It is important to discourage rumors about the *reason* for the suicide. While seeking to place blame on others is a natural response, it's not helpful in the long run. Besides, life is very complicated and there are usually several contributing factors in a suicide death. To think that one person or one event is the sole cause is not consistent with what we know about suicide. We can never know for sure what is going on in another person's mind any more than we can know all the reasons that cause a person to choose suicide. Go to the funeral, no matter what your beliefs or feelings are about suicide, funerals are an important ritual for closure and acceptance of the reality that the person has died. It is a final "goodbye" that we share with each other.

Remembering

It is important for the family to cherish the happy memories that they experienced as a family. I suggest that a bereaved family talk about issues that surround the recent suicide of a loved one. It may be beneficial to join a support group dealing specifically with suicide, or seek out counseling from the police department's EAP office. Denis Adams said that the survivors of law enforcement suicides should seek the help of the EAP. The need to talk with a trained clinician about a suicide in their family is a powerful experience in the healing process. It takes a lot for the family of an officer that dies by suicide to seek help and want to talk about their pain. Trust has to be there for the affected family members of police suicide to open up and express their feelings and emotions. This is a place where the officer's family and children can validate their feelings and heal from the tragedy that they experienced.

 The National Police Suicide Foundation, Inc.
7015 Clark Road
Seaford, Delaware 19973
302-536-1214

June 21, 2012
President Obama
The White House
1600 Pennsylvania Ave. NW
Washington, DC 20500

Dear President Obama,

Our law enforcement officers today are experiencing an ever-growing issue of police officer–related suicides. According to the FBI National Academy, approximately every 17 hours a police officer dies of self-inflicted wounds (Forensic Examiner, Volume 19, Number 3, Fall 2010 "Understanding Police Suicide", Jean G. Larned, National Academy Instructor). Since 1997, we have averaged 166 line of duty deaths of police officers each year, but today, our officers are dying twice as fast by their own hand.

Since 1999, the military has implemented a suicide prevention program for all military personnel; unfortunately, the number of suicides for active as well as inactive personnel continue to grow at an alarming rate. Of our approximately 18,000 law enforcement agencies nationwide, about only 3%–5% of them have any suicide prevention training for their officers. Mr. President, this is not a new issue within our ranks. Our foundation has seen this steadily grow over the past 25 years. Because suicide is considered such a "cultural bias" among our ranks, we find it very difficult to gain support for suicide prevention training among our law enforcement leadership.

I personally and professionally believe that there is a solution, but I strongly seek your attention in addressing this issue within our ranks of law enforcement. I recommend that a Department of Suicide Prevention be established within your administration that would oversee the 18,000 law enforcement agencies within our country and mandate Police Suicide Prevention Training for these agencies as it has been mandated for the military. Our law enforcement officers are warriors here at home and struggle with the same issues of posttraumatic stress disorder (PTSD) as our warriors abroad. We need to break down this "Blue Wall of Silence" concerning this issue of police related suicide.

Mr. President, we are all facing many challenges dealing with the mental health and emotional trauma of our young men and women in the military and we are aggressively striving to reduce this ever-increasing number of suicides on a daily basis, but there is another line of defense within our country that are also experiencing mental health issues dealing with PTSD and cumulative career trauma stress (CCTS) that is also resulting in suicides on a daily basis and that is the young men and women of our law enforcement community. We have a window of opportunity to effectively address this issue today by collectively working together to bring about an awareness that there are serious suicide-related issues within our ranks and that mandated suicide prevention training be implemented in the 18,000 agencies. These brave young men and women officers lay their life on the line every day to protect our rights; the least we can do is help to protect them from the enemy within. I ask you to work together with me to help resolve this problem.

Respectfully,

Robert E. Douglas Jr.
Executive Director, NPSF

References

Illinois COPS Magazine (2013) Closing arguments regarding suicide of a fellow officer's close friend, 1(2), 38.

Nichols, R.H. (2014) Suicide, it can be a sudden and final decision, Article written for LOSSteam.com.

Padar, J. and Padar, J. (2014) *On Being a Cop, Father & Son Police Tales from the Streets of Chicago*, Aviva Publishing, Lake Placid, NY.

Suicide (2013) Hope website, Cheryl Brown, coordinator, www.Finding.com

Law Enforcement Suicide Prevention

10

JOHN MARX*

Contents

* Parts of this chapter have been excerpted from articles written by John Marx on www. CopsAlive.com, and many sections include text from the book "Armor Your Self: How To Survive A Career in Law Enforcement" by John Marx published by the Law Enforcement Survival Institute.

Disclaimer

I am neither a psychologist nor a mental health professional. I am just an ex-cop who lost a friend to suicide and began writing and researching law enforcement wellness after his death. Although I have been a law enforcement trainer for over 35 years, all of the ideas in this chapter are suggestions presented for your contemplation and should be considered with your life and career experience as a guide. If you have further questions or need support, assistance, or additional resources, please visit www.CopsAlive.com or seek the appropriate professional help from a legal, medical, or mental health professional in your area.

Let me start by saying thank you for reading this book about the critically important topics of police suicide, stress, and emotional awareness. Law enforcement suicide is an issue that is long overdue for serious discussion within our profession. We need active discussion, awareness training, and action, because if we don't care about it, who will? We are leaving our police families to suffer because we are too ignorant or afraid to handle the fact that more of our brothers and sisters are falling at their own hands than are being murdered in the line of duty. This is an issue that should be discussed in command staff meetings as much as in roll call sessions in law enforcement agencies and organizations around the world. If you choose, please use the link to CopsAlive.com mentioned in the resource section at the end of this chapter to download a copy of our roll call discussion guide entitled *Law Enforcement Suicide Prevention: Take Charge* (http://www.copsalive.com/suggests?rc10msample/rufo).

I believe that this career of ours is toxic. I think that many of us suffer from its effects in silence. I think that there are *hidden dangers* to this job that no one ever warned me about, and I think it's time that we all talked about them. New people coming into law enforcement need to know exactly what threats they will face. Those of us still on the job, or retired, should do some realistic *threat assessment* to ensure that we are adequately protecting ourselves from all of these threats.

In his book *Flourish: A Visionary New Understanding of Happiness and Well-being*, Psychologist Martin Seligman talks about his work in promoting resilience within the U.S. Army and he writes: "focusing on the pathologies of depression, anxiety, suicide, and PTSD was the tail wagging the dog. What the army could do was to move the entire distribution of the reaction to adversity in the direction of resilience and growth. This would not only help prevent PTSD but also increase the number of soldiers who bounce back readily from adversity."

We can do that same thing in our quest to prevent law enforcement suicides. Let's start with a definition of prevention that will guide us through this exploration. I'm defining prevention here as "the anticipation and recognition of a problem and the initiation of some action to remove or reduce it." I believe that based upon this definition, what we are preventing is not just law enforcement suicide but also the root causes of those suicides.

The Problem

As you have already read here, statistics indicate that somewhere between two and six times more officers kill themselves each year than are killed by the bad guys.

A study of police work patterns and stress has shown a quarter of female police officers and nearly as many male officers assigned to shift work had thought about taking their own lives (*results of the study appear in the October 2008 edition of the American Journal of Industrial Medicine* [source: http://www.news-medical.net/news/2008/10/19/42041.aspx]).

In the research I've conducted since my law enforcement friend committed suicide in 2006, I've discovered that it's hard to find tangible data to be able to predict or even define exactly what the problem is that precipitates a law enforcement suicide. Is it post-traumatic stress or just extreme acute doses of situational stress? Perhaps it involves massive doses of cumulative stress or what would qualify as a clinical diagnosis of depression? We know that it is a very impulsive act that frequently involves the abuse of alcohol or drugs and may be linked to extreme relationship or work-related problems. Despite the information that we have, this is still a very mysterious and hard to grasp issue. Because of this, I believe that we need some common points of reference. I have taken to calling all the issues surrounding the hidden dangers and toxic side effects of a law enforcement career as *blue trauma syndrome* just to create a common term with which we might all be familiar for discussion purposes.

Blue Trauma Syndrome

At the Law Enforcement Survival Institute (LESI), we define the blue trauma syndrome as "a spectrum of negative physical, mental, emotional and spiritual health-effects manifested by a career in law enforcement." Blue trauma syndrome most certainly has its roots in large or cumulative doses of negative occupational stress and manifests many negative physiological, mental, emotional, and spiritual symptoms. My main purpose in utilizing this concept of blue trauma syndrome is not to truly define it, as it is to find ways to prevent its cumulative effects. We can then leave the psychologists and researchers to continue their quest to find the exact root causes and specific effects that lead some officers to commit suicide, others to abuse alcohol or prescription drugs, some to plummet into domestic violence, or still others just to slip into depression. The research is underway but our job here is mainly a preventative one only.

Suicide is a tough thing to prevent because it is an impulsive act. Law enforcement suicides frequently involve alcohol and drug abuse, relationship problems, emotional issues, and/or some personal crisis or trauma. These issues are very complicated and most of their effects are not always discernible from the outside looking into someone's life.

What to Do to Prevent Law Enforcement Suicides?

One of the easiest ways to prevent law enforcement suicides is to separate the taboo from the issue. We need to remove our heads from the sand and openly and consistently address this problem. We need to frequently discuss this topic within our agencies at roll calls, coffee meetings, or choir practices, now! It should be a part of ongoing roll call training and at every level of each of our organizations.

We should be asking the following:

Do you know someone who committed suicide?
Have you ever contemplated suicide yourself?
How should we help someone we think may be contemplating suicide?
What can we do within our agency to prevent law enforcement suicide?

Possible Warning Signs of Impending Suicide

Remember that when looking for the signs of any kind of emotional distress, the behaviors need to be taken in totality and in context. There are no clear and specific signs of suicide unless the person expresses his desire to take their own life. One way or another, it's probably better to error on the side of caution toward wellness and, when in doubt, ask the person if he is contemplating suicide. One of the biggest indicators that something might be seriously wrong with someone is when he shows a massive change in his normal behavior, usually for what a peer would think of as being for the worse. Whether or not it might predict a suicide isn't as important as the fact that it indicates something is wrong and warrants some inquiries from him and possibly the people closest to him.

Other indicators may include the following:

- The person talks excessively about suicide or death.
- The person may make statements such as
  - "I just want to end it all"
  - "I wish I were dead"
  - "I just want this life to end"
  - "Soon you won't have to worry about me"
  - "Nobody would care if I died"
- He might develop a morbid fascination with other suicides.
- He may start to research or discuss methods of suicide.
- He may start saying "goodbye" to friends and loved ones.
- The person may start giving away valuable or sentimental property.
- He seems much more lethargic or depressed than normal.
- All of these things might occur in conjunction with some major life crisis or event.

Warning signs specific to cops are as follows:

- The person might make statements about "going out in a blaze of glory" or "if I died in an on-duty crash, my family would get the benefits."
- He might begin to abuse alcohol or prescription drugs in an expressed attempt to "escape."
- He may make statements about not caring about their police duties to the point of being reckless.
- He might become excessively argumentative, insubordinate, or angry.
- The person might become too passive and show a complete lack of concern for his own safety.
- He might start to take unnecessary risks or become excessively reckless.
- He might become unusually isolated from their peers, friends, and family.
- His uniform and general appearance may deteriorate beyond their normal standards.
- He might begin making statements about feeling out of control or inadequate.

Intervention specialist John Southworth suggests that "if a red warning light goes on in your car most people will take action to correct the problem before it gets worse." Most people believe that preventative maintenance is important for the vehicles, but we don't seem to have the same mentality when it comes to taking care of our cops. Southworth suggested the warning signs for human beings in trouble are relatively simple.

Watch their

1. Behavior
2. Attitude
3. Achievement
4. Attendance

If one or more of these things change, then you should be looking closer for a cause and asking more questions.

For more information and additional warning signs, download the document "Signs Of Excessive Stress & Warning Signs" excerpted from Jack Digliani's *Police and Sheriff Peer Support Team Training Manual* available on the resources page of CopsAlive.com (http://www.copsalive.com/suggests?caresources/rufo).

An addiction to alcohol or prescription pain medications also can be a huge warning sign to problems leading up to a police officer's suicide. A Chicago police department study documented alcohol abuse in 60% of police officer suicides. In many cases other officers are left saying: "Wow, I saw the problem growing and should have done something earlier."

I believe that the effective prevention of law enforcement suicides is based upon a three-pronged approach. Strategies for prevention need to be targeted toward building strength in the individual, the agency, and within our law enforcement culture as a whole. If we are truly going to impact this problem, we must fight it on all three of these fronts. We must strengthen ourselves individually. We must provide the kinds of agency programs and services that encourage wellness and prevention. We must change our culture to be more tolerant of proactive mental health and wellness. We need to have a culture that really walks its talk so that when we say "no one gets left behind" or "I've got your back," we really take care of each other, especially if we are injured physically or mentally from the job. Who needs to be involved in the prevention of law enforcement suicide? We all do! Our efforts should involve our peers, our work teams, a proactive peer support team, psychological services, or an Employee Assistance Program (EAP), as well as supervisors, chaplains, families, and friends.

Strategies for the Individual

Strategies for the individual should begin early in every law enforcement career by having everyone learn to strengthen and condition themselves to withstand the rigors and hidden dangers of this career. In my book and training program *Armor Your Self™: How to Survive a Career in Law Enforcement*, I suggest that everyone in law enforcement, both sworn and civilian employees, learns to strengthen and condition themselves physically, mentally, emotionally, and spiritually. I believe that all four of these areas of your *self* are vulnerable to the toxic effects of this job that wear you down slowly over a career in law enforcement. The targeted goal of our program is also to build Tactical Resilience™. I define this as "a human quality of emotional, physical, spiritual and physiological strength and fitness, that can be developed, and is exhibited through the mind, body, brain and spirit of a police officer or other law enforcement or military professional that allows them to withstand the rigors and hidden dangers of continuous high threat, high stress situations."

We all are familiar with how to train and condition our bodies to build physical strength. I think the modern law enforcement professional needs to go beyond a physical training strategy because I believe the risks and dangers are broader than just physical risks. The dangers and toxic effects strike us mentally, emotionally, and spiritually as well. We as modern professional police *athletes* need to recognize that we are professionals who depend upon our bodies and faculties in order to protect and serve our society. In order to protect and to serve as effectively as possible, we need to strengthen and condition ourselves in all four of these areas of our beings just like professional and Olympic athletes do. As baseball great Yogi Berra once said about his beloved game, "Baseball is ninety percent mental and the other half is physical." I think that success in our profession is also about more than just our physical strength! Having said that, we do need physical strength and fitness to control suspects, chase teenagers, maintain stamina, minimize fatigue, increase reaction times, and withstand the physical effects of excessive and cumulative stress. I encourage you to contact a public or departmental physical fitness trainer to create a comprehensive physical workout that suits your needs.

Beyond the physical, we also need to strengthen and condition the other critical areas of our *self*. We need mental strength and fitness to remember license plate numbers and suspect descriptions, boost our reaction times, solve problems, investigate crimes, and communicate with many diverse populations and to be able to make split-second, life and death decisions. There are many things you can do to enhance your brain function and cognitive abilities, but as you work to build mental strength and fitness, you should be focused upon improving your memory, enhancing your problem solving, cultivating your communication abilities, and speeding up your calculation skills. I recommend using the online brain training resources at www.Lumosity.com to keep yourself mentally sharp.

We need emotional strength and fitness to summon courage, manage fear, control our anger, and be able to do all this job requires and still find happiness and joy in our personal lives. There are many ways to strengthen and condition your *self* emotionally. Any exercise that strengthens your willpower, self-control, or mental toughness will help you build courage, reduce fear, and manage anger. Try a simple daily exercise at home to strengthen and condition your willpower by seeing how long you can go without eating or drinking things that you enjoy but might not be good for you. Consider removing chocolate, fast food, prepackaged foods, or alcohol from your life for 30 days. Keep a journal about how you deal with cravings and handle temptation daily. Simple risk-taking exercises can involve telling someone something that you are afraid to say or maybe asking someone out on a date that you are too intimidated to talk to. Other more advanced exercises can challenge your courage through repeated *safe* risk-taking activities like rope courses, rock climbing, or skydiving. The more you overcome your fears, the more you will be able to draw on those courage reserves when you need them. Research anger management techniques online or start a discussion within your work team.

We need spiritual strength and fitness to ensure our honor and integrity, to bolster our courage, maintain compassion, and establish our faith, whether that be in a higher power or just in our fellow human beings. Spiritual strength and conditioning exercises can be as simple as one-on-one or group discussions of common perplexing issues like where does our inner strength come from, what's the difference between good and evil, and why do bad things happen to good people. Further exploration could involve research, study, contemplation, and even the pursuit of the understanding of higher challenges like what happens when we die, why are some people evil, how will I strengthen my personal integrity, and where does hope come from. I highly recommend you create a chaplain's program within your agency. Chaplains don't just provide spiritual guidance but are trained to support a multidenominational audience by being available for just these kinds of discussions.

All of these topics are discussed with far more detail, along with exercises for each area, in my book *Armor Your Self™: How To Survive A Career In Law Enforcement* as well as being discussed on www.CopsAlive.com.

Know When to Ask For Help

One of the last and most important, but most challenging, objectives that you as an individual can accomplish in your personal growth and development quest is to know when to ask for help. We are immersed in a law enforcement culture that says we need to be independently resilient, self-sufficient, and strong and fit enough to do all that is required of us in this job. That culture also works against us in that it stifles our best self-preservation mechanisms by shaming us into avoiding mental, emotional, and spiritual growth and support that also keeps us from asking for help when we are hurting.

You wouldn't hesitate to see a doctor if you were injured on the job physically. Why then do we not seek mental, emotional, or spiritual first aid when we are injured on the job in those parts of our *self*? Experience has proven that early intervention in mental, emotional, or even spiritual injuries has a much better chance of full recovery than late or no intervention. Why do we defy common sense by not seeking first aid when we have a minor non-physical injury? We are taught to *suck it up* and tough it out, which usually means we wait until that mental, spiritual, or emotional problem has grown too large and unmanageable for us to handle.

If you feel that you are struggling with your own problems, contact your EAP or other health care or support provider as soon as possible.

Consider these resources:

Safe Call Now: (206) 459-3020 or visit their website to learn more: http://www.safecallnow.org/

Safe Call Now was founded and is run by public safety employees. These are people from law enforcement, fire, EMS, corrections, civilian support staff, and families who want to help their peers in crisis. If you need help, call them!

Cop2Cop: 1-866-Cop-2Cop or 1-866-267-2267

Cop2Cop is run by the state of New Jersey Department of Human Services and Rutgers University Behavioral Health Care (http://ubhc.rutgers.edu/cop2cop/main.htm).

CopLine: 1-800-267-5463, http://www.copline.net/index.htm

National Suicide Prevention Lifeline: 1-800-273-TALK (1-800-273-8255) (http://www.suicidepreventionlifeline.org/)

If you are seeking that help for one of your peers that is in trouble, you could ask for assistance from your peers, peer support team agency, police psychologist, or a mental health professional so that your intervention can be a *team* effort with a much higher chance of success. Remember that early intervention, when problems are minor, is so much easier and much more effective than intervention provided too late in the development or compounding of the other person's problems. Intervention beyond the peer support functions is not a simple process. I encourage you to read a little further down to the section entitled "Thoughts on Intervention."

Strategies for Agencies

At the LESI, we believe that in order to support individuals who are trying to care for themselves, agencies should have in place certain support programs that assist individuals in their endeavor to withstand the rigors of a full career and strengthen themselves against its toxic side effects. We call our program *Armor*

Your Agency™, which is both a training program and an ongoing research project looking for best practices in law enforcement health and wellness.

Our Armor Your Agency™ model programs project recommends that all law enforcement agencies have these basic programs for their personnel:

- Wellness program
- Designated fitness trainers
- Psychological services provided by a police psychologist or at least access to an EAP
- Proactive peer support
- Mentoring program
- Family support program
- Survivor support program
- Chaplain's program
- True Blue Valor™ training
- Officer intervention plan
- Critical incident response plan
- Disability insurance and response plan
- Tactical resilience training
- Annual line of duty death prevention training (this includes arrest control, shooting, driving, and self-defense)

All of these concepts, and more, are covered in depth in the Armor Your Agency™ program. A couple of the more important of these that we should consider here are the following:

Establishing Proactive Peer Support

I believe that in order to be preventative and effective, a peer support program should not only be *available*, but it should reach out to people regularly and proactively. Police psychologist, Jack Digliani, PhD, EdD, provides an excellent training program for police and sheriff's agencies, which you can learn more about at CopsAlive.com. There are many peer-to-peer support networks out there and you can find them in many agencies now. Contact yours, or if need be, start a new one. The Critical Incident Stress Foundation or CISM International can offer guidance.

Building a Family Support Network

Build a strong network of support with families of your officers and staff. They are the first line of defense against police suicide and are also an amazing resource for your agency, especially if you build that network early. See the link in the succeeding text to download our free CopsAlive.com suggestions on starting a family support network within your organization or invite our LESI trainers to come to your agency to build a customized program.

Also visit the website of the Law Enforcement Family Support Network (LEFN) at http://lawenforcementfamilysupport.org/. The LEFN advocates on behalf of law enforcement families so that they may have the tools, education, and support needed to remain healthy and connected. They also provide education and resources for officers, family members, departments, and policy makers to understand and address the educational needs and cumulative stress issues of the law enforcement profession. The most important thing about family and peer support networks is that you have to build them now, before a problem arises!

Thoughts on Intervention

An effective intervention strategy should involve a well-planned-out strategy that includes investigating and arranging a treatment facility in advance as well as assembling a team of friends, family, peers, and mental health professionals that can provide the subject of the intervention with specific examples of behaviors that are causing alarm or are self-destructive.

Have a Plan

Even in an emergency situation, you should write out, or at least diagram out, a complete strategy of what you need to do including the place, time, people involved, and words to use during the intervention. You should check to see what insurance coverage is available to the person and what facilities it recommends. You should contact the facility and discuss the intervention with their staff and ensure that they have room for the incoming patient. You should assemble the best possible team of people to help you. Finally, you need to determine when is the good time for the intervention. Offering an unwanted intervention to a law enforcement officer who is armed and perhaps combative might be a recipe for danger and disaster if you don't do some planning and homework first.

Assemble Your Team

Try to assemble the best possible team of people who are family, friends, and coworkers of the person who might have the most influence or be able to offer the most effective emotional support and reassurance to the person in crisis.

You should also always involve the best possible mental health professional(s) that either know the individual or are very familiar with law enforcement mental health issues or both. Some of these people might just help you with the planning for your intervention or might come along during the intervention or be involved in both as well. Always consider the safety of the team, the person needing the intervention and the public.

Arrange Your Resources in Advance

Try to arrange all of your personnel and resources as far in advance of any actual intervention as possible. This will give you the greatest opportunity for success by assembling the best options and resources possible. This might include examining primary insurance coverage, supplemental or other insurance coverage, and applicable departmental policies and procedures. Select a treatment facility and contact them. Ensure they have space available and will accept the person's insurance. Consult with their staff about intervention ideas and options. Arrange transportation to the facility. Provide for security and support not only for the person receiving the intervention but the persons administrating the intervention as well. Weapons issues are critical when dealing with a member of law enforcement. This would include security during the intervention so that the person does not feel so threatened that they would draw a weapon. You should also consider how and where to secure all that person's weapons during the treatment and recovery phases.

Write Your Script to Include Specific Behaviors Depicting the Problem

Getting someone, especially a law enforcement officer of staff member, to accept medical or mental health treatment unexpectedly is an exceedingly difficult task. To enhance your probability of success, I encourage you to find the best people to assist you in verbalizing the need for the intervention. This would include people that are closest to or most trusted by the individual needing help. These people should be patient, calm, and well spoken and should have a *script* of language assembled by all of you that includes very specific behaviors or circumstances that have led you to believe that his intervention is the best, and only, option to help the person. It is most helpful if multiple trusted people can articulate or were present to witness the behaviors or events. Seek the assistance of a mental health professional in developing the language and process for your intervention event.

Some Thoughts on Treatment

I reiterate that I am neither a therapist nor psychologist and defer to the experts when it comes to how to treat mental health issues. I believe that finding the best treatment for emotional issues is no different than arranging the best possible medical treatment. You should ask for advice and referrals and should seek more than one opinion. Remember also that when dealing with someone who is experiencing extreme emotional distress or whose behaviors and conduct are beyond their normal range, there may also be several layers of issues to unravel. Frequently, people experiencing emotional distress turn to alcohol or drugs in an attempt to *self-medicate* their problems. This requires a much more complex treatment methodology than would be needed if we were dealing with only the emotional distress much earlier, when it first became a problem. Having said that, I will refer you to the people at Safe Call Now, if you are trying to find treatment options for any first responders or their family in distress. You can learn about some options by reading some of the many articles we've written on www.CopsAlive.com on this issue. Of note might be our interview with the president of Southworth Associates, John Southworth. As an intervention specialist, John suggests that treatment for alcohol or drug abuse or other emotional disorders might need to last up to 12 weeks in order to be successful, not just the 30 days that insurance companies want you to believe. He believes that we should utilize a case management system for up to 5 years to keep track of people who are trying to make major life changes and that it might take that long with the support of a case management system to not only hold them accountable but give them the support they need as well.

Mr. John Southworth has more than 30 years of both personal and professional experience in the field of substance abuse and mental health. Southworth holds certification as a Certified Alcohol Drug Counselor from the National Association of Alcohol and Drug Addiction Counselors. He is also a nationally certified addictions counselor and an internationally certified advanced alcohol and drug counselor (level) I. He holds membership in the International Certification and Reciprocity Consortium and also is a board registered interventionist (level) II.

Through his personal battle with addiction, Southworth learned that there is no cure for the disease and that it can be fatal, if the appropriate education and steps to recovery are not taken. This knowledge is the driving force behind his motivation to educate others about addiction, and it also plays a major role in Southworth's continued sobriety of over 30 years. The fact that he now works as an interventionist who uses a long-term follow-up system of case management gives him lots of first-hand experience helping lots of people who are battling lots of different addictions, including police officers.

Again, remember that some of his suggestions might seem outrageous such as the fact that treatment might need to last up to 12 weeks in order to be successful, not just the 30 days that your agency or its insurance companies want you to accept. Of major importance is John's accretion that we should utilize a case management system for up to 5 years to keep track of people who are trying to make major life changes. He insists that it might take that long with the support of a case management system to not only hold them accountable but give them the support they need for continued success.

John Southworth is an interesting character, but when you listen to our interview, I think you will find that he has *been there* and now *walks his talk* with information that you can believe. I encourage you to spend 35 min and listen to our interview and then start a discussion at your agency about what you are going to do when it happens to someone you know! You can find our article and listen to the podcast interview here: http://www.copsalive.com/we-need-to-get-serious-about-dealing-with-addictions-in-law-enforcement/.

Strategies for a Positive Wellness Culture

In preventing law enforcement suicide, what's our target?
The questions really are
What is causing the problems that lead to suicide?
How are we going to prevent those problems?

Suicide and suicidal thoughts may be just a symptom of bigger issues. While we support our personnel as they strengthen and fortify themselves against the things that would lead to suicide like alcohol or drug problems, relationship issues, depression, and despondence, we must also recognize that these problems could have their roots in personal disgrace and professional humiliation. Our goal is to become aware of these issues early before they can fester into larger more unmanageable problems.

The third pillar in our comprehensive prevention structure is that of strengthening and conditioning our professional law enforcement culture. Only when we have agency programs in place and start to work on creating a positive and supportive culture of health and wellness can we really start to make inroads into the problem of law enforcement suicide. Strategies to improve our law enforcement culture and make it one of wellness and career survival include making it safe for someone to ask for help, having the support mechanisms in place to provide that help, and creating an environment of support and encouragement that assist in intervention, treatment, and recovery from whatever mental, emotional, or spiritual injuries our personnel are suffering. The culture would also include an understanding of how much teasing and stress are appropriate in training and for the rest of their career. We need to determine how much is too much, so that we are not causing unneeded internal stress rather than providing a supportive environment. We have plenty of bad guys to arrest and dangers to face outside our law enforcement agencies. We don't need to be adding any stress from inside. Many officers report that they feel more stress from inside headquarters than outside on the streets, yet we never fess up to how much stress we absorb from the dark humor, teasing, and downright bullying we get from our peers. If nonbullying policies are appropriate for our children's primary schools, then it should be appropriate for those of us in law enforcement who should hold each other to a higher standard.

Make it Safe

The "Make it Safe Police Officer Initiative" started by police psychologist Jack Digliani, PhD, EdD, creates an environment where officers or other law enforcement professionals feel comfortable asking for help before their problems become extreme. This initiative works to change our policing culture to make it easier and safe for anyone to seek assistance rather than hide their feelings and perhaps suffer a greater second trauma from a critical incident or experience. Digliani gives suggestions about what we have to do to our law enforcement culture to make seeking mental health support for stress-related issues okay.

In his writing and peer support team training, Digliani suggests that the law enforcement profession suffers from two kinds of dangers that he labels primary and secondary danger. Digliani said: "The line of duty fatalities we suffer each year are representative of the primary danger of policing." The primary danger of policing is comprised of the inherent risks of the job, such as working in motor vehicle traffic, confronting violent persons, and exposure to critical incidents. Sadly, there is an insidious and lesser-known secondary danger in policing. This danger is often unspecified and seldom discussed. It is an artifact of the police culture and is frequently reinforced by police officers themselves. It is the idea that equates *asking for help* with *personal and professional weakness* and, in one sense, is truly the number one killer of police officers.

Secondary danger has been implicated in perhaps the most startling of all police fatality statistics, the frequency of police officer suicide. What do we have to do to make it safe for police officers to trust one another enough to be able to ask for help when they need it? What do we have to do to our law enforcement culture to make seeking mental health support for stress-related issues okay? How can we truly walk our talk enough to really *have each other's back* and really *take care of our own*? You can start to *make it safe* in your agency by distributing and discussing this initiative. We must all work to make it safe for officers to ask for psychological support.

The "Make it Safe" Initiative seeks to

1. Make it personally and professionally acceptable for officers to engage peer and professional psychological support services without fear of agency or ridicule or reprisal by a fellow officer
2. Reduce officer fears about asking for psychological support when confronting potentially overwhelming job or other life difficulties
3. Change organizational climates that discourage officers from seeking psychological help by reducing explicit and implicit organizational messages that imply asking for help is indicative of personal and professional weakness
4. Alter the profession-wide law enforcement culture that generally views asking for psychological help as a personal or professional weakness
5. Improve the career-long psychological wellness of officers by encouraging police agencies to adopt long-term and comprehensive officer-support strategies such as the Comprehensive Model for Police Advanced Strategic Support

How serious is police secondary danger? So serious that some officers will choose suicide over asking for help. The Digliani Make it Safe Initiative is comprised of 12 primary components designed to reduce the secondary danger of policing by encouraging

1. Every officer to *self-monitor* and to take personal responsibility for his mental wellness
2. Every officer to seek psychological support when confronting potentially overwhelming difficulties (officers do not have to *go it alone*)
3. Every officer to diminish the sometimes deadly effects of secondary danger by reaching out to other officers known to be facing difficult circumstances
4. Veteran and ranking officers to use their status to help reduce secondary danger (veteran and ranking officers can reduce secondary danger by openly discussing it, appropriately sharing selected personal experiences, avoiding the use of pejorative terms to describe officers seeking or engaging psychological support, and talking about the acceptability of seeking psychological support when confronting stressful circumstances)

5. Law enforcement administrators to better educate themselves about the nature of secondary danger and to take the lead in secondary danger reduction

6. Law enforcement administrators to issue a departmental memo encouraging officers to engage in psychological support services when confronting potentially overwhelming stress (the memo should include information about confidentiality and available support resources)

7. Basic training in stress management, stress inoculation, critical incidents, posttraumatic stress, police family dynamics, and the warning signs of suicide

8. The development of programs that engage preemptive, early warning, and periodic department-wide officer support interventions (e.g., proactive annual check-in [PAC], *early-warning* policies designed to support officers displaying signs of stress and regularly scheduled stress inoculation and critical incident stressor management training)

9. Agencies to initiate incident-specific protocols to support officers and their families when officers are involved in critical incidents

10. Agencies to create appropriately structured, properly trained, and clinically supervised peer support teams

11. Agencies to provide easy and confidential access to counseling and specialized police psychological support services

12. Officers at all levels of the organization to enhance the agency climate so that others are encouraged to ask for help when experiencing psychological or emotional difficulties instead of keeping and acting out a deadly secret

The "Make it Safe" Initiative is dedicated to making it safe for officers to request and engage appropriate psychological support when dealing with difficult circumstances. An officer does not need to be suicidal or experiencing the emotional aftermath of a critical incident to benefit from this change in the police culture. The men and women of law enforcement need to rethink what it means to be a police officer and to consider asking for psychological help when confronting potentially overwhelming stress or experiencing major changes in mood. Take a positive step forward; become part of the Make it Safe Initiative today. If law enforcement officers wish to do the best for themselves and other officers, it's time to make a change. It's time to make a difference. I encourage you to visit www.jackdigliani.com to learn more about police primary and secondary danger and how to implement the "Make it Safe" Police Officer Initiative. I also encourage you to talk to your administrators about the "Make it Safe" Police Officer Initiative and how it can make your agency more effective.

"Make it Safe" Initiative and Concerns about Fitness for Duty

Asking for help does not mean *unfit for duty*.

I asked Jack about his thoughts about how the Make it Safe Initiative would interact with any fitness for duty issues and he said:

> Some officers will not ask for psychological help even when they think they should because they have concerns about being "found out" and perceived as "unfit for duty". Although it is possible for police officers to develop psychological symptoms serious enough to become incapable of safely performing at work, there is no comparison between asking for help and being unfit for duty. Seeking appropriate support and intervention for any reason, be it physical, psychological, emotional, social, or substance-use related does not automatically make an officer unfit for duty. The fear of being found out and perceived as unfit for duty is a manifestation of police secondary danger. Secondary danger is what the Make it Safe Initiative is designed to address.

Use the following action plan for implementing the Digliani "Make it Safe" Initiative:

Initiative implementation action plan:

1. Learn about the initiative.
2. Bring it to the attention of administrators or command staff.
3. Become an advocate.
4. Work with staff to address concerns.
5. Move methodically—first, implement the elements most easily accomplished.
6. Be patient; maintain effort.

Implementing the "Make it Safe" Police Officer Initiative is not difficult. The elements of the initiative are easily implemented by initiating processes, strategies, and programs already well known to law enforcement agencies. The initiative is not an *all or nothing* proposition. Various elements of the initiative can be implemented independently of one another. Although it is best to move forward with the entire initiative, a partial implementation is better than no implementation. There is no *one right way* to implement any element of the initiative. Be creative. Make the Make it Safe Police Officer Initiative work for you. For some thoughts about implementing the initiative, or to learn more about Jack Digliani and all of his programs and initiatives please, visit his website at www.JackDigliani.com. To read our CopsAlive.

com article about the Make it Safe Initiative and download a "Make it Safe" flyer to post on bulletin boards, visit http://www.copsalive.com/make-it-safe.

Consider a Proactive Annual Check-In

Dr. Digliani also recommends that police officer agencies, and other law enforcement professionals, consider doing an annual proactive check-in with their police psychologist, peer support team member, or law enforcement-trained mental health professional. What is a proactive annual check-in (PAC)? The PAC provides police officers and other agency employees with a confidential setting within which to share information about current life circumstances. It is a proactive program designed to offer a positive exchange thoughts, ideas, and information.

Elements of the Proactive Annual Check-In

1. Annual visit with the staff psychologist, a member of the peer support team, department chaplain, private counselor, or other support resource.
2. Confidential meeting that does not initiate any record.
3. No evaluation—It's a check-in, not a checkup.
4. There does not need to be a problem.
5. It's a discussion of what's happening in your life.
6. Participation is voluntary and encouraged.

Agencies can readily implement the PAC in program by utilizing currently available support resources. Disseminate PAC program information by downloading, printing, and displaying the PAC poster available on Jack's website at www.JackDigliani.com.

All of the things we are discussing here are really about all of us learning to take responsibility for the well-being of ourselves, our peers, and our profession. It means we need to actually *walk our talk*. If we say things like "I've got your back" or "no one gets left behind" or "we are all one big family," then we need to mean it. I believe that is part of a code of honor that I describe as "True Blue Valor™."

In our LESI training sessions, we talk about the concept of "True Blue Valor™" as when a cop has the courage to confront a buddy who is slipping professionally and personally and endangering themselves, their peers, and the public. If you think it takes courage to confront an armed suspect, consider what it would take for you to confront one of your friends about their problems, which are affecting their lives and job performance. It takes a system of organizational support and professional leadership to foster and nurture the concept of "True Blue Valor™."

Consider taking the True Blue Valor™ Pledge:

> On My Honor I Pledge:
> To Uphold the Code of True Blue Valor
> First I Will Do No Harm
> I Am A Protector, Not a Bully
> I Will Treat My Coworkers with Respect and Dignity, Because We Are All One Family
> I Will Not Look the Other Way When a Peer is in Crisis
> I Will Offer Support and Encouragement When Needed
> I Will Take Charge and Intervene When Necessary
> I Will Protect and Serve My Country, Community, Family and Peers
> I will Support and Encourage My Brothers and Sisters in Law Enforcement
> I Do All of This Because:
>> I "Walk My Talk" and I say,
>> "We Take Care of Our Own" and On My Watch
>> "No One Gets Left Behind!"

To learn more about this program and download a free copy of our *Honor Code of "True Blue Valor™,"* please visit www.TrueBlueValor.com for more information.

The LESI offers on-site training programs in "True Blue Valor™," or you can license the program to teach it yourself within your agency. The 12 sessions of the "True Blue Valor™" training program include

> Session One "What is True Blue Valor™?"
> Session Two "The Importance of Peer Support"
> Session Three "Fire Spotters & Smoke Jumpers"
> Session Four "The Role of Family Support"
> Session Five "Mentoring in Law Enforcement"
> Session Six "Critical Incident Support"
> Session Seven "Crisis Intervention"
> Session Eight "The Role of the Police Chaplain"
> Session Nine "Resources for Help"
> Session Ten "Taking Care of Yourself"
> Session Eleven "Taking Care of Our Own"
> Session Twelve "The Future of Our Profession"

Learn more at: www.TrueBlueValor.com.

Crisis Hotlines

Remember if you or someone you know needs help, call now!

Safe Call Now (206) 459-3020 or visit their website to learn more: http://www.safecallnow.org/.

Safe Call Now was founded and is run by public safety employees. These are people from law enforcement, fire, EMS, corrections, civilian support staff, and their families who want to help their peers in crisis. If you need help, call them!

Cop2Cop 1-866-Cop-2Cop or 1-866-267-2267

Run by the state of New Jersey Department of Human Services and Rutgers University Behavioral Health Care (http://ubhc.rutgers.edu/cop2cop/main.htm)

CopLine: 1-800-267-5463 (http://www.copline.net/index.htm)

National Suicide Prevention Lifeline: 1-800-273-TALK (1-800-273-8255) (http://www.suicidepreventionlifeline.org/)

Resources for Follow-Up Training and Support

LESI training at www.LawEnforcementSurvivalInstitute.org

Pain Behind the Badge at www.ThePainBehindTheBadge.com

Safe Call Now at www.SafeCallNow.org

The National Police Suicide Foundation at www.psf.org

Sources of Information on Police Suicide

National Police Suicide Foundation at http://www.psf.org

Badge of Life at http://www.badgeoflife.com/suicides.php

Pain Behind the Badge at www.thepainbehindthebadge.com

CopsAlive.com at www.CopsAlive.com

For Your Own Further Research, Please Investigate These Books

Anderson, W., D. Swenson, and D. Clay. *Stress Management For Law Enforcement Officers*. Englewood Cliffs, NJ: Prentice Hall, Inc., 1995.

Digliani, J., Ph.D. *Jack Reflections of a Police Psychologist*: Bloomington, IN: Xlibris Corporation, 2010.

Douglas Jr., R. E. *Hope Beyond The Badge*. Pasadena, MD: Keener Marketing Inc., 1999.

Gilmartin, K. M. *Emotional Survival For Law Enforcement*. Tucson, AZ: E-S Press, 2002.

Hackett, D. P. and J. M. Violanti, Ph.D. *Police Suicide*. Springfield, IL: Charles C. Thomas Publisher, 2003.

Kates, A. R. *CopShock: Surviving Posttraumatic Stress Disorder* (PTSD), 2nd edn. Holbrook Street Press, Tucson, AZ, rev. 2008.

Kirschman, E. *I Love A Cop: What Police Families Need To Know*. New York: Guilford Press, 2006.

Marx, J. *Armor Your Self: How to Survive A Career in Law Enforcement*. Westminster, CO: The Law Enforcement Survival Institute, 2014.

Paris, C. A. and D. Grossman. *My Life for Your Life*. Pain Behind The Badge, 2011. http://thepainbehindthebadge.com/shop/life-life-book/.

Seligman, M. E. P. *Flourish: A Visionary New Understanding of Happiness and Well-being*. Atria Paperback, New York, 2011.

Violanti, J. M. *Dying for the Job: Police Work Exposure and Health*.

Links to CopsAlive.com Articles and Resources

For our CopsAlive.com resources page, visit http://www.copsalive.com/suggests?caresources/rufo. Our CopsAlive.com 10 Minute Roll Call Discussion Guides are single-topic training sessions designed to enable you to provide short but powerful training on a variety of topics in as little as 10 min. This makes it easier to fit training into busy shift schedules and give officers a chance to discuss important, job-related, or self-improvement topics.

For our CopsAlive.com 10 Minute Roll Call Discussion Guide "Law Enforcement Suicide Prevention—Take Charge," go to http://www.copsalive.com/suggests?rc10msample/rufo.

For our CopsAlive.com 10 Minute Roll Call Discussion Key "The Police PTSD Paradox," go to http://www.copsalive.com/suggests?rc10mptsdparadox/rufo.

For our CopsAlive.com 10 Minute Roll Call Discussion Key "Rx3x" 3x Prescription for Stress Management in Law Enforcement, go to http://www.copsalive.com/suggests?rx3xrc10m/rufo.

Homework and Follow-Up Research

If your agency doesn't have a peer support team, start one. Visit either CopsAlive.com or JackDigliani.com for more information and resources. If your agency doesn't have a suicide prevention training program, create one. Consider any of the resources mentioned in this chapter: CopsAlive.com, The Pain Behind The Badge, Safe Call Now, The National Police Suicide Foundation, etc. If your agency doesn't have a family support network, build one. Download our CopsAlive.com document "Suggestions for the

Implementation of a Family Support System within your Organization" at http://www.copsalive.com/suggests?cafamilysupport/rufo.

If your agency doesn't have informational signs for a first-responder Crisis Hotline posted, post them. I recommend Safe Call Now because of their national network and privacy protections.

Above all, don't let one more police suicide occur. Do your part today to protect your friends and loved ones. CopsAlive was founded after one of my peers committed suicide, and I wish that I had known more and done more before that happened. I founded CopsAlive.com to provide information and strategies to help police officers successfully survive their careers. Our motto is "Saving the lives of those who save lives." We help law enforcement officers, their families, and their agencies prepare for the risks that threaten our existence.

Conclusion

11

RON RUFO

Contents

> The difference between a strong man and a weak one is that the former does not give up after defeat.
>
> **Woodrow Wilson**

> Hold yourself responsible for a higher standard than anybody else expects of you. Never excuse yourself. Never pity yourself. Be a hard master to yourself-and be lenient to everyone else.
>
> **Henry Ward Beecher**

Dr. Bruce Handler* said that sometimes officers feel more at ease talking about their colleague's suicide as accidental. Support groups, anonymous help lines, and peer-to-peer support are some ways of bringing out important facts and addressing the emotional suffering those left behind are dealing with while continuing in a stressful job, dealing with family issues, and staying healthy. Crisis Intervention Team training addresses police issues honestly and openly rather than suffering in silence with what's been, up to now, a taboo and embarrassing subject.

10 Points Necessary When Dealing with a Suicidal Person

1. Assess the seriousness of the threat and danger he is in.
2. Allow ventilation and disclosure of the problem.
3. Accept and acknowledge that there is a problem, and identify what led up to the problem.

---

* Handler, Bruce, Personal interview.

4. Have patience and serenity, be honest and sincere, and be nonjudgmental.
5. Be an active listener, establish rapport, and be objective.
6. Use open-ended questions to let the distressed person express their feelings.
7. Be compassionate, understanding, and receptive. Introduce choices.
8. Let him or her reflect on his or her anguish and pain, and let him or her know that he is not alone.
9. Instill optimism and confidence.
10. Encourage that life is worth living.

Dr. Frank Campbell* said that training law enforcement in suicide prevention is imperative. We know it works. The concept is similar to a person drowning. If you train everyone to be a lifeguard, you will have fewer people drown. Police departments across the nation will need to relay the message of suicide prevention to their personnel. We can begin to understand suicide by offering 2-day workshops that would reveal officers at risk with the reality that help can be provided. Dr. Carl Alaimo said that the numbers do not lie. Today, the evidence and the research present that, focusing on law enforcement suicide, the numbers remain significantly higher compared to any other profession. The lack of ongoing educational training increases the stress of the job.

Robert Douglas Jr.† reiterated, "As mental health professionals, we need to raise awareness so that everyone is on the same page regarding the issues that officers deal with and experience continuously. We need to also identity and evaluate the best practices that are effective and mandate training that is essential in preventing the growing epidemic of police suicide." World Health Report on Suicide (2009) said that the prevention of police suicide has not been adequately addressed due to basically a lack of awareness.

According to Suicide: Finding Hope (2013), law enforcement officers are tasked with protecting our communities. They are the first people we call when we need help. On September 11, 2001, thousands of people ran from the twin towers to safety, but law enforcement officers ran toward the towers to rescue those who were injured. Who rescues our law enforcement officers when they need help? Who can they trust with their fears and traumas? How do we as a society support these men and women who are put in harm's way every day? To reduce the suicide rate among law enforcement officers, training must begin in the police academies with periodic in service training throughout an officer's career. It must also entail a change in the law enforcement culture by supporting officers who may need psychological counseling

---

* Campbell, Frank, PhD, Personal interview.
† Douglas, Robert Jr., Personal interview.

as well as medication. The suicide rate will not decline until law enforcement administrators implement policy change to help officers affected by the trauma of this profession.

My Thoughts

Thank you for taking the time to read this book. Many of my colleagues have asked me why I am writing a book about police culture and police suicide. After working as a peer support team leader for most of my career and seeing the trauma, anxiety, and frustration that police work does to an officer, I truly believe that police culture is a major factor in many of the issues that lead to police suicide. Officers become entrenched in police culture. It not only changes the person emotionally, but law enforcement changes a person's entire way of thinking and living the moment they put on the uniform, badge, and gun belt. The change is not by accident, it comes with the territory, and it is the nature of the beast.

Police officers encounter many disturbing situations throughout their careers. They are routinely exposed to human suffering, tragedy, fatal accidents, and death. They are often seen as almost robotic, a cast iron frame, and devoid of emotion or feeling. The facade of their outside appearance is undaunted and unwavering. Police are known for taking care of other people's problems, but rarely face their own demons. When people are running from gunfire or danger, officers are running toward the disturbance. Officers are taught to be in control. An officer does not want to be the weak link in the chain. Police officers encounter many disturbing situations as they officers are forced to make split. They often make life or death decisions with the constant pressure to always be correct in everything they do and for every situation they respond to.

The fact is that police officers cannot be correct 100% of the time; they are human and falter like everyone else. No other occupation risks their life both physically and emotionally by making a mistake on the job. We as officers are judged differently than anyone else, and we play on a different playing field than any other profession. Officers are held at extremely high standards by the community in which they serve, the law enforcement agency in which they work, and themselves. No matter what, the street cop is still human underneath their bulletproof vest—and they should take the time to occasionally communicate their feelings and vent their frustrations. A typical response from an officer in crisis is, "Are you kidding me, I don't need help, or to talk to someone, we just don't do that, besides I have a reputation to uphold."

Who is minding the officer's well-being? The rate of divorce and the rate of suicide is higher than the average across the United States for anyone that has made law enforcement their life's journey. A police officer's emotional well-being needs to be taken into consideration. An emotionally balanced officer is what law enforcement needs today. Emotional well-being is just as important as the tactical training that the officers receive, but somehow the importance of emotional survival has never ever been highlighted, either by accident or on purpose. As police officers we can control our own destiny; in particular, we can monitor and regulate our own emotional survival. If we get hurt on the job, we seek medical attention; when we are feeling down or depressed and in need of an emotional time out, there are many avenues and professionals where we can seek out help without fear of losing our job. Speaking with a professional is not a sign of weakness, but in all reality, it is a sign that as police officers we are not superhuman as we perceive ourselves to be; we are human beings with limitations and shortcomings especially working in a career that deals with a different side of humanity.

My philosophy is not to have a small problem or issue develop into a larger dilemma. We take care of everyone's problems in our community, we need to reach out and take care of our own. My message is unmistakably clear; the time is now to get involved and talk to someone who may be having emotional issues because the help is out there. For those officers who work in the law enforcement field every day, who have survived the beleaguered battlegrounds of the streets, and are now retired, I sincerely hope that you take the time to schedule an appointment with your department's Employee Assistance Program or a member of peer support just to talk about your emotional well-being. For the most part, this service is free to police officers and their immediate families. Police suicide has become a silent statistic that plagues every agency in every city and state in our nation. Police officers who take their own lives leave a tremendous void in their personal family as well in their police family.

I believe that many officers at one time or another have envisioned taking their own lives at weak moments. But it is the officers who continually contemplate taking their own lives and painstakingly plan their deaths that often succeed in doing so. Police officers often suffer emotionally in silence, and those who cannot distance themselves from the heartache of the job often succumb to the temptation of suicide. Police suicide has become a silent statistic that plagues every police department within every city in the United States. Committing suicide is not the answer. *Communication* and *awareness* are the only remedies. God bless and be safe, not only on the street, but emotionally as well!!!

Sincerely,
Dr. Ron Rufo

Reference

Suicide: www.Finding Hope website (2013), Cheryl Brown, coordinator.

Index